ABOUT THE AUTHORS

Sarah Owen began her career in journalism in 1994 at *Cosmopolitan* magazine, before going freelance and writing health and wellbeing features for a range of newspapers and glossy magazines, including the *Express, Daily Mail, Sunday Times, Marie Claire* and *Psychologies*. Sarah has also been involved in creating online content and patient support programmes to help people manage long-term health conditions.

Amanda Saunders has worked as a writer, editor and senior communications professional for almost thirty years. This has included writing for the National Childbirth Trust and working as head of internal communications at the London School of Economics, before more recently becoming a deputy director of communications at the House of Commons, a non-political role.

The authors are first cousins and four members of their close family (Amanda's mum; Sarah's sister and late dad; their shared grandfather) have bipolar disorder.

PRAISE FOR *BIPOLAR DISORDER*

'If you have experienced bipolar disorder – or are close to someone with experience of the condition – then you should read this book.'

Professor Ian Jones, Professor of Psychiatry at Cardiff University and Director of the National Centre for Mental Health

'Like the previous volume, the second edition of *Bipolar Disorder – the Ultimate Guide* will provide a valuable resource for all of us who wish to understand bipolar disorder and how it affects all those who experience and live with it.'

Professor Allan Young, Chair of Mood Disorders at King's College London and Director of the Centre for Affective Disorders, Department of Psychological Medicine at the Institute of Psychiatry

'*Bipolar Disorder – the Ultimate Guide* is the A–Z guide you need to get a comprehensive understanding of the condition. Our team regularly use it as a reference and we recommend it to all our peer support volunteers. Sarah and Amanda have compiled the latest research and thinking on bipolar in an accessible format that is appropriate for friends, families, professionals and, of course, for people living with bipolar.'

Simon Kitchen, Chief Executive Officer at Bipolar UK

'When the first edition of this book was published in 2008, it became a core text for anyone living with or affected by bipolar. Amanda and Sarah provided, in a single volume, the tools for people to begin to navigate this most complex and challenging of conditions. A decade on, this updated second edition is just as useful as ever with its comprehensive mix of information, support and guidance imbued with great humanity and compassion.'

Professor Steven Jones, Professor of Clinical Psychology at Lancaster University and Director of the Spectrum Centre for Mental Health Research

'A wonderful and comprehensive resource, answering all the questions that arise when a person is given a diagnosis of this confusing and often misunderstood condition. I thoroughly recommend it.'

Dr Juliet McGrattan, author of the award-winning book
Sorted: The Active Woman's Guide to Health

'This is the one book I wish I'd had in my pocket for each and every time when I've had to try describing myself and my oddness to anyone I love. It is quite possibly the most comprehensive and enabling guide I've come across to date, remarkably accessible, friendly and nourishing for anyone needing to know about people like me. Us.'

Paul Abbott, BAFTA-winning scriptwriter and creator of
Shameless, Clocking Off and *No Offense*

'I wish I that this superb book had been around when I was growing up with a father with bipolar. It is packed with practical advice for those with the condition and their families on every aspect of the illness – and some astonishing first-hand accounts. It will provide a huge amount of comfort – and help.'

Martin Townsend, former editor of the *Sunday Express*
and author of *The Father I Had*

'Should I ever worry about myself or another close family member developing the condition, this book will answer any questions that I might have in the most friendly and uncomplicated style. It really is *Bipolar Disorder – the Ultimate Guide* – a unique and approachable reference book for those with the condition and their loved ones.'

Jo Crocker, sister and PA to Stephen Fry

'This excellent guide to bipolar is structured around the kind of key questions that anyone encountering the condition for the first time would want to ask.'

***Pendulum* (Bipolar UK)**

BIPOLAR DISORDER -the ultimate guide

SARAH OWEN   AMANDA SAUNDERS

ONEWORLD

A ONEWORLD PAPERBACK ORIGINAL

First published by Oneworld Publications 2008
This fully revised and updated second edition published 2019

ISBN 978-1-78074-543-5
eISBN 978-1-78074-007-2

Text design and typesetting by Tetragon, London
Printed and bound in Great Britain by Clays Ltd, Elcograf S.p.A.

Pathway of Care diagram on p. 66 reproduced by kind permission of Michel Syrett

Oneworld Publications
10 Bloomsbury Street
London WC1B 3SR

Stay up to date with the latest books,
special offers, and exclusive content from
Oneworld with our newsletter

Sign up on our website
oneworld-publications.com

MIX
Paper from
responsible sources
FSC
www.fsc.org
FSC® C018072

Contents

With thanks ...   xi

A word from Paul Abbott   xv

A word from Jo Crocker   xviii

A word from Professor Steven Jones   xxi

INTRODUCTION: IS THIS BOOK FOR YOU?   1

CHAPTER ONE: CAUSES, SYMPTOMS AND DIAGNOSIS   21

Q1. What is bipolar disorder?   21

Q2. Why was manic depression renamed bipolar disorder?   22

Q3. What is the difference between Bipolar I, II and III?   23

Q4. What is cyclothymia?   24

Q5. Is there an age or gender profile for people with bipolar disorder?   24

Q6. What are the symptoms of bipolar disorder?   25

Q7. What is depression?   28

Q8. What is hypomania?   31

Q9. What is a manic episode?   32

Q10. What is psychosis?   35

Q11. What are the mixed features of bipolar disorder?   37

Q12. What are the less recognized symptoms of bipolar disorder?   38

Q13. Are the symptoms of bipolar disorder linked to the symptoms of seasonal affective disorder?   41

Q14. What is schizoaffective disorder?   43

Q15. What is borderline personality disorder?   43

Q16. What is the link between bipolar disorder and addiction?   45

Q17. What impact does bipolar disorder have on someone's physical health?   46

Q18. Can bipolar disorder cause thyroid problems?   48

Q19. What causes bipolar disorder?   48

Q20. Is there an increased risk of bipolar disorder for other family members?   50

Q21. Is it possible to have genetic testing for bipolar disorder?   52

Q22. Is it possible for a child to have bipolar disorder?   54

Q23. Are the symptoms of bipolar disorder different in children?   57

Q24. Is bipolar disorder ever diagnosed in older adults?   59

Q25. Why is bipolar disorder often misdiagnosed?   60

Q26. What can someone do if they think a loved one might have undiagnosed bipolar disorder?   63

Q27. How is bipolar disorder usually diagnosed?   64

Q28. What happens once a diagnosis of bipolar disorder is made?   67

CHAPTER TWO: TREATMENT   71

Q29. What is the most effective way to treat bipolar disorder?   71

Q30. Are there official treatment guidelines for bipolar disorder?   73

Q31. What is psychological treatment, such as cognitive behavioural therapy?   75

Q32. How can someone with bipolar disorder get psychological treatment?   84

Q33. What drugs are used in the treatment of bipolar disorder?   87

Q34. What does someone with bipolar disorder (or someone with a family history of bipolar disorder) need to know about antidepressants?   93

Q35. What new drugs are in the pipeline for bipolar disorder?   95

Q36. Does someone with bipolar disorder need to take medication for the rest of his or her life?   97

Q37. Will drugs encourage weight gain?   100

Q38. How can someone with bipolar self-manage their treatment?   102

Q39. What is electroconvulsive therapy?   104

Q40. What is repetitive transcranial magnetic stimulation?   107

Q41. How can the symptoms of seasonal affective disorder be effectively treated?   107

Q42. What is the best course of action if a child shows symptoms of bipolar disorder?   108

Q43. Does treatment need to be different for older people who have bipolar disorder?   111

Q44. What is an 'advance decision'?   112

CHAPTER THREE: SUPPORT

115

Q45. What professionals support someone with a bipolar diagnosis?   115

Q46. What is an advocate?   127

Q47. What role do family and friends play in the recovery of someone with a diagnosis of bipolar disorder?   128

Q48. On a practical level, how can family and friends help someone with a diagnosis of bipolar disorder?   131

Q49. On an emotional level, how can family and friends help someone with a diagnosis of bipolar disorder?   134

Q50. If someone with a bipolar diagnosis feels suicidal or is self-harming, what is the best course of action?   136

Q51. What is the best way for a loved one to cope during the really tough times?   144

Q52. What support do mental health charities offer?   149

CHAPTER FOUR: HOSPITAL CARE   152

Q53. What are psychiatric hospitals like?   152

Q54. What is an 'informal' patient in a psychiatric hospital?   160

Q55. What does it mean if somebody is sectioned?   160

Q56. Are there different types of sectioning procedures?   164

Q57. Can someone refuse to be sectioned?   166

Q58. What are a person's rights if they have been sectioned?   166

Q59. Who looks after patients in a psychiatric hospital?   168

Q60. What is a 'nearest relative'?   172

Q61. How can friends and family support a loved one in a psychiatric hospital?   173

Q62. How can friends and family forge a good relationship with those who care for their loved one in a psychiatric hospital?   176

Q63. Do psychiatric hospitals allow smoking?   178

Q64. What happens when a psychiatric patient is well enough to leave hospital?   179

Q65. What are the pros and cons of being treated in a psychiatric hospital?   181

CHAPTER FIVE: LIFESTYLE CHOICES 184

Q66. Can a healthy lifestyle lower the chance of relapse for someone with bipolar disorder and reduce the risk of developing it in the first place? 184

Q67. What is the link between stress and mood swings? 185

Q68. How can regular sleep patterns help to control symptoms of bipolar disorder? 187

Q69. How does exercise affect bipolar symptoms? 191

Q70. Can complementary therapies help control bipolar symptoms? 192

Q71. How can meditation and mindfulness help control bipolar symptoms? 196

Q72. What dietary changes can help control the symptoms of bipolar disorder? 198

Q73. What is the 'Mind Meal'? 204

Q74. Can nutritional supplements minimize the symptoms of bipolar disorder? 206

Q75. Can herbal remedies help control bipolar symptoms? 212

Q76. How does nicotine affect bipolar symptoms? 213

Q77. How does caffeine affect bipolar symptoms? 216

Q78. How does alcohol affect bipolar symptoms? 219

Q79. Can over-the-counter medications be harmful for someone with bipolar disorder? 222

Q80. Can prescription drugs taken for conditions other than bipolar disorder influence recovery? 223

Q81. How do recreational drugs affect those with a bipolar diagnosis? 223

CHAPTER SIX: LIVING WITH BIPOLAR   229

Q82. Is there still a stigma around bipolar disorder?   229

Q83. What is the best way to explain to a child that their parent
has been diagnosed with bipolar disorder?   235

Q84. Is a person with a bipolar diagnosis legally obliged to inform
their employer?   237

Q85. What is the most sensible way for a woman with bipolar
disorder to approach pregnancy?   242

Q86. What is the most sensible way for someone with bipolar
disorder to approach university life?   244

Q87. How can someone with bipolar manage their money?   247

Q88. What is a 'lasting power of attorney'?   248

Q89. What is the best way to make a complaint about any aspects
of care?   249

Q90. Where can somebody with a bipolar diagnosis get insurance?   251

Q91. Is it ever unsafe for someone with a bipolar diagnosis to drive?   252

Q92. What well-known people have/had bipolar disorder?   253

Q93. Can a diagnosis of bipolar disorder ever be a positive thing?   261

Q94. What does the future hold for bipolar disorder?   263

Extra resources   267

Glossary   281

Index   287

With thanks ...

This book would not have been possible without the amazing people who came forward to be interviewed about their personal experiences of living with bipolar disorder. We thank each and every one of you for your courage, eloquence and willingness to share your private experiences just because you wanted to help others who find themselves in the same boat ... We can't thank you all enough.

People we interviewed who have a diagnosis of bipolar:

- Amanda B
- Amy
- Ashley
- Carl
- Dave
- Debbie
- George
- Helen
- Jude
- Keith

- Lesley
- Marissa
- Neil
- Paul
- Rachel
- Reka
- Richard
- Sharron
- Sue
- Tamara

People we interviewed who love and/or look after someone with bipolar:

- Alison, mother
- Charlie, brother
- Doreen, daughter
- Gill, mother
- Ingrid, daughter
- Jackie, wife
- Jane, partner
- Jayne, daughter
- Jo, partner
- Juan, father
- June, mother
- Paula, ex-wife

Some of the people we interviewed asked us to change their names. We hope that one day in the near future, no one with mental illness in their life will feel they have anything to hide. Until that day, we have, of course, respected each individual's right to privacy.

We would also like to thank all the people who gave up some of their valuable time to share with us their expert knowledge and opinions, provide useful information and answer infinite questions. In alphabetical order, enormous thanks go to:

- Clare Armstrong, NHS Operations Manager in Ayrshire and Arran, Scotland
- Gillian Connor, Head of Policy and Development at Rethink Mental Illness
- Professor Nick Craddock, former head of the Cardiff University Psychiatry Service
- Professor Guy Goodwin, Senior Research Fellow, Department of Psychiatry, University of Oxford
- Ian Hulatt, Mental Health Advisor to the Royal College of Nursing for 13 years
- Professor Ian Jones, Professor of Psychiatry at Cardiff University and Director of the National Centre for Mental Health
- Professor Steven Jones, Professor of Clinical Psychology and Co-director of the Spectrum Centre for Mental Health Research at Lancaster University

- Terence Ketter, MD, Emeritus Professor of Psychiatry and Behavioral Sciences at the Stanford University School of Medicine
- Professor Peter Kinderman, Professor of Clinical Psychology at the University of Liverpool and honorary Consultant Clinical Psychologist with Mersey Care NHS Trust
- Simon Kitchen, Chief Executive Officer at Bipolar UK
- Juliet Mabey, co-owner of Oneworld Publications
- Dr Ian Maidment, Senior Lecturer in Clinical Pharmacy at Aston University
- Professor Richard Morriss, Professor of Psychiatry and Community Mental Health at Nottingham University
- Dr Michael Miller, Senior Editor for Mental Health Publishing at Harvard Health Publications
- Kay Redfield Jamison, Professor of Psychiatry and Behavioral Sciences at the Johns Hopkins School of Medicine, Maryland, and author of *An Unquiet Mind: A memoir of moods and madness*
- Martha Sajatovic, Professor of Psychiatry and Neurology at Case Western Reserve University School of Medicine, Cleveland
- Dr Arghya Sarkhel, Consultant Psychiatrist at Living Mind
- Michel Syrett, author and former editor of *Pendulum* magazine
- Dr Sara Tai, Senior Lecturer in Clinical Psychology at the University of Manchester and Consultant Clinical Psychologist at Cheadle Royal Hospital and Greater Manchester West Mental Health NHS Foundation Trust
- Professor Sir Graham Thornicroft, Consultant Psychiatrist for the South London and Maudsley NHS Foundation Trust and Director of the National Institute for Health Research
- Professor Mark Weiser, Chairman of the Department of Psychiatry at the Sackler School of Medicine in Israel
- Dr Jo Williams, general practitioner since 1992
- Professor Allan Young, Chair of Mood Disorders at King's College London and Director of the Centre for Affective Disorders, Department of Psychological Medicine at the Institute of Psychiatry

We would especially like to thank the hugely talented and supportive trio who agreed to write a foreword for the book, each representing a different viewpoint on bipolar:

- **Paul Abbott**, TV screenwriter, has written episodes of *Coronation Street* and *Cracker* and the dramas *State of Play, Clocking Off, Touching Evil, Linda Green, Shameless* and *No Offence*. He has won numerous BAFTAs and Royal Television Society awards, as well as an Emmy and the Writer's Guild of Great Britain Award. He revealed that he has bipolar disorder during a radio interview in 2007.
- **Jo Crocker** is sister and PA to actor, broadcaster, director and writer Stephen Fry. Stephen, who was diagnosed with bipolar in 1995, wrote in his autobiography *Moab Is My Washpot*, 'Jo runs my life more efficiently and more sweetly than is credible, and knows that were she not there I would be as a balsa twig in a tornado [...] My life could neither have been led nor written without her.'
- **Professor Steven Jones** completed his PhD and clinical training at the Institute of Psychiatry, and since 2008 has been Professor of Clinical Psychology at Lancaster University and Co-director of the Spectrum Centre for Mental Health Research. His research focuses on developing new interventions for people with bipolar and includes online self-management support and intensive face-to-face psychological therapy using CBT to encourage personal recovery. His professional life is dedicated to improving the lives of people with bipolar.

With more thanks ...

To our families, friends and all those who have given us both so much support over the years, we send our deepest thanks and love. We couldn't have written either the first or the second edition of this book without you.

AMANDA AND SARAH XX

A word from Paul Abbott

The first my family knew about me being a writer, or even wanting to be, was when they saw my photo in our local paper, aged 16, wielding the trophy I got that day for my story in the Lancashire Literature Festival competition. Their congratulations came instantly laced with discomfort and suspicion about me not being quite a full shilling, because I hadn't told a soul about this, nor, for that matter, much about myself at all for a good long while.

It wasn't uncommon for one Abbott or another to be splashed across the Court Report pages, to reactions of tormenting laughter at being so thick as to get caught at all! ... never mind the gimpish reputation it inflicted on the family name by making it into the bleedin' paper!

Being way down the pecking order in our big, chaotic family, I reckon I took up writing as a means of communicating without being contradicted. Truth being, I never consciously took up writing at all. I wanted nothing else but to be a surgeon in an outfit like Médecins Sans Frontières. The writing thing crept up silently and *it* found *me*, like a latent self-defence mechanism rallying to jumpstart its host, having detected early warnings for the jet-black, depressive tailspin that was heading for me like thunder.

This wasn't the first time I'd done something bizarre and unpredictable. The last event was attempted suicide and being sectioned at the age of 15. Somehow, winning a writing competition was more embarrassing and inexplicable than a suicide slam. This heralded the beginning of the end of my relationship with the wider orbit of my family.

I hadn't deliberately kept secrets from anyone. But I had no clear memory of doing this. I don't mean amnesia – I remembered the anxiety of writing that story and rewriting with a mission, knowing I needed higher than average quality to stand a hope in hell of succeeding, or face scorching humiliation if I bodged the job in public. I couldn't fail. Mustn't. So I won, which was great. But to this day I don't know what possessed me to seek out combat of any sort, never mind a scrap on this scale.

Years later when I found myself doing something equally bonkers and 'out of character' it dawned on me that I had a regular, cyclical pattern for doing stuff like this behind my own back, seemingly without my authorization – those 'I swear, it wasn't me!' periods.

Actually, it was. It was the same me I'm no longer ashamed to recognize, the me I have learned to feel proud of and take credit for, the one winning regular BAFTAs and gongs for outstanding achievement. Then lifetime achievement awards I've received for maintaining high standards in my work which, in turn, racks up the reputation of British drama in the outside world. I'm paraphrasing the prize-giving eulogies here, not trying to show off! Point being – nearly all those BAFTAs and various prizes for outstanding achievement came from material I wrote during periods of manic propulsion, vivid cycles of accelerated behaviour that I now, but only recently, have learnt to come to terms with being *the way I am*.

After 30-odd years of this, I've obviously grown a fairly hefty CV. These ordinarily get updated by your agent or a PA so I don't need to be involved, but when I did look at it properly for the first time, it was like a shrink's X-ray, a disappointingly predictable, graphic demonstration of my bipolar phases – some more volcanic than most, but in stark black and white print, revealing a correlation between my mood swing cycles and achievements. During my last manic cyclone, I created and produced not one but two full primetime drama series – *State of Play* and *Shameless* – in a 12-month period. Proud as I am of both those titles, output like that isn't just 'not quite normal', it's as barking and demented, and as riddled with potentially dangerous consequences, as it can get in this Non-Full-Shilling Club!

I can only describe these manic cycles as some kind of protracted convulsions that can last weeks, months or sometimes years before I get to stop for a breather, look back and check out what the fuck I've been up to *this* time. I can only dream of being as brave and clever as it might appear on the outside.

I am now able to do this with a bit more admiration for the results I produce, and with a better understanding that all of this stuff comes from me – well, parts of me that ultimately form a full shilling, eventually! You can't blame me for loving the volcanics as much as I do on occasions. They're always odd. Same here!

I was delighted to be asked by Amanda and Sarah to contribute a foreword to this book, *Bipolar Disorder – the Ultimate Guide*. I'm pretty sure they regretted this the day we first met in London. They arrived armed with a dozen questions for me, but never stood a chance of airing a single one of them. I talked non-stop for a good two hours, then waved them off. Only after they'd gone did I realize I didn't know what either of them actually sounded like! Well, they did ask!

This is the one book I wish I'd had in my pocket for each and every time when I've had to try describing myself and my oddness to anyone I love. It is quite possibly the most comprehensive and enabling guide I've come across to date, remarkably accessible, friendly and nourishing for anyone needing to know about people like me. Us.

A word from Jo Crocker

Jo who exactly? I hear you wonder – well, a fairly ordinary Jo, really, but I have an extraordinary brother. His name is Stephen Fry and in 1995 he was diagnosed with bipolar disorder. Some of you may be familiar with this. In 2006 he presented a two-part documentary, *The Secret Life of the Manic Depressive*, in which he told his story of diagnosis and understanding of the condition woven throughout the stories of both well-known and not so well-known sufferers of the illness and the impact of the condition on them and their loved ones. Each and every personal account was heartbreakingly moving.

I have been Stephen's Personal Assistant for 20 years. He often introduces me as his Personal Sister which, I think, neatly sums up our sibling and professional relationship, both of which fill me with pride. The impact of the documentaries was perhaps naively and massively unexpected by me in terms of the public reaction via letter, email, telephone calls, text and posts to the forum on his website. My very small part in the two films (a discussion of his dramatic exit of a West End play and brief few weeks missing abroad in 1995 that led to his eventual diagnosis) had in turn a huge impact on me and my understanding of what I had always subconsciously known was different about my brother. The impact of Stephen's disorder on our family and myself has been very real.

I was seven when I discovered my brother after he made his first suicide attempt. I remember the ambulance arriving, the family upset and finally, thankfully, Stephen returning home, stomach pumped and apparently restored. Stephen's story of his adolescent years and varied subsequent troubles is well documented, but looking back I can see that the impact of these testing times led to troubles of my own. The most trying on my parents must have been my phase of feigning illness at school so as to come home and demand attention from my poor mother, who had more than I could possibly realize to deal with and worry about at the time.

Much more positively it was during these years that I made up my mind to 'look after' Stephen, come what may, and of course I had no inkling that his spectacular career would allow me to fulfil this ambition to such great personal satisfaction.

His diagnosis allowed me to look back on the subsequent years of being in his close proximity assisting him (I shared his house in London in the late 1980s and early 1990s) and realize that I subconsciously and instinctively read his moods. I have to say, nothing hugely dramatic but the diary never lied about the enormous scale of personal and professional commitments he would undertake. I would, and still do, sternly point out when there is a full two weeks or more of engagements morning, noon and night. Most are unavoidable but some can be gently rearranged for a later and less fraught time ahead.

I particularly worried when he was away for long periods alone writing or filming and we were out of physical contact, especially because I knew he was 'self-medicating' in perhaps not the healthiest way (thankfully this is not the case now). I would find excuses to call him early in the morning with some daft reminder (that he was perfectly capable of remembering himself), just to check. Just to check...

Watching the documentaries, it was a shock to learn that the condition is hereditary and can strike at any age, perhaps as the result of certain stressful triggers – which finally, hurrah, brings me to talking about this wonderful book, written by two such warm and compassionate cousins as ever you could hope to meet, who both have close family members with bipolar disorder. Should I ever worry about myself or another close family member developing the condition, this book will answer any questions that I might have in the most friendly and uncomplicated style.

It really is *Bipolar Disorder – the Ultimate Guide* that stands as a unique and approachable reference book for those with the condition and their loved ones, who more often than not are their prime carers, who are most concerned for them and all aspects of their welfare.

So many of the truly remarkable letters from bipolar sufferers written to Stephen following the documentaries thanked him for 'being one of us', and those from their loved ones told movingly of how the programmes had helped them understand the condition more fully and got them talking openly about it for the first time. I thank Sarah and Amanda, Amanda and Sarah (they deserve equal billing) for writing this book for all of us who need to understand more about the illness and, armed and empowered with this knowledge, spread the word that bipolar disorder, indeed *any* mental illness, is not an embarrassment to be hidden behind closed doors.

Stephen answered the final question put to him in his film emphatically that he wouldn't change his condition 'not for all the tea in China'. I know how lucky I am that this is his response. I wouldn't change him either, not for all the Jimmy Choo handbags in the whole wide world. I hope Stephen will know, frivolous though it is, how much this truly means.

A word from Professor Steven Jones

I am a clinical psychologist by training and became interested in the early 1990s in exploring how people living with bipolar might be supported through psychological therapy. At that time, there were very limited treatment options and there was a high degree of professional scepticism about whether people living with bipolar could benefit from non-drug approaches. I recall one medical colleague asking me what the point was of offering talking therapy for bipolar disorder as people were either too acutely unwell to benefit from it, or between episodes and not in need of it. Gradually, I am pleased to say, this situation has improved, although there is still a long way to go.

Today there is much greater awareness of the complexity and variety of experiences among those living with bipolar disorder, during mania and depression and in the periods in between. It is now recognised that a range of talking therapies (e.g. psycho-education, cognitive behaviour therapy, behavioural family therapy) can be effective in reducing the risk of future episodes of mania and depression. In the UK the National Institute for Health and Care Excellence (NICE) specifically recommends that these approaches are offered to people with bipolar disorder. Furthermore, the UK Department of Health funded a 3-year national project on improving access to psychological therapies for people with bipolar, psychosis and personality disorders (IAPT-SMI). This demonstrated that it was possible to deliver effective psychological treatments as part of routine NHS care for bipolar disorder.

Recently there has been increasing interest in supporting personal recovery in bipolar disorder. This contrasts clinical recovery (absence of symptoms) with personal recovery (ability to live an engaged life with personal meaning). This approach highlights the importance of helping people living with bipolar to flourish rather than just exist, to harness their skills, talents and resilience to help themselves and those around them, but also contribute to the wider world. Not all people living with bipolar are talented artists, comedians or writers but there is an established link with creativity, which can manifest itself across all levels of the professions if people are given the necessary help, support and freedom.

When the first edition of this book was published in 2008, it became a core text for anyone living with or affected by bipolar. Amanda and Sarah provided, in a single volume, the tools for people to begin to navigate this most complex and challenging of conditions. This second edition continues to use a series of evidence-based lifestyle Q&As to help support people with bipolar in their personal recovery journeys.

A decade on, this updated second edition is just as useful as ever with its comprehensive mix of information, support and guidance imbued with great humanity and compassion.

INTRODUCTION

Is This Book for You?

If you've been diagnosed with bipolar disorder, there's no doubt that life has dealt you a challenging hand. When symptoms spiral out of control, living with this condition can be a complete and utter, seemingly never-ending nightmare – both for the person with bipolar disorder and for those who live with and love them.

If bipolar disorder is in your life, this book will be useful to you in three ways. First, it aims to answer all the questions – practical and emotional – that you will inevitably have. Second, it will offer hope because more has been discovered about bipolar disorder since the mid-1990s than was discovered in the 50 years before that. Also, there's increasing evidence to show that this sometimes debilitating condition can be kept under control with the right combination of psychological therapies, medication, support and lifestyle choices. However unpromising the outlook, it *is* possible to lead a healthy, happy life with a diagnosis of bipolar. Last, but definitely not least, this book will help end the stigma and feeling of shame that often come hand in hand with mental illness. There's no shame in breaking a leg or being diagnosed with asthma. Why the shame of bipolar? One day there will be none. This second edition of our book is yet another step closer towards that day.

We want to stress, though, that this book has not been written just for those with a diagnosis of bipolar disorder. It is equally intended for their family and friends – the network of those who care for loved ones with the condition. Bipolar has a huge ripple effect. If you're a mother, father, husband, wife, partner, sister, brother, son, daughter or close friend, you probably suffer in silence from the loss, the unpredictability, the helplessness, the loneliness, the ignorance of others, the shame and the fear. This book will help you offer them your love and support in the most helpful ways possible, without losing your own sanity in the process. And if you're a blood relative, it will also show you how to minimize your own risk of developing the illness.

The bottom line? This book is the emotional equivalent of a good friend who's just researched all there is to know about bipolar disorder. It's brimming with useful, practical advice gleaned from the very latest research and the wisest individuals (psychiatrists, psychologists, psychiatric nurses, pharmacists, therapists) on the planet who have devoted their lives to making bipolar easier to live with. And the book has many other voices too – people with bipolar, and relatives of those with bipolar. Not impersonal 'case histories' or 'studies', but real people, real voices, all speaking out to tell the world what it's *really* like to live with bipolar disorder, helping to dispel the ignorance that often surrounds the condition.

Amanda is a writer and editor, and Sarah is a health journalist, with over 45 years' professional experience between us. First cousins, we share three close relatives with bipolar disorder (Amanda's mother, and Sarah's sister and late father). It's probable our late grandfather had bipolar too.

This book is dedicated to anyone whose life has ever been touched by bipolar disorder.

Amanda's story

Our family's bipolar fault line reached my mum Irene when she was 51, but you can trace the roots of it deep into her past.

She doesn't talk much about her early childhood, but I've heard enough to know it was desperately unhappy. Impoverished too: she was born and brought up in the grimy heart of 1940s Birmingham, with its Victorian slums of back-to-back houses. But poverty wasn't the worst part. My mum and her younger brother Jim (Sarah's father) were physically and emotionally neglected by their parents. A few vivid and terrible details have filtered down to me – the children so starving they scavenged in bins, they walked barefoot to school, they were abandoned for hours outside pubs where their parents drank all evening. And when my mum was 12, the family broke down completely – their mother walked out to start a new life with someone else, and then their father, struggling to cope, left them too.

My mum's teenage years were spent in care: first in a children's home, then with foster parents. She was separated from Jim, who was fostered with an aunt, and their father disappeared from her life altogether. And although they still lived in the same city, and would do for the next 20-odd years, my mum never saw her own mother again, even though Mum wrote letters begging her to visit. So she was all alone in the world – until a cold and rainy January evening, when (aged 16) my mother went to the Co-op youth club and first met my father, Gordon. She's described how, as she hovered uncertainly in the doorway and saw the handsome, dark-haired 19-year-old glance up from the pool table, it was as if her life only began at that moment. In fact I can't picture my mother's face before then – I've never seen photos of her as a child. Maybe they're lost, or maybe none were taken. In the earliest one I have, she's perched on my dad's lap at a New Year's Eve party, smiling up at the camera, a new engagement ring sparkling on her hand clasped in his. When they married at Birmingham Registry Office in 1961, my mum just 18 years old, she was welcomed into my dad's loving family, and her rescue from the past seemed, at the time, to be complete.

My brother Andrew was born in 1963, and I followed in 1965. We grew up in a neat semi-detached house in Sutton Coldfield, a quiet suburb of Birmingham, and I guess we fitted the description of an average suburban family – two hard-working parents (Dad at a printing company, Mum in a department store), two kids at local state schools, a fortnight in a traditional English seaside town every summer (never 'abroad'). To us, our family just appeared to be like everyone else's on our leafy road – happy but ordinary. But to my mum, after the chaotic unhappiness of her own childhood, our cosy life must have seemed utterly extraordinary and wonderful. Of course I didn't realize any of this at the time, but when I think of the model of parenthood she'd been given, our 'normal' upbringing appears nothing short of a miracle.

Did Mum show early bipolar symptoms during my childhood? I've tried hard to recall any mood swings or erratic behaviour, but none come to mind. When I look back, I can only see a confident woman, always smartly dressed, handling the complex logistics of family life with infinite care and organization. But bipolar disorder did flash up on our family's radar when I was still at school and my mum's younger brother Jim returned to Birmingham from Kent. He was already ill, and spent most of his time in a psychiatric hospital, where my mother would visit him every week (until his death in 1987). She drove him back to our house for tea a couple of times, which as an insensitive teenager I resented because she would be so upset afterwards. Also I was afraid: partly because no one ever discussed Jim's illness with my brother and me (or even gave it a name), but also because I could sense my mum was afraid too. 'If your Uncle Jim ever turns up here when you're alone,' she would say to me over and over again, 'don't let him in. Just tell him you have to go out.' It's so sad to think that she was frightened of her own brother, or his illness – and it planted an unwarranted fear and stigma about him in my mind. I wonder now if she was also afraid of developing bipolar disorder herself.

If so, then her fears were realized in 1993 when she was 51 – triggered by hormone changes during her menopause. During that spring and summer, my mum's familiar, loving personality flipped. She became suspicious, despairing and irrational, accusing my poor bewildered dad of having affairs and plotting to leave her, and finding hidden meaning in every irrelevant detail – the whole world, she declared, was whispering about her. In October, Mum was diagnosed with a depressive 'breakdown' and for a couple of weeks was admitted as a voluntary patient to a psychiatric unit. She was prescribed antidepressants, which initially seemed to work, so she came back home, quiet but stable. But within weeks her mood shifted again – at first we thought it was only the depression lifting, but she swung upwards even further, not just happy now but euphoric, rapidly shedding her inhibitions and culminating in a full-blown manic episode.

At the time, I was living and working in Bristol, 100 miles away. Mum had sounded agitated on the phone, so I drove up to Birmingham for a flying visit one November day, when Dad was still at work. As soon as I arrived at their house, she began to unravel right in front of me. She flung her clothes, jewellery, shoes, family photos, all her most personal possessions, out of the bedroom window, then ran downstairs to hurl herself repeatedly against the living room walls, shouting that the IRA were coming to kill us. I tried to grab her arms and stop her, but she fought back, and I remember looking into her eyes, and realizing she didn't recognize me as her daughter. One of her close friends rang in the middle of this – 'I'm brilliant, I'm feeling bloody brilliant!' my mum yelled down the phone before throwing it at me. Her GP turned up, but by then she was far beyond his help. She took him hostage in a bedroom, and in a ghastly parody of her engagement picture, sat on his lap and tried to kiss him. That evening, Mum was sectioned. My dad, my brother and I watched helplessly as she was carried out shrieking, and driven away to be held down and medicated.

Eventually, after weeks of treatment, my mum came home – but normality never really has. For the last 20 or so years, she has swallowed a daily cocktail of drugs, including lithium, with partial success: the mania is largely kept at bay, but the depression (mixed with agitation) is not. When she sinks into this mixed state, she becomes depressed, irrational and paranoid, and her typical behaviour pattern is then to refuse all her medication. Sometimes she says she's dying of some mystery disease, so the drugs are useless. At other times she believes the drugs are laced with poison because the doctors want to kill her. 'It's too late,' she says over and over again. 'It's too late for me.' And then she'll spend days and nights pacing the house, crying, unable to rest or sleep, eat or drink, and fixated on her imminent death.

Stopping the medication so abruptly only worsens her fractured mental state – she has tried to kill herself twice and she's been sectioned back into her local psychiatric unit 13 or 14 times (we've lost track) over the years. Even when Dad knows that sometimes hospital is the best place for Mum (and as years have passed, he has come to accept this), he dreads it because he misses her so much. He can't bear to go upstairs to bed, because she's not there – he'll just crash out on the sofa, with the TV blaring away for company, filling the silence of their house. The first few days are especially rough for them both. At first, as she struggles with her mood swings, she's often hostile and says hurtful things or orders him to leave. But he still visits her every day. He spends hours just sitting quietly with her, as close as she'll allow him, waiting for the bipolar cloud to lift from her mind, however long that takes.

Sometimes Dad opens up and talks to me about how he feels, but then he'll stop himself and shake his head angrily and say, 'I shouldn't feel so sorry for myself ... I have no right, I'm not the one who's ill – I'm not in hospital, am I?' He finds it hard to accept that his feelings are valid and that he does have the right to think about himself. I have tried to get him to understand that there is no league table of suffering where he is somehow 'not allowed' to think of his own needs. The impact of bipolar is huge on carers too. Both my parents live with enormous tension, always wondering what each day will bring. It can start well, but no one knows how it will end. One Christmas a few years ago, we spent a great morning around my dining table, playing daft board games with my children: Mum was laughing, the kids were laughing, we were all happy. Twelve hours later, her mood had swung into the familiar drug-refusing depression and agitation, and my brother and I were struggling with her on my driveway, trying to 'persuade' her into my dad's car so he could drive her back home to the care of her psychiatric team in Birmingham, who know Mum so well. Even after all these years, as we fought to close the car door so that Dad (tears streaming down his face as he pleaded with her) could lock it and drive away, we were still shocked at the speed of her mood change.

And as she's grown older, the frequency of her episodes has accelerated, until really there is no defined beginning or end, just a blurred spectrum of 'bad days' or 'better days'. She is now permanently unwell, or what might be called (on a good day) a fragile 'managed well'. The decades of mixed state symptoms in particular have taken their toll, sapping her confidence and her cognitive abilities. Fearful of the outside world (getting her out of the house is a major event), she now has symptoms of early onset dementia too – identified by research as a common comorbidity bedfellow for people with bipolar as they age. So she is forgetful and easily confused, struggles with balance and coordination, and finds it hard to follow conversations – my once talkative, gregarious, confident mum. It's said that grieving for the living is often harder than grieving for the dead. My family feels the sting of this sad truth every day.

I have been totally honest with my three children about bipolar disorder. They've heard all about their grandma's illness (and other family diagnoses too), what the symptoms are, and why she sometimes goes to hospital. It has become the everyday wallpaper of our family – it's just a physical fact, like the dark hair and eyes running in our genes. And they're completely cool about it. The great thing about telling kids is that their generation hasn't absorbed all the old stereotypes about mental illness – as far as they're concerned, the brain is just a physical organ that can 'get sick', like any other part of the body. They don't see a stigma. How fantastic it would be if the rest of the world felt the same.

Talking about bipolar disorder, and bringing it into the open, is one of the best forms of protection I can offer my children, who need to understand how to lessen their risk in our family's bipolar lottery. If we collude with the old taboos surrounding mental illness, how can we treat it effectively, and protect ourselves and those we love?

Sarah's story

My late father Jim was born in 1945 and grew up in Birmingham in extreme poverty. The only word I can use to describe his parents is 'dysfunctional' – Amanda has described what little we know about his and his sister Irene's neglected childhoods. Dad was a 'Barnardos boy' for a while before being fostered by an aunt, although he never talked about his early years. He trained to be a chef and then married my mum in 1969. They moved from London to the Kent coast and had two daughters – me in 1971 and my sister Rebecca in 1974. Sadly the marriage began to break down and, with hindsight, that was probably the catalyst for his first manic episode and later diagnosis of bipolar (or manic depression as it was then called). Dad was working as a chef on a passenger ferry at the time and, years later, I discovered that he lost touch with reality in Germany, convinced he was a spy for the English government.

He was brought back home and all I can remember before he moved back to Birmingham months later are a few snippets of the effect the illness had on our family. At the age of six or seven, I came downstairs in the middle of the night to find a doctor sedating my obviously distressed father in our dining room. My mum hurried me back to bed, explaining that 'Daddy isn't feeling very well'. Another time, I remember him losing his temper and punching a hole in the dining room wall – my mother lifted my sister and me over the fence into our neighbours' garden. I wasn't frightened because his anger wasn't directed at anyone in particular and because there wasn't any obvious build-up to the outburst. One minute he was in his normal calm mood, the next minute he was shouting out and punching a wall. All I can recall about the aftermath of the event is being excited at the prospect of seeing the inside of the neighbours' house for the first time! By the time my sister and I were taken home, everything was back to 'normal' and the incident was never mentioned again. In the summer of 1978, Dad had a few days off work and decided to organize a jumble sale in our front garden in aid of the Save the Children Fund. Mum was working at the time. He made hundreds of posters and we plastered them all over town. The next day, we set up several big tables in the front garden. Dad was so excited, infecting my sister and me with the feeling that something really amazing was about to happen. The trouble was we only had a few tatty old things to sell – two or three pieces of old crockery, a few old books and some half-used balls of wool. We spread them out over the tables, although Dad kept re-arranging them. I'll never forget the ear-burning shame I felt when I heard two ladies from down our road laughing at him. Another thing I remember was that he had a pair of the brightest blue and red shoes – sort of casual trainers, a bit like bowling shoes. He loved them, but my mum absolutely hated them, naming them his 'Joey' shoes after Joey the kangaroo. She did have a point ... They made his feet look enormous and looked ridiculous poking out from under seventies brown flares. Looking back, I suspect they were a symbol of his manic frame of mind.

My parents finally divorced, and Rebecca and I would speak to Dad once a week on the phone and visit him once or twice a year in a psychiatric hospital in Birmingham – it couldn't be more often because we didn't own a car and the train was expensive. The memories from those visits are indelible in my mind: a smoke-filled pool room; the smell of urine; horrible strong tea in Styrofoam cups; Dad wearing his pyjamas, stepping from side to side because of the medication he was on; squirrels climbing trees in the hospital grounds; Dad's friend Malcolm who thought he was Jesus; Dad's comfort items on a table – a transparent plastic lighter and a green packet of Wrigley's spearmint gum side by side on top of a black packet of JPS Superkings. Rebecca and I would clamour to sit on his knee in the common room or hold his hand as we walked around the hospital grounds. He was our dad and we loved him. I didn't think any of this was particularly strange. This was my normality. You don't question things as a child, you just accept them.

In December 1987 my dad was walking down a road in Birmingham and was tragically knocked down by a drunk driver. He died the day before my sixteenth birthday. Since then I've mourned the years his premature death stole and I'm still mourning the years his illness stole. I can hardly remember my dad as a well man. It took me a long time and a lot of tears to get to this point, but now it gives me a lot of comfort to imagine how happy he must have been walking my mother down the aisle and holding his two new baby daughters in his arms. I can picture him teaching me how to ride a bike and sharing with me his love of word puzzles. I can conjure up an image of the two of us making cheese straws, and another time fish cakes, together. I can remember him cheering and thumping the living room floor with joy when Ipswich won the FA Cup in 1978. Of course his neglected childhood and diagnosis of 'manic depression' as it was then called had a huge impact on him, but he did know happiness, as well as immense sorrow, in his life and I give thanks for the happy memories I have.

My sister Rebecca was diagnosed with bipolar disorder at the age of 22 – the catalyst for her first manic episode was, believe it or not, my wedding.

We later discovered that an overwhelmingly happy event is often a trigger. There I was soaking up the Jamaican sun on honeymoon while my mother had doctors, social workers and policewomen round the house one evening, trying to persuade my psychotic sister to get into an ambulance to transport her to a psychiatric ward. I'll never forget visiting her for the first time in hospital. Rebecca had aged ten years in two weeks. I found it hard to reconcile the beautiful bridesmaid in my wedding photos with this girl – her skin pale, her eyes sunken and vacant, her fingers trembling as she tried to light a cigarette. How guilty I felt – and sometimes still feel – that I was the one fate had spared ...

With hindsight, Rebecca had symptoms of bipolar disorder long before the official diagnosis. She was one of those children who always seemed to be getting into scrapes. She had obsessive tendencies – spending literally hours listening to the same pop records over and over again. She had a volatile temper. At school, she was labelled 'trouble' and left without a single qualification, even though she's very bright. My mum asked our GP if Rebecca could have the same condition as her father, but he said categorically that, no, manic depression wasn't hereditary. Yet things got progressively worse. The summer after our father's death, at the age of 13, she started bunking off school, drinking and smoking. She had relationships with a string of unsuitable boyfriends. She was brought home by the police for being drunk and disorderly more than once. At the time, perhaps not surprisingly, we all thought that her unruly behaviour was an expression of grief. She found it extremely difficult to cry about Dad's death, bottling up everything. Mum was at her wits' end. Rebecca was on a path of self-destruction and it seemed there was nothing anyone who loved her could do about it.

The year before Rebecca's first breakdown, fate dealt her two enormous blows. Her 19-year-old cat died. And then our nan, our mum's mum, to whom Rebecca had always been very close, died from a stroke while Rebecca was at her side. At the time, Rebecca was working 100 miles from home, only returning for occasional visits and then for my hen party and wedding, which, it seems, turned out to be the final straw in her stress load.

In one way, the diagnosis brought relief because it helped to explain why Rebecca's life had been so turbulent. Yet naming the problem didn't really make the journey any easier. Since her diagnosis, I have witnessed my sister go to the depths of hell and back again several times. She has been sectioned several times and has made various suicide attempts (taking different combinations of pills and once throwing herself in front of a car). It seems like she's tried one hundred and one different types of medication with varying success. She's been psychotic, paranoid and as low as you can go – one winter she found it hard to get out of bed for weeks at a time. She spent almost a year in a secure unit where she wasn't allowed in the garden or to have a cup of tea without permission; that was where we 'celebrated' her thirtieth birthday. My mum brought in a party tea and we laid it out on the pool table. I don't think I've ever felt as desperately sad in my entire life as I did while standing in that psychiatric common room eating Twiglets.

I have always loved my sister. She knows that. But the hours and hours of research, interviewing experts, reading books, talking to people touched by bipolar and immersing myself in the bipolar world, helped me understand her better. As I've delved further into the subject, I've understood more and more how huge the struggles are she's had to face; how hard her life really has been. In the past, I've envied sisters sharing secrets over lunch in restaurants and mourned the absence (both emotional and physical when she's in hospital) of mine. During the rough patches, she can be there, but not really there, and that makes me feel so sad and empty. I feel like I've lost her to the illness, that I'm grieving for her. I just miss her so much. I think that's why I've always felt so frustrated at the fact that she goes to the pub sometimes to drown her sorrows and blot out reality. I used to think – why can't she live a healthy life and then it's more likely she'll stay well? But now that I understand a bit more, I'm asking, how the hell has she survived through so much without drinking herself into oblivion?

There's no denying that bipolar disorder has cast a huge shadow over Rebecca's life. She's had to stop work – her job in a travel agency proved to be too stressful. Her relationships have never been straightforward or stable. But as she's got older, her entire attitude towards her own well-being has changed. She's accepted that she does have a condition that needs careful controlling. She knows she can't party every night of the week and deprive herself of sleep without suffering the consequences. She turns down invitations or requests because she knows she has to put herself first rather than say yes to please. She no longer forgets to take her medication. In other words, she's now taking more responsibility for her own mental health.

In a logical sequence of events, I suppose, I've come to admire my sister. I admire how she copes with Christmas family get-togethers when all she really wants to do is hide under the duvet. I admire how generous and loving she is to my three sons when all she really wants is to have children of her own, but at 44 knows that's pretty unlikely – especially as she hasn't yet found the right relationship. I admire how she's managed to pick herself up after a dark, dark depression more than once. I admire how she has (reluctantly sometimes, I admit) come back down to earth after one of her incredible highs. I admire how she gets back up time and time again after being floored by this sometimes devastating illness.

I cannot tell you how much impact bipolar disorder has had on my mother Rose's life. Not only did she lose her husband to 'manic depression' nearly 40 years ago, she has been my sister's main carer far beyond the 18 years of official childhood. My mum is there for my sister 24/7. On a practical level, Mum does Rebecca's washing and cooking. Yet from what Mum tells me, it's not the practical side of being a carer that she finds challenging, it's the emotional toll. Mum's the one who mood monitors and calls the psychiatric nurse if Rebecca's having a wobble. She's the one who can't relax if Rebecca's mobile phone is switched off for an afternoon, who phones the ambulance after a suicide attempt. And during the rough patches, my mum experiences guilt, frustration, helplessness, sorrow and exhaustion in equal measure. There is no love like the love a mother feels for her child. My mother is unequivocal proof of that.

I can't remember a time in my life when bipolar disorder hasn't caused my family pain. By writing this book, and its second edition ten years on, Amanda and I hope to turn those decades of pain into something infinitely more positive.

Amanda and Sarah's journey

Because of the geographic distance between us (Amanda in Birmingham and Sarah in Kent), we saw each other very rarely when we were growing up, and the six years' age difference seemed wider too. We last met as children when Amanda was 13 and Sarah was 7, and both of us have happy memories of building a snowman together in Sarah's back garden.

Sarah saw Amanda's parents Irene and Gordon at her dad's funeral, although Amanda was away at university. After that, our only link was the exchange of Christmas cards between Sarah's mum and Amanda's parents.

Fast-forward almost 20 years, and Amanda's mum casually mentioned to Amanda (by now married with children) that Sarah and her husband had just had a baby boy. Husband? Baby? What had happened to the blonde seven-year-old cousin? On impulse, Amanda wrote a letter to Sarah, and a few days later, when Sarah phoned, the years and distance fell away. We clicked immediately.

The added dimension to this new friendship was discovering our shared experience of bipolar disorder. Amanda knew nothing about Rebecca's illness, and hadn't realized that her Uncle Jim's mystery illness from her childhood had been the same as her mum's. Sarah knew that Irene had been 'unwell' but didn't know it was bipolar. It was a shock to realize that three of our close relatives had all developed bipolar, but ultimately, the realization helped, knowing that our similar experiences could be a source of mutual support. Ever since that first phone conversation, whenever Irene or Rebecca goes through an unstable patch we talk a lot on the phone. It is such a relief to be able to talk to somebody who *really* understands.

So although officially the journey of the first edition of this book started in October 2006 – when Amanda's mum had just been sectioned again, and Stephen Fry's brilliant two-part documentary *The Secret Life of the Manic Depressive* was aired on BBC1 – the journey really began when we reconnected in 1999.

When we wrote the first edition it was for our relatives with bipolar (and those who care for them). But through talking to experts, we came to understand that genetics play a much bigger part in bipolar disorder than we realized and the purpose of the book evolved. We began to write it for ourselves. Before we began the research, we had neatly cordoned off our relatives into a bipolar box. In our minds, we had always blamed Irene and Jim's upbringing as the main reason why they both developed bipolar disorder. The early environment they had shared seemed the obvious culprit. Then, the divorce of Rebecca's parents, the death of her dad when she was 13 and the grief she found impossible to express, seemed to confirm this view – Rebecca must have developed bipolar because of a difficult childhood, we thought. But, whilst their childhood experience was probably a factor, we began to see it was only one part of their bipolar profile. We discovered that Irene's and Jim's father – our grandfather – who had bouts of mental illness, probably had bipolar too. In fact, his alcohol addiction was most likely a form of self-medication.

Yes, challenging events in their lives probably did nudge them further along the road to bipolar, but genetics played a huge part too. And this new-found knowledge opened our eyes to the fact that we were also writing the book for our wonderful children: Amanda's Ben, Hannah and Will, and Sarah's Harry, Jonah and Luke. We realized our family history meant our children had a greater risk of developing the condition than any old Joe Bloggs who doesn't have a relative with bipolar in sight. Yet, far from filling us with fear and foreboding, arming ourselves with information on their behalf was an empowering experience. We saw that it's possible to live a happy and fulfilling life with a diagnosis of bipolar. With the right combination of medication, psychological therapies, support and lifestyle choices, we saw that the negative impact of bipolar disorder on a life is much smaller than once thought possible.

Writing the first edition of the book helped us see that stress alone, genetics alone, or both stress and genetics can lead to mental illness and we saw clearly there wasn't a big brick wall dividing and protecting us from the possibility of bipolar. We saw that anybody, yes, *anybody* can be touched by it. To reflect the reality that 'mental illness does not discriminate', we spoke to men, women, young, old, rich, poor, teachers, cleaners, students, partners, mothers, fathers, sons, daughters. People just like you and us. Nobody is immune. There is no bipolar wall. There is no 'them and us', only 'all of us'. Rebecca was diagnosed with bipolar at 22, Jim at 32, Irene at 51. It can strike at any time.

Ten years ago, we said: 'If bipolar comes knocking on our family's door again, we're certainly not saying it will be easy, but we will seek help and support from all available sources and rise to the challenge in the wisest way possible. As far as feeling ashamed is concerned, we genuinely would feel no more shame than if one of us had hay fever. We passionately hope that everyone around us would feel the same. Bipolar disorder will never be a dark shameful secret in our houses – we will talk about it openly and trust that others will follow our lead. And at least we'll have this book – the book we wish we'd had sitting on our bedside tables when Jim, Irene and Rebecca were diagnosed with bipolar all those years ago... '

Not one word of what we said then has changed.

So what *has* changed?

In the decade or so since we wrote the first edition of this book:

1. BIPOLAR DISORDER HAS BEEN ON SCREEN A LOT

Loads of different characters spring to mind, including Pat in the Oscar-winning film *Silver Linings Playbook* and CIA agent Carrie in the award-winning TV drama *Homeland*. And don't forget Tony in *The Sopranos*, Ian in *Shameless*, Sonny in *General Hospital*, Andre in *Empire*, Maria in *Lady Dynamite* and Marlo in *Rookie Blue*. In Canada, there are Craig and Eli in *Degrassi: The Next Generation*. In the UK, there are TV soap characters Jean and Stacey in *Eastenders* and Gina in *Coronation Street*.

In the States, there's even an annual awards evening (the PRISM Awards) set up to applaud creators who use their power and influence over their audiences to show accurate stories involving substance abuse and mental illness. They want to encourage programme makers to inform and entertain. They call it 'the art of making a difference'.

Opinions are divided about whether this proliferation of characters with mental illness is a good thing. For instance, some viewers praise *Homeland* writers for the realistic portrayal of Carrie's symptoms, while others think the storylines sensationalize the illness for the sake of melodrama. Research shows that most people form their ideas about mental illness based on what they see in mass media, and that television is especially influential. So do all these characters help to promote understanding about bipolar or do they reinforce damaging stereotypes?

It's impossible to generalize because accuracy is so variable from scene to scene and from show to show. Overall, however, we think there's a definite trend towards more three-dimensional characters. And if, at the very least, the storylines get a conversation going, we reckon that's a positive step forward in normalizing mental illness.

2. THE STIGMA SURROUNDING MENTAL ILLNESS IS LIFTING

Although the stigma surrounding mental illness still very much exists, more celebrities than ever – the likes of actor Dwayne 'The Rock' Johnson, writer J.K. Rowling, actor Kristen Bell, former political aide Alastair Campbell, TV host Ellen DeGeneres and Princes William and Harry – have been talking about their struggles. The other noticeable big difference is the increasing number of anti-stigma campaigns – there's more information about these in question 82, p. 229.

We think both of these factors are helping to show the general public that mental illness doesn't discriminate, that it can happen to absolutely anyone. It also helps people who have been diagnosed realize they're not alone.

While there's a long way to go before society views and treats physical and mental illness in the same way, the gap is closing. The statistics are pretty clear – the stigma is lifting. It's lifting slowly, but lifting nevertheless.

3. WE'RE ALL USING THE INTERNET MUCH MORE

The internet was around ten years ago, of course, but there's been a dramatic increase in the way we use it. Most of us go online daily now and we use the internet in all sorts of ways to support our mental health:

- we look for answers to questions – research shows almost three-quarters of American adults use the internet to search online for health information each year
- we connect with people going through similar experiences – as well as hosting websites and having social media profiles, many mental health charities run a moderated forum or community where people can share ideas and experiences in a safe online space
- we buy books online or download books electronically rather than go to a bookshop – so access is easier than ever.

And while some research shows that the overuse of social media can sometimes trigger or exacerbate bipolar symptoms (especially during a manic phase), on balance we think the access to information and support can be a positive mechanism for recovery and a lifeline for people who feel lonely with their experiences.

4. TREATMENT IS MORE 'HOLISTIC'

Frustratingly, someone with bipolar is diagnosed and treated in more or less the same way as they were ten years ago. The process for reaching a diagnosis is the same. The medication is the same. If only we could write about a 'groundbreaking new test for bipolar' or the 'exciting new treatments for bipolar' available now! Sigh. Maybe in the next update? Let's hope so, especially as there are some promising new treatments on the horizon – for more information about these, see question 35, p. 95.

In the meantime, at least it seems like we're moving even further away from the 'medical model' of the 1970s and 1980s, where people with a mental illness were given medication and nothing else. Guidelines now strongly recommend that someone diagnosed with bipolar is treated with a three-pronged approach – medication, psychological support and social support. Although healthcare professional attitudes can still be old-fashioned and resources can be locally variable (to say the least), from our experiences with our family there's definitely a positive shift towards a more rounded package of care.

And what's changed closer to home?

AMANDA'S UPDATE

When we wrote the first edition of this book, Sarah mentioned her six-month period of mild postnatal depression. I, on the other hand, had experienced nothing more than two brief episodes of stress, which I'd shaken off without the need for either therapy or drugs. So I felt very fortunate (and perhaps even a little smug) that I had escaped the grasp of our family's genetic fault line.

I was wrong. Four years ago, those lurking genes were kick-started by personal trauma, workplace stress and a heap of related issues, and a long bout of mental illness toppled my world.

Insight can be one of the first casualties of depression. Your senses gradually dull as the fog creeps in and swallows your self-awareness. So despite witnessing my mum's depressive episodes so many times, it took me several months to realize what was happening. I dragged myself to my GP but it was already too late to stop it, and I sank even deeper. Below are fragments from the journal I tried to keep at the time:

It has come for me. I didn't spot the cloudy-eyed stranger sidling up to me, slipping a blanket over my head. So slyly done ... Depression is a tricksy bastard. I have been caught unawares, smothered by degrees, by stealth. I'm invaded. It's taken over my personality, thoughts, behaviours, everything. I do not exist as me.

Mornings are the worst. I hate opening my eyes. It hurts so much. Moving my body is like dragging a dead horse through sand ... The pain overwhelms me, crashing through me in black waves. When it peaks, I can feel a stone throbbing hard inside my chest, expanding, pulsing relentlessly, until I think it will punch a hole in my lungs. This morning I lay on my bedroom floor, face down, eyes clenched, breathing into the carpet, until the pain receded a bit. It took hours.

And as my depression deepened, mood swings and agitation (which I later realized were already scratching at the door) shifted and accelerated. It was like despair on speed:

 I get in my car and drive and drive and drive. As if I can outrun the pain. Or outrun myself. Or lose myself completely. Today I spotted lots of friendly-looking trees and ditches, then looked at my hands on the steering wheel, and thought how easy it would be to just spin it sideways. Not that I want to die. I just want to make the pain stop.

I'm fuelled by a burning, impulsive energy. I've done some reckless things in this frame of mind – way out-of-character, paranoid, risky – without being able to stop myself. I'm drifting in and out, in and out, in and out, of self-awareness. I don't entirely trust what I may do or say next ...

A psychiatrist's diagnosis of cyclothymia (see question 4, p. 24) was inevitable, given my family history, and also a relief. It was the first thing that had made sense in a long time. By this point, I was so ill I'd been signed off sick from work and was a daily outpatient at a local psychiatric unit, undergoing months of intensive cognitive behavioural therapy (CBT) sessions, group counselling and drug therapy. It's a jumble of memories now, but this treatment package (which I know I was very lucky to have) eventually worked. My depression began to lift, just as the mood swings and agitation gradually subsided to a murmur. I stopped noticing friendly trees. I stumbled back to reclaim my life.

There is a much, much longer story about the lead-up to and aftermath of this episode in my life – but it belongs elsewhere, in another book. How am I now, as I co-write our second edition? I'm well and working full time in central London, doing a job I love. I have avoided any relapses and my mood is stable. Even though I still regularly drive past the hospital where I was treated, it's fair to say I've travelled some distance from it, and from that dark period four years ago.

But I am forever changed by it. One positive is that I've developed a much deeper understanding of mental illness. After more than 20 years since my mum's and my cousin Rebecca's bipolar diagnoses, as well as co-writing this book and supporting friends with depression, I had felt well informed about mental illness, for a non-medical person. But just as antenatal classes can't prepare you for the visceral reality of childbirth, nothing prepared me for the impact of depression and mood disorder every single hour of every day. As my journal recounts, the physical effect was savage – my whole body, not just my mind, was battered by my breakdown.

This experience has of course added new insight to writing the book's second edition. You could say I've been out doing (very) personal fieldwork.

And mental illness leaves a watermark, even when its waves have receded. Vulnerability lies just under my skin, like a bruise. I guess it's a little like being a recovering alcoholic, and so when I say I'm 'well', I mean I'm 'currently well'. I try to stay balanced with the twin support of regular psychotherapy and a low dose of daily medication – just to mute the cyclothymic demons and keep them at bay. Alcohol is not my friend, not even in small amounts, and so I now avoid it altogether. Sleep, on the other hand, most definitely is, and my years of proclaiming I only need five hours a night are over. My current job is busy, enjoyable but sometimes stressful, with multiple priorities to juggle, so I pace myself, delegate and try not to over-promise my time.

It's now hard to imagine that four years ago I was lying in the gardens of a suburban psychiatric unit, sobbing into the weeds. To prevent a rerun, and stay as 'currently well' as I can, I've made life changes. I owe it to myself and those who love me, to value myself more and do everything I can to avoid sliding into full-blown bipolar. So far, it's working. I'll never be a completely calm person (ask my kids) but right now my cyclothymia remains a manageable background murmur.

In other words, I have learnt to live by the book. Our book.

CHAPTER ONE

Causes, Symptoms and Diagnosis

Q1. *What is bipolar disorder?*

Bipolar disorder is a serious mental illness that's thought to be caused by an imbalance in the way brain cells communicate with each other. This imbalance causes extreme mood swings that go way beyond the normal 'ups and downs' of everyday life, wildly exaggerating the mood changes that everyone has. Someone with bipolar can have long or short periods of stability, but then tends to go 'low' (into deep depression) or 'high' (experiencing mania or psychosis). They can go into a 'mixed state' too, where symptoms of depression and mania occur at the same time.

According to a World Mental Health survey by the World Health Organization (WHO), bipolar disorder affects a total of 2.4% of the world's population. The survey found that the US has the highest rate of bipolar spectrum disorders (4.4%), while India has the lowest rate (0.1%). In the UK, the mental health charity Bipolar UK estimates that 1% to 2% of the country's population experience a lifetime prevalence of bipolar disorder.

Q2. *Why was manic depression renamed bipolar disorder?*

'Bipolar disorder' has now replaced 'manic depression' as the official name for this condition. The term 'manic depression' was first coined in 1896 by Emil Kraepelin, a German doctor, and was widely used in the psychiatric world throughout the twentieth century, until the American Psychiatric Association renamed it in 1980 as 'bipolar disorder' – to reflect what it called the 'bi-polarity', or dual nature, of the illness (the highs and lows).

> I prefer the term 'bipolar' to 'manic depression' as bipolar sounds more medical and less scary. Manic depression seems to carry an undeserved stigma. I was speaking to someone I used to work with when I said my daughter had bipolar – she asked what that meant and I was able to explain. On a separate occasion that same day, I used the term 'manic depressive' to see if that was understood, and the reaction I received was of shock.
>
> *(ALISON)*

However, not everyone is as enthusiastic, including actor and writer Stephen Fry who presented two BBC documentaries about bipolar disorder in 2006 – *The Secret Life of the Manic Depressive* – in which he openly talked about his own bipolarity. In the foreword to the book *You Don't Have to be Famous to Have Manic Depression*, which was published at the same time, he comments:

> Bipolar isn't quite right – the condition isn't really just about two poles, there are mixed states in between. Besides, why not give it a title that names the effects?

Another writer with a bipolar diagnosis, Julie A. Fast, also dislikes the term bipolar disorder and suggests an alternative in her book *Loving Someone with Bipolar Disorder*:

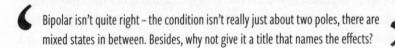

> Bi-polar disorder is a bit of a misnomer. Yes, people with the illness do go up and down, but doesn't it seem as if they also go sideways or do little corkscrews as well? Maybe if it were called MULTI-polar disorder, people would understand the illness a little bit more.

We agree that the term 'multipolar disorder' describes the condition more accurately because there's so much more to bipolar than simply being up or down, at one pole or the other. In fact, the psychiatric world recognizes that the current labels used (such as Bipolar I and II) don't always reflect the wide range of bipolar symptoms. But the answer lies not in dispensing with the labels, but using them as a starting point to decide how people are treated. We might move towards talking, for example, about 'bipolar spectrum disorder' or a 'continuum of bipolarity'. In other words, experts will be less likely to focus on a concrete diagnosis in the future ('let's forget what the illness is called') and concentrate more on an individual's unique set of symptoms.

Q3. *What is the difference between Bipolar I, II and III?*

There are 'types' of bipolarity, known as Bipolar I, Bipolar II and Bipolar III.

To be diagnosed with Bipolar I, a person will have experienced at least one full manic episode in their lifetime, along with at least one major episode of depression. Around 1% of the general population is thought to develop Bipolar I at some point during their lives.

Bipolar II is diagnosed when someone's mood swings between major episodes of depression and periods of hypomania rather than manic episodes. The incidence of Bipolar II is estimated to be about 4–5% of the general population.

According to the latest Diagnostic and Statistical Manual of Mental Disorders or DSM-5 (the fifth version of a manual published by the American Psychiatric Association, which is used in the UK and US for categorizing and diagnosing mental health problems), the main difference between Bipolar I and Bipolar II is full mania for seven days versus hypomania for four days. Once a person experiences a full manic episode, they will receive a Bipolar I diagnosis.

Bipolar III is not in the official handbook, but is used by some mood experts in the United States to refer to hypomania that emerges only when a patient has been given an antidepressant (known by doctors as treatment-emergent mania/hypomania or TEMH). There is more about this in question 34, p. 93.

In the US, Bipolar II and III are sometimes referred to as 'soft' bipolar.

Q4. What is cyclothymia?

If a person's depressive and manic symptoms last for two years but are not severe enough to qualify as bipolar disorder, they may instead be diagnosed with 'cyclothymia', which is a milder form of bipolar. According to UK charity Bipolar UK, 'Individuals experience mood swings but at a much lower level. Symptoms must last for a period of at least two years, with no period longer than two months in which there has been a stable state and no mixed episodes.' However, a strong family history of bipolar, as in Amanda's case (see p. 18), can lead to a much quicker diagnosis.

There is evidence that for some people with cyclothymia, the mood swings will worsen over time until they develop Bipolar II or Bipolar I. Confusingly, cyclothymia is also sometimes referred to as Bipolar III.

In terms of diagnosis, this is a tricky area, because where do you draw the line between sad or irritable behaviour that's considered 'normal' and the kind of ups and downs that warrant a diagnosis of cyclothymia? Even the world's leading experts on mental health can't agree and probably never will. After all, what is normality?

Q5. Is there an age or gender profile for people with bipolar disorder?

Gender

Bipolar disorder tends to affect equal numbers of men and women overall, although research carried out at the Institute of Psychiatry at King's College in London does show gender differences in the way bipolar tends to run its course:

- The researchers found that in early adult life (defined as 16–25), there were higher rates of bipolar disorder in men than in women.
- Throughout the rest of adult life (26 years and over), the rate of bipolar disorder was higher in women than in men.
- Women are thought to have a higher chance than men of developing rapid-cycling bipolar disorder (in which changes in mood occur more rapidly) and mixed state (mania in which a low mood is predominant).

Age

In the mid-1990s, the average age of people being diagnosed with bipolar was 32. But this has dropped to under 19, and is expected to fall even further. The reason for this decrease is not known but is probably due to a number of factors, including an increased awareness of the disorder among the public and mental health practitioners, increased drug abuse, changing sources of life stresses and a huge jump in the number of children diagnosed with bipolar disorder in the USA.

But although the age of diagnosis has dropped, the illness affects people of all ages. In fact, in 2015 the International Society for Bipolar Disorders (ISBD) published findings showing that nearly 25% of people in the world with bipolar diagnoses are 60 and older.

Q6. *What are the symptoms of bipolar disorder?*

People with bipolar disorder tend to swing between depression and mania. But there's no 'typical' pattern of symptoms. Every person with bipolar is different, and the length of time they spend at either extreme of mood (high or low) is very variable – it can be days, weeks or months. And a person with bipolar can have any number of episodes of highs and lows throughout his or her life. There can be periods of normal mood in between the two extremes, but some people can swing between depression and mania quite quickly without a period of stability in the middle. The DSM-5 states that the four main symptoms of bipolar disorder are: depression, hypomania, mania and mixed state. Diagnosis is based on the presence and pattern of these symptoms over specified periods of time.

To reflect the fact that bipolar can be very different in frequency and an individual's specific symptoms, the DSM-5 also describes various subtypes that can be 'tagged on' to a diagnosis. So someone can be diagnosed with Bipolar I or II and then one or more of the following descriptors can be added to give a fuller, more accurate picture:

... with anxious distress

This means that during the most recent or current mood episode (depressive, hypomanic or manic), at least two of the following symptoms were present: feeling keyed up or tense, feeling unusually restless, difficulty concentrating because of worry, fearful something bad will happen, or feeling on the edge of self-control. Anxious symptoms improve as the underlying mood episode resolves. There's more about anxiety in question 12, p. 38.

... with mixed features

This describes the presence of depressive symptoms during a manic or hypomanic episode, or hypo/manic symptoms during a depressive episode. In the previous edition of the Diagnostic and Statistical Manual of Mental Disorders (DSM-IV), this came under a separate category for 'mixed state' episodes, which required meeting full criteria for both poles at the same time. There's more about mixed features in question 11, p. 37.

... with rapid cycling

This means four or more mood episodes of any kind within a 12-month period. Some people who rapid cycle can have monthly, weekly or even daily mood swings (this is known as 'ultradian cycling').

... with catatonic features

This is used to describe certain extremes of physical activity and speech happening during a mood episode, including lack of response to stimuli, not moving or speaking, repeating words or movements of another person, or frantic movement with no purpose.

... with psychotic features

This means that paranoia, delusions or hallucinations have been present at any point during a mood episode. There's more about psychosis in question 10, p. 35.

... with melancholy features

This describes a depressive episode that's characterized by an almost complete lack of ability to feel pleasure even when something good happens. Typically, there is also insomnia and a significant slowing of speech and activity.

... with atypical features

This applies to a depressive episode in which the person sleeps and eats more than usual, often gaining weight. Other traits include feeling sluggish and being abnormally affected by rejection. If there is low mood, spirits may lift in reaction to a positive experience.

... with seasonal pattern

This is used for depressions that recur during certain seasons – usually in autumn or winter – that can't be put down to events like school starting or seasonal unemployment. More rarely, some people experience a pattern of summertime depressions. There's more about seasonal affective disorder (SAD) in question 13, p. 41.

... with peripartum onset

This indicates that mood episodes began during pregnancy or in the months after giving birth. This replaces 'postpartum onset', the term used in previous DSM editions, to reflect the fact that many women have mood symptoms before giving birth, as well as after the birth. There's more about the risk of bipolar during and after pregnancy in question 85, p. 242.

When making a diagnosis of bipolar disorder, a doctor must also take into account that comorbidity (when two or more conditions exist in one patient) can be high. For example, it is estimated that around 50% of people with bipolar have a substance abuse problem, plus there are other physical and personality disorder issues that can make diagnosis and treatment challenging.

Other 'unofficial' symptoms of bipolar disorder include low self-esteem, libido problems and self-harm. There are more details about these in question 12, p. 38.

Q7. *What is depression?*

How many times do people say they're depressed about their job, their relationship or even the weather? Yet what does depression really mean?

The DSM-5 states that a diagnosis of depression must be based on at least five of the following symptoms, occurring over the same two-week period, and must include either the first or second symptom listed below:

- a depressed mood for most of the day
- markedly diminished interest or pleasure in almost all activities
- significant changes (loss or gain) in weight and appetite
- insomnia or hypersomnia nearly every day (difficulty in falling asleep, or excessive sleep)
- physical slowing, or agitation
- fatigue and loss of energy
- feelings of worthlessness
- excessive feelings of guilt
- poor concentration levels
- recurrent thoughts of death and suicide.

Someone can experience either 'unipolar' or 'bipolar' depression. There are some differences between the two:

- In bipolar depression, the average duration of symptoms is three to six months, but in unipolar depression it is six to twelve months. The shorter the depression, the more likely it is to be bipolar.
- Compared with unipolar depression, post-natal depression is more common in bipolar disorder.
- The more episodes of depression you have, the more likely you are to have bipolar rather than unipolar. More than 95% of people with bipolar have recurrent episodes, versus people with unipolar, of whom two-thirds have recurrent episodes.
- The earlier the onset of the depression, and the more people in the family with bipolar, the more likely it is to be bipolar disorder (rather than unipolar depression).

And although mania or hypomania are the defining characteristics of bipolar disorder, people with a diagnosis tend to spend much more time depressed than manic during the course of the illness. In fact, it's been estimated that people with Bipolar I spend three times longer feeling depressed than manic and are depressed around a third of the time. People with Bipolar II have been found to experience an even higher proportion (50%) of time feeling depressed rather than manic.

Statistics aside, for those who experience depression in all its terrible, crushing reality, this is how it actually feels:

> I feel very detached and as if nothing is real. I feel like I am a camera and I'm watching every action, and everything is really slow. Then it just turns into this absolute nothingness. I can't locate a cause, I just feel incredibly tired all the time, I sleep 22 hours a day, or I don't sleep at all, but I'm sort of on the edge of sleep. I don't want to eat, I don't want to move.
>
> *(TAMARA)*

> What happens these days is that my body literally starts to give way. Suddenly walking to the shop becomes like climbing Mount Everest, and it's just ridiculous and I just can't do it. It's literally like somebody has pulled the plug on me. And there's this sense of impending doom, and my thoughts start to change drastically. I'll be obsessed with death thoughts. I don't get suicidal, but my mind is full of anything to do with death or decay or waste, and it's like, 'Here it comes … the winter of my mind.'
>
> *(ASHLEY)*

> For months on end I spend days and days shut in my room. I don't want to do anything. I don't want to see anyone. I hate everyone around me and hate myself more than anyone. I didn't speak to my dad for four years. It was a nightmare.
>
> *(PAUL)*

Sarah vividly recalls Rebecca's deepest depression during one long winter:

> For a period of six or seven months, Rebecca cocooned herself in her bedroom under her duvet. Her life became TV and cigarettes – nothing more. And for much of the time the TV wasn't even on. The curtains were drawn, the shelves cluttered with mugs and ashtrays and the air smoky and stale. Rebecca stopped taking calls

from friends and wouldn't have eaten if Mum hadn't brought up meals on a tray. It was impossible to connect with her during this time.

Q8. *What is hypomania?*

The most recent DSM-5 says that mania is 'the cardinal symptom of bipolar disorder. Without the mania, [the diagnosis] would be considered depressive disorder.'

Hypomania is sometimes described as 'mania lite', and people who experience hypomania rather than full-blown manic episodes tend to be diagnosed with Bipolar II rather than Bipolar I. The DSM-5 calls it 'a distinct period of abnormally and persistently elevated mood' and there is usually a heightened sense of well-being. A hypomanic person feels confident, creative, productive and full of energy, whilst the rest of the world seems sluggish and dull. One 12-year study found that people with Bipolar II are in a state of hypomania for approximately 1% of the time.

 Hypomania begins with agitation and then just builds, and I become very impulsive, and create strange connections between things that don't exist. And sometimes I absolutely love it. I'm really active and productive. Sometimes I have energy in a way that other people just don't, and I get quite cross because I find them quite apathetic about things, whereas I will see something simple like a light on water which will completely light me up, and I just see the beauty – you get ultimate clarity about things. I've sat down and written essays and got really good marks, and I've written them when I haven't exactly been 100% stable. But I've just had the creativity to do it, and I read them back now and think, 'No way did I write that!' I write poetry and see connections between people and music. I guess sometimes it can actually be a gift.

(TAMARA)

Normal daily life is not necessarily disrupted – in fact, a person with hypomania can put their extra energy, creativity and mild euphoria to good use.

The artist with hypomania will create more pictures (Ashley painted 120 pictures in six weeks) or the hypomanic saleswoman (see Reka's story below) will smash through her quarterly target with ease. But the downside is that someone with hypomania can become easily irritated by other people, and disputes can erupt if they feel they're being challenged:

> I'm very hypomanic. I get very excited; I think I'm very talented, better than everyone else. It's a beautiful feeling. All of my achievements, all of the good things in life, I've basically done when I've been hypomanic. If I'm high, I think I'm the best salesperson ever, and because of my great belief in myself I'd make really good deals … It made me very confident – I'd walk around as if I owned the place. I'd see myself as an equal to the managing directors … It caused a lot of friction with the management and the directors. And often I'd end up walking out.
>
> (REKA)

And although some people (usually those with Bipolar II) will remain hypomanic, for others – if they don't recognize the warning signs – hypomania can herald an escalation into full-blown mania.

Q9. *What is a manic episode?*

In the DSM-IV, a manic episode was described as an 'elevated, expansive and irritable mood'. In the more recent DSM-5, as well as elevated mood, 'changes in energy and activity levels' have been added. The definition was widened because changes in energy and activity are easier to spot and report in the early stages of the illness. The reasoning behind this decision? To improve diagnostic accuracy and to make early detection and treatment easier. A manic episode usually lasts for more than seven days, and has a severely disruptive impact on normal activities. Without intervention, someone in the grip of severe mania will often need hospital treatment. Common symptoms of mania include:

- unnaturally high, euphoric mood
- inflated sense of self-importance
- extreme irritability
- incoherent, racing thoughts
- excessive, rapid speech
- easily distracted, can't concentrate well
- reduced need for sleep
- excessive risk-taking, such as extreme spending sprees, irresponsible sexual behaviour, or overuse of addictive substances such as alcohol or street drugs
- lack of inhibition.

> A manic episode feels fantastic, almost beyond any experience that you've ever felt. The sensations are greater than you've ever experienced. The pizza is always the best pizza ever. Everything's just magnified to such intensity. And you don't understand when people close to you treat you completely differently to strangers ... strangers don't know you from Adam, and so they want to be with you and have a laugh. You're the life and soul of the party, and yet your friends and family are having a hard time dealing with it.
>
> (*NEIL*)

A manic person will rush headlong into what seems like a great idea, acting on impulse with no thought to the consequences:

> In the grip of a manic episode, Tom would leap over things, climb trees, and jump out of windows. He thought he could stop traffic.
>
> (*JO*)

> At the moment I can go high on a daily basis. Last night at 2am I was waxing the bathroom floor. I get up, pick up the dog I'm looking after for a friend, I then dig up a huge rose bush, then dig up a tree. Then I pick up a birthday present and go to the supermarket. I did actually rip our chimney breast out a few weeks ago. My husband Dave was a little bit shocked to say the least. We hadn't discussed doing

> it. The idea just popped into my head. The poor neighbours! I hadn't covered any furniture. They came round as they heard the banging. It took me two days. I was covered in soot. Me with a sledge hammer. 'Use the force,' that's my favourite saying. Another time, I chopped down 18 trees at the end of the garden in one day. And when I was in my mid-30s I moved to Rhodes on a high and lived there for 18 months. I thought, 'I know, I'll be a holiday rep.'
>
> *(SHARRON)*

Someone experiencing a manic episode usually has no insight into their condition and so has no idea how difficult their wild behaviour can be for their family and friends, even if it causes terrible problems. One common problem is excessive overspending, which can lead to long-term financial difficulties:

> Whenever I'm high, I will spend anything that's going. It's led to so many problems in my marriage. When I was undiagnosed, my wife just assumed I was really selfish, especially as we haven't got a lot of money. I can easily go and blow £3,000 or £4,000 on a credit card. Electronic goods are my thing. It's making a big buy that creates excitement.
>
> *(PAUL)*

> Credit card bills started arriving. My husband David had taken out about eight credit cards, and he owed in excess of £30,000. The funny thing was that it must all have happened at the same time, because they all started demanding money at the same time. And then he left us within the week, just walked out. To this day, I have no idea what he spent it on.
>
> *(PAULA)*

Another common manic symptom is the delusion of grandeur:

> During one major high, I impulsively got on a flight from Newcastle to London and booked a room at the Park Lane Hilton. I got on the Tube, but it wasn't good enough for me. I felt like I deserved better. You think you're entitled to the best.

Lots of friends call me Lord George. I thought I ought to have servants. In the hotel reception I was told that the room would be many hundreds of pounds per night, plus VAT. I was annoyed because I hadn't been told about the VAT on the phone. 'I'm terribly sorry, Sir, you can have a suite,' said the receptionist. 'This will do me nicely,' I thought. They sent me a valet who dry-cleaned and ironed my trousers. I bought all the chambermaids into my room and told them to have five minutes rest and a glass of champagne. Once, having lunch, I asked them to get me the chef. I had bought a bottle of fine expensive wine and offered him a glass. I went to Bond Street and found a fabulous tailor and got kitted out with clothes. I spent £2,000 in there. What a wonderful way to shop. I didn't need to carry the bags home because, when I got back to the hotel, all the clothes I had bought were hanging in the wardrobe. I rented a Rolls Royce with a chauffeur to get me round London. I stayed there for five or six days and spent thousands on the credit card. I was having such a great time. I wish you could leave me on a high with an American Express card. It took me years to pay it back.

(*GEORGE*)

Q10. *What is psychosis?*

Sometimes an episode of mania can become so extreme that the manic person experiences wild delusions, extreme paranoia and hallucinations – these can be 'auditory' (where someone is hearing voices), 'visual' (where someone is seeing things that aren't there) or 'sensory' (where someone is feeling something that isn't there). Losing touch with reality in this way is called 'psychosis'. It's not uncommon for the fun of mania to tip over into this state – in fact, research shows up to 70% of people with bipolar have psychotic symptoms during a period of mania:

 I get a train of thought that seems very logical at the time. For example, last summer I just thought, 'I need some space, I need to get out of here, it's too much' ... so I was thinking, 'Where am I going to go? If I stop taking my tablets I'll go off the planet – so that's what I'll do.' I'm then thinking, 'Where shall I go in space? I'll go to Saturn because that's got the nice rings around it, and it'll be fun to sit on the rings and swing my legs.' And I'm thinking, 'Well, there are no shops there, so I need to take enough stuff with me.' It basically went on like that until I went into a local shop and said, 'I'm going to live on Saturn and I need to take enough stuff to last. I'm planning to live until I'm 90, so I need enough shampoo, conditioner and shower gel ... can you work out how much I'll need?' They laughed at me because they thought I was having a joke and I got very annoyed because they weren't taking me seriously. In the end, they very tactfully said, 'It's going to take us a while to work out – if you come back next week we'll have it all worked out for you.'

(SUE)

Someone in the grip of a psychotic episode may think that the TV is sending them messages, or believe that other people are reading their mind or controlling them. Religious delusions are common – someone might have a psychotic belief that they have been sent a message from God, that they have superhuman powers, that they're a special being sent on a mission to solve the world's problems, and/or that there are forces of evil plotting against them.

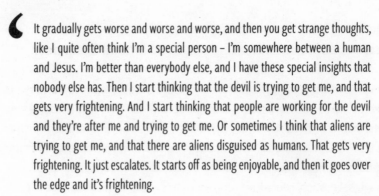

It gradually gets worse and worse and worse, and then you get strange thoughts, like I quite often think I'm a special person – I'm somewhere between a human and Jesus. I'm better than everybody else, and I have these special insights that nobody else has. Then I start thinking that the devil is trying to get me, and that gets very frightening. And I start thinking that people are working for the devil and they're after me and trying to get me. Or sometimes I think that aliens are trying to get me, and that there are aliens disguised as humans. That gets very frightening. It just escalates. It starts off as being enjoyable, and then it goes over the edge and it's frightening.

(SUE)

It's also not uncommon for someone in a psychotic state to hear voices giving them instructions – even to harm themselves.

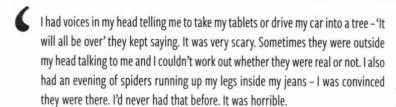

I had voices in my head telling me to take my tablets or drive my car into a tree – 'It will all be over' they kept saying. It was very scary. Sometimes they were outside my head talking to me and I couldn't work out whether they were real or not. I also had an evening of spiders running up my legs inside my jeans – I was convinced they were there. I'd never had that before. It was horrible.

(DEBBIE)

Psychosis doesn't need to occur for a diagnosis of bipolar disorder to be made, but it can often accompany a manic episode, especially if the mania is not treated effectively.

Psychosis can also occur during a depressive episode – at least half of people with bipolar experience psychosis during a period of depression. People who experience psychosis during a depressive episode commonly feel guilty, worthless or even that they don't exist.

It's also worth noting that in the general population, marijuana use doubles the risk of developing psychosis and this risk is especially high if someone has a particular form of the 'BDNF' (brain-derived neurotrophic factor) gene, a protein that protects neurons and that is important for learning and memory. For more information about bipolar and cannabis, see question 81, p. 223.

Q11. *What are the mixed features of bipolar disorder?*

Someone with bipolar can experience 'mixed features', when they have symptoms of mania and depression simultaneously – so they can be depressed and agitated at the same time, or 'tired but wired'. In previous editions of the DSM, this was called a 'mixed state'. Any mix of the symptoms of mania and depression can occur at once – for example, someone may have racing thoughts, agitation, overactivity and unrealistic ideas, but feel worthless, guilty and suicidal. It's estimated that approximately two-thirds of those diagnosed with bipolar experience mixed features at some point in their illness.

Amanda often sees her mother Irene in this mixed state, depressed and despairing but also agitated and paranoid:

I can only describe my mum's mixed episodes as despair on speed. There's none of the wild euphoria of mania, or the lethargy of depression. Her mood spirals downwards but she also becomes terribly agitated and restless, and can't even sit down. She just paces around the house for hours, as waves of paranoia and irrational fears flood her mind.

It's a dangerous combination of moods. Someone with mixed features can have depression without the usual tiredness and lack of motivation that can go with it, whilst their agitation gives them enough energy to put suicidal thoughts into action – both of Irene's suicide attempts have been during mixed state episodes.

Q12. What are the less recognized symptoms of bipolar disorder?

People with a diagnosis of bipolar often have some less recognized symptoms, such as anxiety, low self-esteem, libido problems and a tendency to self-harm.

Anxiety

Anxiety is an umbrella term used to encompass a wide range of symptoms, including excessive worrying, paranoia, a racing heartbeat, feelings of dread and fear, sweating, shaking, breathing difficulties and obsessive tendencies, such as collecting objects, repetitive actions and an inability to leave the house without making endless safety checks. Some studies suggest that more than a third of people with bipolar also have an anxiety disorder.

 Because of my condition, I can never judge whether I should be worried about something or not. I always try to question, would someone without bipolar be worrying or feel anxious about this? For example, we're refurbishing the house and I worry that the house looks like a tip. My husband doesn't seem to worry.

Any stress at all is like a double stress. It makes me feel as though I'm the only person worrying in the world.

(*SHARRON*)

I don't feel I can teach well and I feel anxious a lot. That's why I've got a stammer at the moment.

(*JUDE*)

When I was first dating David, he was very paranoid. I didn't realize he was ill at the time, but he would phone at 3am to make sure I was on my own, and turn up at odd times. He was convinced I was married, and was trying to catch me out. He also has a lot of obsessive symptoms and collects things. I've since found out that this is typical bipolar behaviour. David will have 20 cans of the same deodorant in the cupboard, all with a millimetre of deodorant left, but I'm not allowed to throw them out in case he needs them. He will also buy lots of things exactly the same – shoes, shirts and trousers. When we moved, I had three bags of brown boots labelled 'Brown boots', 'More brown boots' and 'More bloody brown boots'!

(*JACKIE*)

I was hospitalized on two occasions when I was 22 after I'd had panic attacks, which I now recognize were tied in with me going hypomanic.

(*LESLEY*)

When Mum is low, she won't even go out of the front door, and is frightened to speak to anyone, let alone have any workman round the house.

(*INGRID*)

Low self-esteem

Self-esteem is an individual's assessment of their own worth. Does someone recognize their own qualities and talents or do they believe only negative statements about themselves? Those with a mental illness, including bipolar disorder, often have very low self-esteem, which can lead to a number of problems, including dysfunctional relationships and unfulfilled potential. Many fear revealing their true self to the outside world.

> I believe bipolar people wear this amazing mask outside the house. Most days it is possible to put on a mask for a certain amount of time and be normal. Some close friends I only told recently about my diagnosis said they never would have believed it.
>
> *(DEBBIE)*

> David's self-esteem was so low that he didn't believe that anyone would like him for himself, and so he had to create a persona.
>
> *(PAULA)*

Libido problems

Some people with bipolar disorder experience a disrupted sex life. Problems include: a lack of libido during depressed periods, excessive libido or 'hyper-sexuality' during periods of mania, a general lack of affection because the bipolar symptoms can prevent a fulfilling and loving relationship, and the side effects of medication.

> Bipolar has had a huge impact on my sex life. First of all, you don't feel good about yourself, so you don't feel like sex. When I'm low, in my mind I'm wondering 'why does he want me, I'm just being used, why do I do this?' Then there's the other angle – when you're on a high, you just want sex all the time. It confuses the life out of your partner because they don't really understand. One minute you're refusing, the next minute you're all over them.
>
> *(SHARRON)*

> Before I got my bipolar under control, one of my symptoms was that I became very sexualized. It was really out of character – I'd gone from being like a nun to being a promiscuous after-work wine drinker. My libido was rampant.
>
> *(MARISSA)*

Self-harm

Sometimes referred to as deliberate self-harm (DSH), self-harm is a way of coping with distress. People self-harm in many ways, including destructive lifestyle habits, such as excessive drinking, taking recreational drugs and overeating. However, DSH is taken to mean self-harming in ways such as cutting, burning, scratching, taking overdoses and swallowing inedible objects. According to UK charity Mental Health Foundation, the UK has the highest self-harm rate of any European country, with estimates of 400 in 100,000 people self-harming. Many people who self-harm have had traumatic, abusive childhoods and/or have psychiatric problems such as bipolar disorder.

For a list of organizations that can support someone who is self-harming, see question 50, p. 136.

> I've self-harmed a lot. I used to cut the back of my legs using any surgical implement I could find – usually razor blades or scalpels. I wanted to cut myself open, turn myself inside out and put myself back together again feeling less stressed. I'd go through periods of doing that – anything from two weeks to one year.
>
> (*SHARRON*)

> I do self-harm a fair bit. I cut my arms with a razor or a Stanley knife blade. I tend to do it when I'm feeling horribly anxious because it seems the only way to clear the anxiety. I know this sounds ridiculous, but because the anxiety makes me think something bad is about to happen, harming myself is the bad thing that happens, and then the anxiety goes because I can convince myself that nothing else bad will happen.
>
> (*PAUL*)

Q13. *Are the symptoms of bipolar disorder linked to the symptoms of seasonal affective disorder?*

Seasonal affective disorder (SAD) is a type of winter depression that affects approximately one in every 15 people in the UK between September and

April, according to findings published by the National Health Service (NHS). Symptoms can be particularly acute during December, January and February. Key features of SAD include the desire to sleep more and eat carbohydrate foods.

SAD seems to develop from inadequate bright light during the winter months, and is thought to be caused by a biochemical imbalance in the hypothalamus, the part of the brain that controls mood, appetite, sleep, temperature and sex drive. In the US, it's estimated that SAD affects 4% to 6% of the population.

The DSM-5 doesn't regard SAD as a separate condition, but as a seasonal pattern for depression and bipolar disorder. According to John McManamy in his book *Living with Depression and Bipolar Disorder*, people with mood disorders are far more likely to be affected by seasonal changes. John also advises that, 'At all times, those with bipolar need to pay regard to the fact that our illness is defined by our cycles. Typically, we tend toward winter depressions and summer manias, and these cycles are regulated by the availability of light.'

Many people diagnosed with bipolar disorder report symptoms of SAD:

> About November, I can feel the symptoms coming on, and about March I begin to pick up again. And that's been pretty constant now for quite a good few years. I really collapse, and it's like there's an on/off switch in my brain, and it's 'goodnight'. And I just want to hibernate – for the first few weeks of that period I sleep and sleep and sleep and sleep. It was a running joke amongst my friends in my twenties. They'd just hammer on my doors and windows, and nothing was going to wake me. I'd be in bed 18 hours a day. And I can't go out. What I need to do is rest, massively. It's almost as if the rest of the year has caught up on me, as if I've burnt out my year's worth of energy.
>
> (ASHLEY)

> I have noticed over the years that Mum's high periods coincide with the fine weather from April to September and her low periods are usually from October through the winter months to April.
>
> (INGRID)

For information on how to treat the symptoms of SAD, see question 41, p. 107.

Q14. *What is schizoaffective disorder?*

Schizoaffective disorder is a mental health condition characterized by mania, depression and psychosis. In the UK, less than one in 100 people are likely to have schizoaffective disorder in their lifetime. However, schizoaffective manic patients make up 3% to 5% of all patients admitted to a psychiatric hospital.

The DSM-5 lists schizoaffective disorder under 'schizophrenia and other psychotic disorders,' but some experts say it could easily sit in the 'mood spectrum disorders' section because so many of the symptoms overlap with bipolar. In fact, there is a school of thought that schizoaffective disorder sits in the middle of a spectrum, with schizophrenia at one end and bipolar disorder at the other. To put it another way, some experts view schizoaffective disorder as a form of bipolar with 'heavy-duty' psychosis.

Regardless of how it's labelled or how it emerges in an individual, schizoaffective disorder can be treated effectively – usually with a combination of antipsychotic, antidepressant and mood stabilizing medication, and psychological therapy.

Many of the areas we cover in this book – relapse prevention with healthy lifestyle choices and dealing with stigma, for instance – are just as relevant for someone with schizoaffective disorder as they are for someone with bipolar disorder. The Royal College of Psychiatrists has a useful leaflet about schizoaffective disorder. You can find it online at www.rcpsych.ac.uk – look under 'health information'.

Q15. *What is borderline personality disorder?*

Borderline personality disorder (or BDP) is a mental illness characterized by lots of widely varying symptoms. It is sometimes called just 'personality disorder'. According to UK charity Mind, you might be given a diagnosis of BPD if you experience at least five of the following things, and they've lasted for a long time or have a big impact on your daily life:

- You feel very worried about people abandoning you, and would do anything to stop that happening.
- You have very intense emotions that last from a few hours to a few days and can change quickly (for example, from feeling very happy and confident to suddenly feeling low and sad).
- You don't have a strong sense of who you are, and it can change significantly depending on who you're with.
- You find it very hard to make and keep stable relationships.
- You feel empty a lot of the time.
- You act impulsively and do things that could harm you (such as binge eating, using recreational drugs or driving dangerously).
- You often self-harm or have suicidal feelings.
- You have very intense feelings of anger, which are really difficult to control.
- When very stressed, you may also experience paranoia (thinking and feeling as if you are under threat even though there is no or very little evidence that you are) or dissociation (where you feel disconnected in some way from the world around you or from yourself).

BPD is a common condition – a large study in 2006 found that about one in 20 people in the UK have a personality disorder. Researchers also say that many more people have traits of a BPD, but not the full disorder.

Because some people with BPD can act impulsively or aggressively and experience extremely changeable moods (symptoms that can overlap with bipolar disorder), BPD can sometimes be confused with or misdiagnosed as bipolar disorder. In fact, while it is widely agreed that some people can have both conditions at the same time, others argue that bipolar disorder and BPD are 'variations on a theme' and on the same spectrum.

Either way, BPD is treatable with a combination of medication and psychological therapy. Getting the correct diagnosis is important because the treatments for bipolar disorder and BPD can be very different. Saying that, much of the 'stay well with a healthy lifestyle' advice for people with bipolar disorder in Chapter 5 of this book also applies to someone with a diagnosis of BPD. The Royal College of Psychiatrists has a useful leaflet about personality disorder. You can find it online at www.rcpsych.ac.uk – look under 'health information'.

Q16. *What is the link between bipolar disorder and addiction?*

According to the charity Action on Addiction, one in three people in the UK is addicted to something. Common addictions include alcohol, nicotine, recreational or prescription drugs, sex, gambling and, increasingly, video gaming.

Addiction is a disease that impacts regions of the brain involved in mood regulation, decision-making, willpower and motivation. When someone abuses a substance, such as drugs or alcohol, or keeps repeating an unhelpful behaviour, such as inappropriate sexual activity, gambling or excessive gaming, in the long term pathways in the brain are altered and a dependency can be formed. Brain chemicals (dopamine, norepinephrine, and serotonin and neurotransmitters) that help to transmit feelings of pleasure in the brain are increased, and over time, the brain may depend on their presence in order to function normally. This is when someone can lose control over the substance or the behaviour – not having or doing it causes withdrawal symptoms, or a 'come down'. Because this can feel unpleasant, it's easier to carry on having or doing it, and so the cycle continues.

Addictive tendencies are more common in people with bipolar disorder – one survey in the US found that over half of people with bipolar had experienced addiction to drugs or alcohol at some time. A Canadian study found that people with bipolar disorder were more than twice as likely to have a gambling addiction as someone in the general population.

The first sign that my teenage son was becoming unwell with bipolar was that we found it increasingly difficult to get him off his Xbox. Even though he'd agreed to come off earlier, he'd always say, 'Just one more game.' It was compulsive. Eventually he stopped sleeping altogether and played 24/7 until he was so manic he had to be sectioned.

(*JUAN*)

The good news is that addiction is a treatable condition and studies have shown that brain chemistry linked to addictive behaviour can be rebalanced. Getting the right support, whatever the addiction, is the first step. There's more information at www.actiononaddiction.org.uk, or on 0300 330 0659.

For more information about giving up ...

- ... nicotine, see question 76, p. 213.
- ... alcohol, see question 78, p. 219.
- ... recreational drugs, see question 81, p. 223.
- ... gaming, see www.gamequitters.com.

Q17. *What impact does bipolar disorder have on someone's physical health?*

The harsh reality is that life expectancy among adults with bipolar disorder is estimated to be 15–20 years lower than for the general population. People with bipolar have higher rates of cardiovascular disease, respiratory disease, diabetes and obesity.

One large study published in the *British Journal of Psychiatry* found that people with bipolar are more likely to have certain conditions compared to people with unipolar depression. For example, 23.7% of people with bipolar disorder had migraines compared to 21.9% of people with unipolar depression. The odds were similarly higher when comparing rates of asthma, high cholesterol, hypertension, thyroid disease and osteoarthritis between the two groups. The risks are especially high if someone has a history of anxiety disorder, rapid cycling mood episodes, suicide attempts or mood episodes with a typically acute onset. In other words, having bipolar disorder doesn't just affect your mental health but your physical health too.

Why? It's thought this increased risk is due to a combination of unhealthy lifestyle choices (smoking, drinking alcohol, recreational drug use, lack of exercise) and medication, particularly antipsychotic drugs as they stimulate appetite and slow down metabolism, which causes weight gain.

The light at the end of the tunnel?

Although on the face of it this research seems nothing but bleak, it is possible to view it more positively.

1. Knowing the increased risk of obesity, diabetes and heart disease means you can make a conscious decision to make healthy lifestyle choices and lower that risk. There's more information about exercise, nutrition, alcohol and recreational drugs in Chapter 5, starting on p. 184.
2. Based on this research, your healthcare team has a duty to monitor your physical, as well as your mental, health. Indeed, NICE recommends that adults with bipolar disorder have a physical health assessment at least annually. This is to check your:

- blood pressure
- weight
- nicotine and alcohol intake
- blood sugar levels
- cholesterol levels (if you're 40 or older).

Plus, if you are taking lithium, you will need a lithium level check every three to six months, and a blood test for thyroid and kidney function and calcium levels at least every 15 months.

This means any physical health problems can be picked up earlier and treated straight away, reducing the risk of long-term complications. In other words, forewarned is forearmed.

Q18. *Can bipolar disorder cause thyroid problems?*

Situated at the front of the neck, the thyroid is a gland that produces the hormone thyroxine. This hormone is very important for many of the body's functions and also influences moods. It's been found that people with bipolar disorder quite often have abnormal thyroid function. The usual problem is that the thyroid gland doesn't produce enough thyroxine, leading to hypo-thyroidism, symptoms of which include slow body movements and speech, tiredness, weakness, poor concentration and memory problems (which can mimic depression). People with rapid cycling bipolar disorder may be particularly prone to problems with their thyroid gland. The problem is usually corrected by taking thyroid pills in addition to the usual medication for bipolar disorder.

In a chicken-and-egg situation, it's not yet known for sure whether bipolar disorder causes someone to be more prone to thyroid problems or whether having thyroid problems means someone is more prone to bipolar disorder.

Even more confusingly, taking the mood stabilizer lithium can cause low thyroxine levels in some people, also resulting in the need for thyroxine supplementation – see question 33, p. 89, for more information.

Q19. *What causes bipolar disorder?*

People often ask if mental illnesses are caused by either genes ('nature') or environment ('nurture'). Many research studies show that there's a tendency for bipolar disorder (along with other mental illnesses) to run in families. So is it all down to someone's genetic 'blueprint'?

No. All human characteristics are a combination of genes and experiences. And it's now widely recognized that environmental factors can affect both the structure of our brain and our mood – both on a day-to-day basis and in the long term. Of course, all individuals differ in their life experiences and in the genes they inherit from their parents, so the relative importance of genes and environment will vary from person to person.

And having a genetic predisposition to bipolar disorder in the family doesn't mean somebody is destined to develop it. The best way of illustrating this is to look at studies of identical twins – if one twin has bipolar disorder, their genetically identical sibling has a 60% chance of developing the illness and a 40% chance of staying bipolar-free. If bipolar disorder was purely genetic, both twins would be diagnosed 100% of the time.

So if the cause of bipolar disorder can't be purely genetic, what environmental factors are in the mix?

- Upbringing may play a part for some people, such as the traumatic childhood shared by Amanda's mum Irene and Sarah's dad Jim.
- Stress – positive, as well as negative events – is known to be involved in triggering bipolar and other mental illnesses (see question 67, p. 185).
- The use of street drugs such as cannabis can also trigger bipolar and other mental disorders (see question 81, p. 223).
- Persistent lack of sleep can be a trigger (see question 68, p. 187).
- Hormonal changes can be a factor, particularly for women after childbirth (see question 85, p. 242) or who are going through the menopause as in the case of Amanda's mum.

In extremely rare cases, a head injury can also be an external trigger for bipolar disorder because head injuries can cause damage to some systems in the brain that are involved in the condition.

Q20. *Is there an increased risk of bipolar disorder for other family members?*

This is a question that looms large for us, as we consider the risk for ourselves and our children. At first glance, the straight answer is not an optimistic one. According to research presented by an international team at the European College of Neuropsychopharmacology (ECNP) neuroscience congress in Vienna in 2016:

- If a brother or sister has bipolar disorder, then their siblings are four times more likely to develop bipolar disorder or other psychiatric disorders.
- The more relatives with bipolar someone has, the greater the risk, going from about 5%–6% when they have only one affected first-degree relative to more than 50% when they have four.
- Children of a parent with bipolar have a 30% chance of a mood disorder developing.
- Children who have two parents with bipolar have a 70% chance of developing the condition.

'These results are important clinically, as they encourage mental health workers to be aware of the increased risk of psychiatric disorders in siblings of patients,' says lead researcher Professor Mark Weiser, Chairman of the Department of Psychiatry at the Sackler School of Medicine in Israel.

 My father was bipolar, though he was never actually diagnosed – he committed suicide. His mother spent 20 years in an acute psychiatric unit. And his father had 'shellshock' during World War 1 and was an alcoholic. Looking back, I wonder if there was more to it.

(*SHARRON*)

Saying that, a more optimistic way of looking at it is that even when the risks are higher on paper, it does not automatically mean bipolar disorder will develop. Even if the genetic cards are unfavourably stacked, it's not necessarily inevitable – far from it, in fact, as life events and lifestyle choices can make all the difference.

To explain the risk more clearly, think of this analogy: if you're born with fair skin, you're more at risk of sunburn than someone with dark skin, but if you protect yourself (using sun protection cream, staying out of the midday sun and wearing a hat in summer, for instance) then you're far less likely to get burnt. And on the flip side of the coin, being born with dark skin means you have a lower risk, but does not eliminate the risk of sunburn altogether (if you spend time in the Australian outback with no protection, for instance). It's the same with bipolar risk. You can be born with a higher genetic leaning towards bipolarity, but if you protect yourself (generally making wise lifestyle choices), then you're far less likely to become unwell. And, similarly, if you're born with a low genetic risk yet don't protect yourself, you may become unwell with bipolar symptoms.

Of course, it's far from possible to control everything in life (parents divorcing, stress in childhood, bereavement, to name but a few). Luck plays a part in whether bipolar puts in an appearance or not. But it's reassuring to know that a high genetic risk doesn't necessarily mean that developing bipolar disorder is inevitable.

 I really hope my daughter hasn't inherited my bipolar. She's nine. She doesn't seem to have the personality that goes with it. As a child I was already very impatient, very moody, I didn't listen to anyone, I did what I wanted to do. My daughter is very much more like her dad.

(*REKA*)

Worth a mention...

If you have a first-degree relative with bipolar, you not only have a higher risk of developing bipolar but also of developing unipolar depression. Research at the University of Manchester found that someone with a parent who has bipolar disorder is twice as likely to experience depression – this is because characteristics often shared by people with bipolar are also found in the children of parents with bipolar, even if they don't have bipolar disorder themselves, as Professor Steven Jones, Professor of Clinical Psychology and Co-director of the Spectrum Centre for Mental Health Research at Lancaster University, explains: 'We found in individuals with diagnoses of depression and also individuals with bipolar that there is a tendency towards a "ruminative" coping style (thinking over problems repetitively without moving to problem solving), and in people with a bipolar diagnosis this is also paired with a risk-taking coping style, particularly for dealing with negative mood ... And what we found in the children of bipolar parents was that they also showed a pattern of more rumination and more risk taking. Another thing that we found in the psychological research into people with a diagnosis of bipolar disorder is that instability seems to be a key characteristic, which is detectable in different ways. One reliable observation is that people with a bipolar diagnosis appear to have more unstable self-esteem. And what we found in children of bipolar parents again is that there was greater instability of self-esteem, and also higher levels of negative mood.'

The research also looked at the sleep patterns of children who have a parent with bipolar disorder, which found that they reported poor sleep even when test results showed that they had in fact gone to sleep more quickly and had slept for longer than the control group (people who don't have a parent with bipolar). This would suggest that the children of a parent with bipolar need more sleep than the general population to feel refreshed – which in turn suggests that they might share the same vulnerability (to bipolar disorder being triggered by routinely disturbed or shortened sleep) as their parent with bipolar.

Q21. *Is it possible to have genetic testing for bipolar disorder?*

Every so often a headline in a national newspaper declares that the 'bipolar gene' has been discovered and that we're one step away from the definitive bipolar test. But it's not as simple as that. There's not just one, or even just a few, genes involved in the development of bipolar disorder, but many.

In short, the answer is no, it isn't possible to have genetic testing for bipolar disorder. Not yet at least. Although there's a great deal of research being done at the moment to understand the genetics of bipolar, the purpose of this is not to test people to see if they are personally at risk of developing it. Instead, the gene research is focused on trying to understand the brain processes involved in the illness, which will hopefully lead to more individualized and generally better diagnosis and treatment.

'With regard to understanding the role of genes, a lot has changed in the last decade,' says Professor Ian Jones, Professor of Psychiatry at Cardiff University and Director of the National Centre for Mental Health (NCMH). 'Whereas previously researchers were competitive, working in isolation on their individual projects, we realized we could only move forward if we started working together. A global collaboration – the Psychiatric Genomics Consortium (PGC) – has linked up researchers from around the world to make progress. In the UK our Bipolar Disorder Research Network (BDRN) has brought together researchers, clinicians and over 7,000 people with lived experience of bipolar disorder for research. Along with tens of thousands of other participants from around the globe we are starting to understand more about how genes influence risk. So far about 30 variations in the genome have been shown to play a role, nudging up the risk of bipolar.

'It's early days though. There are probably hundreds or even thousands of these genes because the condition is an incredibly complex interaction of genetic, biological, psychological and social factors. But it's a promising start and there is real potential for more advances in the next few years and decades. We are extremely grateful to everyone who has given their time to join in – without their help the research would not happen. What we need next are some even bigger studies. To find out how to take part, go to: www.ncmh.info.'

Q22. *Is it possible for a child to have bipolar disorder?*

This is an extremely controversial subject area, to say the least. According to the UK mental health charity YoungMinds, one in ten children between the ages of one and 16 in the UK has a diagnosable mental health disorder. Yet the medical profession is divided into two camps when it comes to diagnosing children with bipolar.

The 'yes' camp

A report from Harvard Medical School states that symptoms of bipolar disorder first appear in childhood or adolescence at least one-third of the time. 'Childhood bipolar disorder is a real and serious illness that should be recognized and treated as early as possible,' says Dr Michael Miller, Senior Editor for Mental Health Publishing at Harvard Health Publications.

Bear in mind, though, that there's a *much* higher tendency in the US to diagnose children with bipolar than in the UK. According to a 2014 study, led by University of Oxford researchers and published in the *Journal of the American Academy of Child & Adolescent Psychiatry*, US children receive a diagnosis of bipolar at a rate of 100.9 per 100,000, compared with UK figures of 1.4 per 100,000.

The 'no' camp

Until the 1990s bipolar disorder was regarded as an adult disease, only thought to affect people in their early 20s or older, and many psychiatrists are still reluctant to 'label' or medicate children. In fact, according to a report in the British journal *New Scientist*, one US paediatric psychiatrist says that only 18% of children referred for a second opinion actually have bipolar disorder. Similar results are reported by other specialists. In other words, more children are being diagnosed with bipolar, but many experts believe they're being misdiagnosed.

The middle ground

Professor Nick Craddock, former head of the Cardiff University Psychiatry Service, agrees that children can display signs of bipolar illness, but advocates a more cautious approach to diagnosis: 'Although I believe it's impossible to diagnose children as young as two (which is increasingly seen in America) and that clear-cut bipolar in children is still uncommon, the number of cases does seem to be going up. This is probably due to a combination of the fact that we're more alert to the possibility and that there is a true increase, although we can only guess as to why this increase has happened. But we're coming to a point where we can identify certain behaviours in children that are indicative of a future likelihood of bipolar.'

Perhaps as a reflection of this more cautious approach, the most recent version of the DSM-5 says children who experience extreme irritability, anger and frequent, intense temper outbursts may now meet the criteria for a new disorder called 'disruptive mood dysregulation disorder'. This is officially categorized as a depressive, rather than a mood, disorder. It means that children who might have previously been given a diagnosis of bipolar disorder in the US now won't receive one, so maybe the high rates of diagnosis in the US will go down.

Why is making a diagnosis in childhood so difficult? A definite diagnosis in childhood is so difficult because every single person with bipolar disorder has a completely different experience of when and how the condition manifests. There is no typical pattern. For example, although Amanda's mum, Irene, didn't display any symptoms until she was in her 50s, Sarah believes with hindsight that some of her sister Rebecca's behaviour as a very young child were clues to a future diagnosis. When she was about six, Rebecca would say she had a 'speedo' and that when it was switched on she could do everything really fast. She hated school, partly because she found it so difficult to sit still and concentrate. She was always getting into trouble.

Would a diagnosis in childhood have made a difference to Rebecca's experiences? We certainly don't believe that throwing medication at a problem solves everything, particularly because little is understood about how drugs can affect a developing brain. But at least if Rebecca had had a diagnosis, she might have been given support and understanding, rather than labelled as naughty and disruptive. And although medical opinion is divided, many people have first-hand experience of symptoms showing up in childhood...

The National Institute for Health and Care Excellence (NICE) guideline for the treatment of bipolar (published in 2014 and revised in 2017 – see question 30, p. 73) stresses that a diagnosis of bipolar in children or young people should be made only after 'a period of intensive monitoring by a healthcare professional or multidisciplinary team trained and experienced in the assessment, diagnosis and management of bipolar disorder in children and young people, and in collaboration with the child or young person's parents or carers.'

As well as this long period of monitoring and consultation with a child or young person's family, healthcare professionals also take into account a family history of bipolar disorder or other mental health conditions when they're making an assessment or diagnosis.

> I suffered from depression at school and took my first overdose aged 11. The teachers just thought I had attitude problems and saw me as arrogant. I was always a strange child. I didn't mix or play games with others. I used to watch rather than join in. I felt like an alien who just couldn't fit in anywhere. Once, I went round all the ladies toilets and took all the taps off. I still don't know why I did it even now. Maybe it was a cry for help. I was diagnosed with bipolar disorder at the age of 30.
>
> (SHARRON)

> My symptoms probably started, looking back now, at the age of 12. I can pinpoint that's when my behaviour started to change. The first time I self-harmed – I'm a cutter – I was 12. When I was about 16, I was found by my teacher lying in the middle of a main road. I didn't know why ... I was diagnosed when I was 24.
>
> (AMY)

> My daughter Laura was always fighting with other children and in trouble at school. I was always being phoned and written to by the teachers. She wouldn't go to bed.

She would throw things out of windows. When we were out shopping, she would always get into physical fights. She was generally very destructive, but there was literally nothing I could do to change it. I couldn't go anywhere with her. Looking back, I think these were definitely symptoms of bipolar at a very early age. I also believe that the behaviour left unmanaged led to more stressful conditions in her life, which in turn opened the door to bipolar, although she was also genetically susceptible due to my ex-husband's family history.

(*JUNE*)

I was quite cross after my diagnosis at the age of 20 that someone hadn't picked it up sooner. I was completely off the wall at times. I was really miserable around the ages of 13 and 14. And as a child I could be quite hyperactive.

(*TAMARA*)

My daughter Vicki's diagnosis at the age of 14 has been a positive thing, because she knows I'm looking into it all the time to help her. It makes her feel as though she's not abnormal. She can think, 'I feel this way for a reason ... I'm not weird or freaky, this is just the way my body works.' She does accept it. She's my little trouper ... I'm very proud of her.

(*ALISON*)

Q23. *Are the symptoms of bipolar disorder different in children?*

The NICE guideline for the treatment of bipolar disorder states that for bipolar to be diagnosed in children:

- Mania must be present.
- Euphoria must be present most days, for most of the time (for at least seven days).
- Irritability is not a main reason to diagnose bipolar disorder.

The US-based Child and Adolescent Bipolar Foundation (CABF) goes much further. According to CABF, children are more likely to have continuous, mixed state mood cycles and without the clear periods of wellness often seen in adults. Symptoms in children may include:

- an expansive or irritable mood
- depression
- rapidly changing moods lasting a few hours to a few days
- explosive, lengthy and often destructive rages
- separation anxiety
- defiance of authority
- hyperactivity, agitation and distractibility
- sleeping little or too much
- bed wetting and night terrors
- strong and frequent cravings, often for carbohydrates and sweets
- excessive involvement in multiple projects and activities
- impaired judgement, impulsivity, racing thoughts and pressure to keep talking
- 'daredevil' behaviours
- inappropriate or precocious sexual behaviour
- delusions and hallucinations
- grandiose belief in their own abilities that defy the laws of logic (ability to fly, for example).

CABF also states that the 'symptoms of bipolar diagnosis can emerge as early as infancy. Mothers often report that children later diagnosed with the disorder were extremely difficult to settle and slept erratically ... and often had uncontrollable, seizure-like tantrums or rages out of proportion to any event.'

How much these behaviours may be due to developmental issues, instead of a disorder such as bipolar, can be difficult to judge. But other sources point to specific symptom patterns in children that may suggest they have bipolar. Demitri Papolos MD, Clinical Associate Professor at the Department of Psychiatry and Behavioural Sciences at the Albert Einstein College of Medicine in New York, is also the co-author of *The Bipolar Child*. In his view, 'children appear to experience such rapid shifts of mood that they commonly cycle many times within the day. This cycling pattern is called ultra-ultra rapid or ultradian cycling and it is most often associated with low arousal states in the mornings (these children find it almost impossible to get up in the morning) followed by afternoons and evenings of increased energy.'

Q24. *Is bipolar disorder ever diagnosed in older adults?*

Perhaps because the average age of diagnosis of bipolar disorder has dropped in recent years to 19, the condition is sometimes seen as a 'young person's illness'. However, the symptoms can start at any age, and can be recognized and diagnosed at any age. Our own family shows this only too well – Sarah's sister Rachel was diagnosed at 22, her dad Jim was diagnosed at 32 and Amanda's mum Irene was diagnosed at 51. And a diagnosis in older adults is far from rare.

I first remember Mum getting seriously depressed in the early 1980s when she was around 60. She had several long bouts of depression, sometimes lasting years rather than months, continuing up to when she died in 2003. She did have the 'highs' when she eventually came out of each period of depression, which probably only lasted for a few weeks before she settled down. The time between her bouts of depression varied, sometimes lasting a few months, other times a few years. Mum had all sorts of treatment. She was put on various antidepressants. She had several periods in hospital and had some courses of electric shock treatment which, although horrible, did seem to bring her out of the depressions. She was also put on lithium which she took for the rest of her life. My dad found it extremely hard to cope. Before Mum had her depressions, she was very outgoing and loved looking after everyone and Dad really never had to do anything in the home. Like many elderly people, he really couldn't understand mental illness and didn't see why she couldn't just snap out of it, so he was very impatient with her. He then became very demanding and expected me to be there far more than I could manage. It was particularly difficult as during one of Mum's stable periods they moved much further away from us (against everyone in the family's advice), which made it hard to visit very often once she again became depressed. Later on we persuaded them to move near to us which made life a little easier. We are convinced that Mum's illness was triggered by some personal problems in her early life which she kept hidden from us for many years and was scared of us discovering. We feel that it would have helped her enormously if she had been able to talk about her problems more. It is a very hard illness to cope with. I felt that I really lost my mum many years before she died as she was so changed. It was wonderful each time she came out of her depressions to have her back to normal, but we were always worried because we never knew how long it would last.

(DOREEN)

Q25. *Why is bipolar disorder often misdiagnosed?*

It's hard to imagine living with any other type of chronic long-term illness without appropriate treatment – yet people with bipolar disorder are often undiagnosed (or misdiagnosed with another condition) for far too long. In 2016, researchers from the University of New South Wales and Italian colleagues published an international study in the *Canadian Journal of Psychiatry*, pulling together the results of 27 bipolar and mental health research projects from across the world. They discovered that it takes an average of six years for someone with bipolar disorder to receive the correct diagnosis, and many patients experience distressing symptoms for years before being given the right treatment. The trouble is, unlike a 'physical' condition such as diabetes, there isn't a simple test to determine whether or not someone has bipolar. Often, the diagnosis is only made when a severe manic episode occurs – often involving sectioning under the Mental Health Act and a stay in a psychiatric unit (see question 55, p. 160). So why isn't bipolar diagnosed before such a desperate crisis point is reached? There are two main reasons:

1. Bipolar disorder is often diagnosed as depression

The first clue that someone has bipolar disorder is often a depressive episode. If someone seeks help from their family doctor at this point, and if no mention of previous mania or a family history of bipolar disorder is mentioned by the patient, the doctor is likely to make a diagnosis of, and suggest treatment for, depression. On the other hand, first experiences of mania are not always reported. A manic episode, especially in the early stages, often feels so enjoyable that the person experiencing it can't see what the problem is. Their family and friends may be alarmed and try to intervene, but for the manic person, feeling euphoric and invincible, it seems as if everyone else is trying to spoil their fun: 'Why should I go the doctor? There's nothing wrong with me!'

In fact, there's huge overlap between bipolar disorder and depression and it can be extremely difficult for medical professionals to distinguish between the two during the depressed phase.

In 1993, Amanda's mum Irene went through the all-too-common scenario of being misdiagnosed with depression, and others have had a similar experience:

> I was only treated for depression for years. I would go to the doctor, get some antidepressants, take them for a while, stop taking them and then go back. I took a variety of antidepressants, long term, but things just weren't getting any better, the antidepressants just weren't working.
>
> *(SUE)*

> At 17 I was diagnosed with recurrent depressive disorder and only got my diagnosis of bipolar at the age of 22.
>
> *(RACHEL)*

> My bipolar started during a period of stress at work. Three years later nobody had really diagnosed it properly. The doctors thought it was depression and I was prescribed antidepressants.
>
> *(RICHARD)*

> I was diagnosed with depression at the age of 20 and finally diagnosed officially with Bipolar II when I was 33.
>
> *(LESLEY)*

> The first two times I was in hospital in my twenties I was diagnosed with depression. Even though my dad has bipolar disorder, my psychiatrists didn't put two and two together.
>
> *(CARL)*

> After David had a car accident ten years ago, he was diagnosed with post-traumatic stress disorder (PTSD). At first he threw the antidepressants down the toilet. Then he was diagnosed with clinical depression and became suicidal 99% of the time. I knew what was wrong with him 12 months before he was diagnosed at the hospital because I went to the library and picked up a few books. I knew he had bipolar, but the professionals refused to listen to me.
>
> *(JACKIE)*

Many studies suggest that roughly a third of all depressions have a bipolar course when followed over time. To help prevent misdiagnosis, NICE recommends that GPs look for symptoms consistent with bipolar when they're diagnosing depression by using 'The Mood Disorder Questionnaire', a simple screening tool that indicates whether or not bipolar might be considered.

2. Bipolar sometimes gets misdiagnosed altogether

> After my first major manic episode at the age of 24, I was diagnosed with schizophrenia which was way off course.
>
> *(GEORGE)*

> Five years ago I had a complete physical collapse for a few months. I couldn't function at all. I was just physically exhausted, could hardly get out of bed, or if I went to the shop I would have to fall into bed again afterwards. A specialist diagnosed me with chronic fatigue syndrome.
>
> *(ASHLEY)*

Professor Nick Craddock, former head of the Cardiff University Psychiatry Service, explains why this kind of misdiagnosis happens: 'What we know is that lots of people are told they have schizophrenia or a personality disorder, and then it turns out they have bipolar disorder. It's not that suddenly things change completely or that psychiatrists are stupid. It's because we're trying to use simple labels for something that's much more complicated.'

But he does believe that misdiagnosis will become less common in future. He says: 'As we understand more, we'll get a lot better at diagnosing and target treatments better.'

There is more information about conditions people with bipolar sometimes get misdiagnosed with because the symptoms can overlap – see question 14, p. 43, for information about schizoaffective disorder and question 15, p. 43, on borderline personality disorder.

Q26. *What can someone do if they think a loved one might have undiagnosed bipolar disorder?*

The first step to recovery for someone with suspected undiagnosed bipolar disorder that's causing problems is an accurate diagnosis. If they are in the grip of an extreme mood swing, get immediate help – either call an ambulance and get them to A&E (or the Emergency Room in the US) or phone their family doctor and ask for help from the community mental health team. (There's more information about this in question 45, p. 115.) If they are relatively stable, try to persuade them to see their GP as soon as possible, accompanying them to the appointment if they allow it to describe any worrying symptoms.

Remember that the earlier they are diagnosed the better the long-term outcome will be, as Terence Ketter, MD, Emeritus Professor of Psychiatry and Behavioral Sciences at the Stanford University School of Medicine, explains: 'Early and accurate diagnosis is important in preventing disease-related episodes, which potentially lead to illness progression. It's much easier to treat patients who have had fewer than three episodes; after that bipolar disorder gets incrementally more difficult to treat. If we don't let episodes occur, patients can do exceedingly well.'

Q27. *How is bipolar disorder usually diagnosed?*

As discussed in question 25, a GP or family physician often only sees someone when they're experiencing the depressive symptoms of bipolar disorder, so family doctors don't typically diagnose bipolar disorder. Either he or she will misdiagnose the patient with depression or refer the patient to a psychiatrist who will review medical history, family history and compare symptoms with the official list in the DSM-5.

To gather a list of symptoms, a psychiatrist is likely to ask questions such as the following:

Depression

- How sad do you get and for how long?
- Do you enjoy things?
- Can you imagine what your future will be like?
- Do you feel hopeless or helpless?
- Can you concentrate?
- Do your thoughts feel slow?
- Do you feel tired all the time?
- Do you sleep too much?
- Do you think about death and dying?
- Do you think about killing yourself?

Mania

- Do you have periods of high energy and productivity?
- How happy or angry do you get and for how long?
- Do you have times when you feel you're the best at everything?

- Have you ever got into trouble during these times by spending or borrowing too much money?
- Do your thoughts feel hyperactive?
- Do you sleep too little?
- Do you ever hear voices or believe you have magical powers?

Anxiety

- How much do you worry about things?
- Have you ever had a panic attack?
- Do you think people want to harm you?
- Do you ever self-harm?
- Do you hate social situations or avoid them altogether?

Mental health history

- Have you ever been hospitalized in a psychiatric unit?
- Have you ever been depressed or manic?
- Have you ever taken medication for a psychiatric condition?
- Have you ever seen a therapist?
- Are any family members diagnosed with a mental health condition, including depression, or do any family members have a problem with substance abuse?
- Did you experience depression or manic symptoms as a teenager or child?

Lifestyle

- What's your life like now?
- Are you in full-time education or do you work?
- What's your social life like?
- Do you exercise?
- Do you eat well?

- Do you drink alcohol?
- Do you smoke?
- Do you take any prescribed or recreational drugs?

The psychiatrist is then likely to give an initial diagnosis.

PATHWAY OF CARE

© Michel Syrett, 2006.

Q28. What happens once a diagnosis of bipolar disorder is made?

Once a diagnosis of bipolar disorder has been made, what happens next very much depends on the individual. The first factor involved is whether or not the person has insight into their own condition. This then determines a 'pathway of care' – as brilliantly captured in diagram form by author and journalist Michel Syrett, who himself has bipolar disorder. This diagram (opposite) was originally published in the BBC booklet *The Secret Life of Manic Depression: Everything You Need to Know about Bipolar Disorder.*

Below, Michel Syrett explains how his Pathway of Care diagram illustrates broad stages in the journey to managing bipolar disorder successfully:

Insight

'People with milder forms of the disorder, such as Bipolar II, often have the insight to recognize early symptoms, engage in consultation with their GP and agree to a referral to a psychiatric outpatient unit, which results in an accurate diagnosis.'

Lack of insight

'However, many people who develop a bipolar disorder have a distinct and potentially destructive lack of insight. The symptoms of the disorder are often only spotted with the onset of a crisis in a person's life, sometimes involving the police, a visit to an Accident and Emergency department or compulsory treatment under the Mental Health Act 1983. It is only then that they are referred to a psychiatric unit and diagnosed.'

Towards diagnosis

'Even then someone has to accept the diagnosis. Denial at this stage will lead to a cycle of crisis and re-diagnosis that, not confronted, can last decades.

On the other hand, acceptance will lead to insight which will in turn lead to action and the creation of a self-management plan to help the person control the illness rather than vice versa.'

Life-long acceptance

Just as someone faced with a diabetes diagnosis pre-empts and controls their blood sugar levels, someone with a bipolar diagnosis needs to pre-empt and control mood swings for the rest of his or her life. And it's the 'incurable' nature of the illness that means some people find accepting the diagnosis extremely difficult, including Amanda's mum Irene and her family:

> When my mum was first diagnosed with bipolar in 1993, I don't think she or any one of us really understood what this meant in the long term. Each mood swing episode would last for a few days or weeks, and sometimes she would end up in hospital. But when she was stable and back home again, she hated the bipolar diagnosis so much that she would go into denial, and think that the problem had been 'fixed' – and we would try to believe it too. It sounds so naive now, looking back, but each time, we all so desperately wanted to think that Mum's illness was over. Eventually, as she struggled over the years with recurring mood swings, a realization sank in that for however long she might stay 'well' in between episodes, the bipolar was never cured, only managed.
>
> (AMANDA)

> People say once they're diagnosed they feel relief, but I've never felt relieved – I felt really scared. I've always known you can't cure these things. But somehow I wish there could be treatment without diagnosis. Because once you have a label like this slapped on you, it affects everything from insurance to driving licence. If you're honest about it and actually declare it, it's really hard to deal with.
>
> (TAMARA)

> I was told years ago by a psychiatrist that I suffered from manic depression but I dismissed it. Last year, I became manic but rejected the diagnosis again. My

psychiatrist then explained that I had to accept the diagnosis in order to help prevent relapse, but I felt angry at myself for not being able to control it properly. Now I hope I can become fully stable on medication so I don't swing up and down so often, and that I can make bipolar disorder something I can live with.

(*JUDE*)

At first I was relieved to have a diagnosis because it put a name to my problems. But on the other hand, having a diagnosis has added more of a strain. Although I'm diagnosed and getting treated, my behaviour is still very erratic. It felt like the diagnosis was an easy answer, but it wasn't. The diagnosis isn't the answer to all our prayers. It names the problem but doesn't solve the problem.

(*PAUL*)

Others, though, experience relief when they are diagnosed, because they finally have an explanation for sometimes decades of inexplicable behaviour:

It's early days, but I do feel relief from having the diagnosis. It's been a massive relief to realize that a lot of my behaviour has been completely normal for a bipolar person. And there's relief to know that I can get the right treatment.

(*ASHLEY*)

Laura was diagnosed with bipolar last February. I was very worried. We'd lost the person. When she's well and in a balanced state, she's a very sociable person and great fun. I would say she's like that one tenth of her life as it comes and goes. The rest of the time she's either up or down or aggressive. It was an enormous relief to give it a name.

(*JUNE*)

The bipolar diagnosis has helped me, because it made sense of my previous feelings. I'm comfortable with it. It's not going to define me. It's just some aspect of me that probably made me who I am. Without the disorder, are you the same person? I don't think so.

(*NEIL*)

The important thing to remember, as Candida Fink and Joe Kraynak clearly explain in *Bipolar Disorder for Dummies*, is that a bipolar diagnosis doesn't define you: 'You're not bipolar, you *have* bipolar. This is a huge difference because language conveys powerful meanings. Always refer to your illness as something you're managing, not as a label that identifies you. People say "Pat is bipolar", but if Pat had cancer they wouldn't say "Pat is cancer". Always remember that you're not bipolar disorder but that bipolar disorder is something you have.'

CHAPTER TWO

Treatment

Q29. *What is the most effective way to treat bipolar disorder?*

It can't be said enough times that bipolar disorder is a lifelong condition like diabetes or asthma. The treatment for bipolar is, then, the management of a chronic illness, not a permanent cure.

This isn't necessarily bad news. So much more can be done nowadays to treat bipolar disorder successfully, to reduce or remove symptoms and help someone with a diagnosis to live a happy and stable life. Currently, someone diagnosed with bipolar is typically prescribed medication (usually a mix-and-match combination of antidepressants, mood stabilizers, anti-psychotics and anti-anxiety drugs), offered a form of psychological therapy and taught a range of self-management techniques. In hospital, they might also be given electroconvulsive therapy (ECT) or repetitive transcranial magnetic stimulation (RTMS).

'In the past couple of decades I hope we have come to see the importance of a more holistic approach to the treatment of bipolar disorder,' says Professor Ian Jones, Professor of Psychiatry at Cardiff University and Director of the National Centre for Mental Health. 'There's more recognition that treatment isn't just about medication (although medication is a very important part of treatment for most people), rather it's about a combination of the right medication, self-management and psychological and social support. We've still got a way to go compared to other areas of medicine – people with diabetes are given much more diet and lifestyle advice alongside their insulin, for example. But we're moving in the right direction.'

As for the treatments themselves, although currently it can take time and an element of luck to prescribe the right treatment, new research is emerging all the time that we're hoping will lead to more effective, personalized treatments.

The key here is the phrase 'personalized treatments'. The vision for the future shared by many scientists seems to be that rather than saying to someone, 'You have Bipolar I – here's the standard treatment for it,' a person's treatment will focus on their individual symptoms rather than their diagnosis.

Another growing school of thought is that the treatment of bipolar disorder should include *preventing* symptoms in high-risk people. Professor Richard Morriss, Professor of Psychiatry and Community Mental Health at Nottingham University, believes that it is possible to delay or reduce symptoms so that someone with a high genetic risk is more likely to develop the condition later in life – in their thirties rather than their twenties, for example, which will have huge, life-changing implications: 'Because you can identify a high-risk group (children of a first or second degree relative with bipolar – parent, sibling, aunt, uncle, for instance) it may be possible in the future to prevent or delay the full expression of the illness … If we could identify and monitor closely people at risk – if we had good services, i.e. more supportive, less emphasis on drugs – at least there wouldn't be a long delay before diagnosis. Of course, it is difficult to know how much these things are predetermined. But it would be great to delay or limit consequences. Then at least when symptoms arrive you have more experience, more maturity, you've achieved something, maybe met a partner, you're not involved in drugs, basically you're in a more stable part of your life. There are increasingly ways to identify high-risk behaviours – essentially identifying that people have something like cyclothymia. Then they could seek preventative treatment.'

Preventative treatment for those at higher risk of developing bipolar could include using psychological therapies, as Dr Sara Tai, Senior Lecturer in Clinical Psychology at the University of Manchester, explains: 'There are a number of things we've identified that can help prevent potential signs of bipolar growing into full-blown bipolar. For example, it's natural for everybody to get low or to feel down sometimes. Those who mull and ruminate over why they're depressed are in much more danger of having mood swings, whereas those who think "What can I do to get over this?" are much less likely to get depressed. So that's a coping mechanism, a skill that anybody can learn, regardless of their natural tendencies. Another important factor is how people solve problems. You're not necessarily born with problem-solving skills, but you can learn them.'

Living a healthy life could also help protect someone who has a higher genetic risk of developing bipolar disorder – see Chapter 5, p. 184, for advice on lifestyle choices that protect mental health.

Q30. *Are there official treatment guidelines for bipolar disorder?*

In England and Wales, treatment guidelines are issued by NICE, which was established in 1999 after widespread concern that treatment and care for a wide range of medical conditions was becoming a 'postcode lottery' characterized by local inconsistencies. The NICE guidelines set the 'gold standard' for healthcare services – all NHS trusts are expected to comply, and they are regularly reviewed by the Care Quality Commission (previously known as the Healthcare Commission), the independent regulator of health and adult social care in the UK.

At the time of writing, the most recent NICE guideline for the treatment of bipolar disorder in England and Wales (CG185) was published in 2014 and last updated in April 2018. You can view or download the full or summarized version at www.nice.org.uk – search for 'bipolar disorder' or 'CG185', and you'll find a list of useful topics.

The NICE guideline emphasizes 'person-centred care' and states in the introduction that: 'This guideline offers best practice advice on the care of adults, children and young people with bipolar disorder. People with bipolar disorder and their healthcare professionals have rights and responsibilities as set out in the NHS Constitution for England – all NICE guidance is written to reflect these. Treatment and care should take into account individual needs and preferences. People should have the opportunity to make informed decisions about their care and treatment, in partnership with their healthcare professionals.'

The NICE guideline also recommends that healthcare professionals should 'promote a positive recovery message from the point of diagnosis and throughout care,' and 'build supportive and empathic relationships as an essential part of care.'

A separate NICE guideline on 'service user experience' in adult mental health was published in 2011, with the stated aim of 'improving the experience of care for adults with bipolar disorder using mental health services'. This can also be accessed via the NICE website (search for 'CG136').

If NICE treatment guidelines are not followed – for instance, if psychological treatments or annual health checks are not offered – a patient or loved one can raise this with their family doctor, psychiatrist, support worker, or other members of their community mental health team (see question 45, p. 115). Knowledge is power, and knowing what the recommendations are is the first step towards getting them implemented.

It's also helpful to inform the Care Quality Commission if NICE guidelines aren't being implemented in a local area. The more information the commission has, the better equipped they are to guide health trusts towards positive change – see Extra resources, p. 267, for contact details.

In Scotland, the Scottish Intercollegiate Guidelines Network (SIGN) performs the same function as NICE. They issued a bipolar treatment guideline in 2014, which broadly follows similar principles to the NICE guideline. For more details, contact SIGN via the details in Extra resources, p. 267.

Another resource for health professionals is *The International Classification of Diseases* – a diagnostic manual published by the WHO. It was last updated in June 2018 and includes lots of useful guidelines about the treatment of bipolar.

And all around the world, many clinicians refer to treatment guidelines from the World Federation of Societies of Biological Psychiatry (WFSBP) – a non-profit organization with members from over 50 countries.

Q31. *What is psychological treatment, such as cognitive behavioural therapy?*

More and more evidence is accumulating to show how important psychological therapy can be in the treatment of bipolar disorder. For example, a study published in the journal *Archives of General Psychiatry* showed that patients with bipolar disorder who are taking medication improved faster and stayed well if they also received intense psychotherapy (a generic term which includes CBT as well as other therapies such as family focused therapy). The study, led by David Miklowitz, Professor of Psychology and Psychiatry at the University of Colorado and author of several books on bipolar disorder, monitored patients who received nine months of intense psychotherapy, and others in a control group who received three psycho-educational sessions. During the course of the year, 64% of the patients who received intense psychotherapy became well, compared with 52% of the control group. The study also found that patients who received intense psychotherapy became well an average of 110 days sooner and were one-and-a-half times more likely to be well during any month of the study year than the other patients.

Perhaps not surprisingly, the latest NICE guideline for the treatment of bipolar disorder (CG185) recommends psychological therapies. The guideline's Development Group found that 'individual structured psychological interventions are clinically effective ... Studies support the efficacy of individual CBT.' So the NICE guideline advises that a person with bipolar should be offered:

- a psychological intervention that has been developed specifically for bipolar disorder and has a published, evidence-based manual describing how it should be delivered, or
- a high-intensity psychological intervention (CBT, interpersonal therapy or behavioural couples therapy).

A huge number of experts in the field also believe that psychological therapies are an extremely important part of the treatment jigsaw. Professor Steven Jones, Professor of Clinical Psychology and Co-director of the Spectrum Centre for Mental Health Research at Lancaster University, is one of them: 'Maybe 20 years ago, there was a bit of an assumption that psychological approaches weren't really relevant to bipolar disorder – it was seen almost purely as a biological problem. I think that story is changing gradually, which is good.'

Dr Sara Tai, Senior Lecturer in Clinical Psychology at the University of Manchester, cautions, though, that all therapies might not be equal: 'You have to be careful with the phrase "talking therapies". It doesn't mean you're just sitting there talking. In fact, it covers a wide range of interventions. It's true that some less evidence-based "therapies" might consist of talking and befriending. But the type of psychological intervention that research shows really works is not just about talking, it's about getting people to become more aware of things and make changes in their life so they can understand how their symptoms have developed. It's not necessarily an easy process for people, not straightforward, but the results can be amazingly powerful. And as an added bonus, there aren't really any side effects in the same way that medication might cause side effects.'

The most common psychological treatments offered to those with bipolar disorder are: CBT; family focused therapy; counselling; and group therapy.

So how can they actually help?

Cognitive behavioural therapy (CBT)

One of the biggest buzzwords in psychological treatment in recent years has been CBT. Usually carried out by psychologists in one-to-one sessions with the patient, the theory is that thought, behaviour and mood all affect each other, which means it's possible to teach someone how to change their thoughts and behaviour in order to influence their mood.

The key to CBT is not about mental health professionals telling someone what to do, but about giving them the tools to monitor and control their own behaviour, thoughts and mood. Peter Kinderman, Professor of Clinical Psychology at the University of Liverpool, says: 'What this isn't doing is giving people advice, because you don't sit as a guru and say to someone either, "It is good in life to avoid going to parties – alcohol is a bad thing," or, "I can tell that *you* shouldn't go to parties and *you* shouldn't drink alcohol." What you say is, "When you notice yourself going high, bring yourself down, and when you notice yourself going low, do something about it." It's teaching people to respond to their own internal states in a way that they haven't done before.'

Research shows that CBT is particularly effective for patients with recurring depressive mood swings – here the therapy works on the idea that negative thinking is a bad habit, and that it's possible to learn techniques to break this habit. A patient gains more insight into their condition, learning to step back and look at the evidence for their negative thoughts, recognize these for what they are and then build up new positive ones. They intervene in their own automatic negative thinking about themselves and the world – for example, instead of the depressive train of thought that says, 'I'm hopeless, I can't do anything,' the patient learns how to examine and challenge this thought, and recognize that it's not true.

And for those with bipolar disorder, research carried out at the Institute of Psychiatry shows that CBT can help prevent relapse when used alongside mood stabilizing drugs. The study recruited 103 people with a Bipolar I diagnosis who had frequent relapses, and split them into two groups – half were given CBT treatment as well as medication, and the other half (the control group) received only medication and no CBT. Comparing the two groups over the following 30-month period, results showed that:

- 44% of the CBT group experienced a relapse, compared with a 75% relapse rate for the control group.

- The group receiving CBT spent an average of 27 days experiencing a bipolar episode, compared with 88 days for the non-CBT control group.
- 15% of the patients receiving CBT were hospitalized, compared with 33% in the control group who did not receive CBT.

Research by Professor Jan Scott, Professor of Psychological Medicine at the University of Newcastle, and Honorary Professor at the Centre for Affective Disorders at the Institute of Psychiatry, Psychology & Neuroscience (formerly the Institute of Psychiatry), and Dr Mary Teach, Special Adviser in Crisis to the Royal College of Psychiatrists 2014–17, has also shown that a shortened form of CBT can improve patients' regularity in taking lithium.

As well as the clinical research, there's also a lot of anecdotal evidence around to show that CBT is a good treatment for bipolar disorder:

> I've had a lot of CBT. It definitely works – and really it's the only thing that's ever worked for me.
>
> (SHARRON)

> The CBT has really worked for me, but it's been a very long process. I've been trying to undo 20 years of learned behaviour.
>
> (LESLEY)

> I started a course of CBT on a weekly basis for about 50 sessions and I learnt a lot. I can identify the triggers much better.
>
> (TAMARA)

So how does CBT actually work? For someone with bipolar disorder, the first stage of CBT is a short period of what's called 'psycho-education', giving them information on the cause, diagnosis, symptoms and treatment to help them get a real understanding of their illness.

This is followed by an extended period when they record activities, behaviour and mood fluctuations in a 'mood diary'. This charts the impact of activities on mood, highlighting those that may trigger a mood swing. Another goal, as Professor Steven Jones explains, is to challenge the common trait in people with bipolar to identify personally with their internal experiences and not look for external reasons or activities as explanations for why they may feel or react in a particular way: 'People within the bipolar spectrum seem to be more likely to explain how they are feeling as being to do with something about themselves, rather than something to do with what's going on in their environment. If a person is feeling slightly energized or more alert or aroused than usual, the tendency would be more to think, "I've got more energy, this is the real me," rather than to think, "Maybe I've had a bit too much coffee" or "I didn't sleep so well last night" or that there's some event coming up which is stimulating their interest. People come in and say, "I feel awful, it's come out of the blue, I've no idea why, this proves I've got no control over what's going on for me." And then you look back over their diary for the previous week and the person has been dealing with all sorts of significant and major challenges. Making those links with the person over time can help them detect these patterns earlier, and then they can take steps to deal with those.'

Another huge part of CBT for someone with bipolar is to detect early warning signs for the mood swings. 'What we try and do is to work quite hard to identify what we call early, middle and late signs, and recognize the early ones as early as possible,' says Professor Steven Jones.

So, before a depressive episode, the early warning signs might include:

- lack of energy
- insufficient/interrupted sleep
- feelings of anxiety
- negative thoughts
- low motivation/can't do routine tasks
- withdrawing from social/enjoyable activities
- less interest in food and sex.

And the early warning signs leading up to a manic period might include:

- less need for sleep
- thoughts starting to race
- irritability
- heightened sense of self-worth
- feeling over-excited and restless
- 'goal directed' activities, often impulsive, such as chopping down all the trees in the front garden, applying for 20 new jobs in one week, suddenly redecorating the house
- overspending
- being more sociable than usual.

Yet not all early warning signs are the 'obvious' ones listed above. In fact, often they're very specific to each individual. When Amanda's mum Irene, for example, starts asking Amanda and her brother Andrew if they had a happy childhood, this is usually an early signal that a depressive mood swing is imminent. And when, in mid-conversation, Sarah's sister Rebecca starts casually referring to her plans to become a famous pop singer, this is a sure-fire sign that a manic episode is brewing. Other early warning signs can be just as specific to an individual:

> When Laura's heading for a high, she won't take public transport. Either she takes my car, or if she doesn't have access to a car, she takes a taxi to work even though it costs her £75.
>
> *(JUNE)*

> When I'm starting to go manic, I start to think, 'Oh, I don't really have this illness, and I don't really need to take this medication.'
>
> *(LESLEY)*

> I'm learning to recognize the early warning signs of a manic episode. I start to overbook gigs and take loads of work on and I'm out everywhere wanting to be sociable.
>
> *(ASHLEY)*

So, once these early warning signs are spotted, what action does CBT encourage someone to take?

If the early warning signs point towards a looming depression, someone is advised to:

- take a positive goal-directed step, however small – for instance, sending an email or doing the washing up
- do something enjoyable – call a friend or go for a walk
- speak to a health professional, such as their doctor, psychiatrist or care coordinator
- take extra medication, as previously agreed with their doctor or psychiatrist.

If the early warning signs point towards impending mania, someone is advised to:

- reduce their daily task load
- engage in a calming activity, such as reading or soaking in the bath
- avoid stimulating activities
- take more breaks in the day
- ensure a good sleep routine
- take extra medication, as previously agreed with their doctor or psychiatrist.

Saying that, CBT certainly isn't a quick-fix option. Upward mood swings can sometimes kick in really quickly so there's very little time to spot the early warning signs. During this time, a person's insight can vanish and, of course, because going high can be so enjoyable, it's not unheard of for someone with bipolar to ignore the early warning signs even if they recognize them. But, as Professor Peter Kinderman explains, sensible protective steps can be taken beforehand to help combat this: 'Lack of insight is part of why CBT doesn't always work as well when people go high. The problems that you see with going high are often what the people themselves might not recognize as problems. Cognitive behavioural therapy is less easy then because you've got to persuade people to tell themselves to do something unpleasant – to not go out, not drink, not spend loads of cash, not go on eBay, all sorts of things that are really quite difficult for them to avoid doing. But it's not that difficult to set up a system beforehand where the person can protect themselves – so they could for instance phone up their bank and say, "Can you put a £100 limit on this credit card?" It's not difficult to do this when you're well, but it's very difficult to do this when you're high.'

For details on mindfulness-based cognitive therapy (MBCT), see question 71, p. 196.

Family focused therapy

Family focused therapy aims to foster good dialogue and improved communication within a family group, in this case the person with bipolar and their close family members. Educating family members in the causes, symptoms and treatment of bipolar, and encouraging more shared understanding of the condition, can lead each of them to understand the difficulties of others in relation to the illness, and help them all to develop coping skills and strategies to deal with the challenging situations the illness can create. Sarah and her mother Rose went to six family-focused therapy sessions during one of Rebecca's hospital stays:

 Rebecca had been in hospital for nearly a year when we were offered family therapy once a week. Mum was worrying about how Rebecca would cope after having been in hospital for so long, and we were both concerned about what the future might hold for her. We talked lots of things through – how much we loved Rebecca, yet how frustrating we found her to live with and how difficult we found it to accept some of her life choices. Perhaps the most useful thing of all was that the therapist helped us see that while we continued to treat Rebecca as a child we weren't allowing her to grow up. We learnt that it was important for her to be allowed to make her own mistakes, as only then could she learn from them. And ultimately we learnt that however much we loved her and wanted to rescue her, we weren't responsible for her decisions. The idea was that Rebecca would join us for sessions after she left hospital, but she found the first one overwhelming and we all stopped going. It was a shame, but the timing obviously wasn't right for her. And even though Mum and I only had six sessions, it was really useful and tangibly changed our relationships with Rebecca, as we both took a step back and tried to treat her like an adult.

When my older brother went manic, it was a big shock for me, my brother and our parents. I couldn't get my head around the fact that my sociable, sporty brother had suddenly been taken into hospital. It was like a bomb had gone off in our family. The sessions we had with a family therapist helped us all understand bipolar disorder better and definitely helped me unravel some of the complicated feelings I had about my brother and his illness.

(CHARLIE)

Counselling

Here the patient talks about the difficulties and issues caused by their bipolar disorder to a counsellor, who listens supportively and helps the patient to acknowledge and accept the illness. Sometimes the counsellor is able to give practical advice and suggestions for ways of dealing with these challenges, but his or her main role is to listen. Bear in mind that anyone can call themselves a counsellor, which means that qualifications, training levels and experience can vary considerably.

Group therapy

People diagnosed with the same condition, such as bipolar disorder, can be invited to take part in group therapy sessions, which allow people to share the experiences of others with the same problems and realize that their experiences aren't unique. Mutual support and understanding, and the sharing of coping strategies, can also be very beneficial to group therapy members.

Q32. *How can someone with bipolar disorder get psychological treatment?*

Anyone diagnosed with bipolar disorder (or any other mental health condition) can ask their GP or their community mental health team (CMHT) for a free referral to a clinical psychologist, and it may in any case be recommended as part of their care plan. But, as with many healthcare services, the national availability of psychological treatment through the NHS is patchy. Back in 2007, when we were writing the first edition of this book, the report *We Need to Talk* (produced by the UK charities Mind, Rethink, the Mental Health Foundation, Young Minds and the Sainsbury Centre for Mental Health) highlighted that despite the government's good intentions and the 2006 NICE recommendations for more psychological treatments to treat mental illnesses, availability was still far from adequate. Waiting times of over six months were common – a huge shame because evidence shows that the longer the wait between someone developing bipolar and receiving psychological treatment, the less effective the treatment.

In response, the UK government launched its 'Improving Access to Psychological Therapies' (IAPT) programme later in 2007. This increased funding for psychological therapy, with over £170 million earmarked for psychological therapy and a target of 3,600 newly trained psychological therapists. This was followed by their 'No Health Without Mental Health' strategy in 2011, which aimed to ensure that mental and physical health conditions are treated equally in the NHS. The government also reaffirmed its dedication to IAPT by publishing *Talking Therapies: A Four-Year Plan of Action*, which made clear commitments to improving access and continuing the roll-out of IAPT until 2015, backed by a further £400 million for the IAPT programme.

But has it been enough? Mind's 2013 follow-up report, *We Still Need to Talk*, recognized the progress the UK government had made within NHS psychological therapy provision in England, especially the commitment to improving the IAPT programme. However, the report also highlighted that waiting times, equity of access and choice of therapies were still far from adequate – a view later backed up by the report 'Psychotherapy provision in the UK: time to think again', published in *The Lancet* in 2015 and jointly produced by the UK Council for Psychotherapy (UKCP) and the British Psychoanalytic Council (BPC). It seems that demand for talking therapies continues to outstrip supply massively – 94% of (BPC) therapists surveyed for the report said they regularly saw clients privately who felt let down by the NHS.

If you do have enough funds or private health insurance, you can seek private CBT treatment from a clinical psychologist or professional counsellor. The best way to find one is to request a referral (or a list of suggestions) from your GP, get a personal recommendation from someone you know, or go via a professional body, such as the British Association for Counselling and Psychotherapy (www.bacp.co.uk) or the British Association for Behavioural and Cognitive Psychotherapies (www.babcp.com).

Online CBT

Online CBT can also be helpful, especially if face-to-face therapy is not easily available.

The online CBT course 'Beating the Blues' was developed by the Institute of Psychiatry, King's College London, as part of the government's IAPT pro-gramme. The course consists of eight one-hour sessions helping to pinpoint and change unhelpful ways of thinking and develop more effective ways of solving problems. Research from independent randomized controlled trials, published in the *British Journal of Psychiatry*, has shown that Beating the Blues is an effective treatment for depression. You can find out more at www.beatingtheblues.co.uk.

Another online option is 'Moodgym', an interactive online CBT programme, developed and evaluated over 15 years by researchers at the Australian National University in Canberra. According to its website, Moodgym can help users prevent and manage their depression symptoms by teaching skills based on CBT. You can register for Moodgym at www.moodgym.com.au – the programme is free, secure and confidential.

Too many drugs, not enough psychology?

The frustrating thing about the poor availability of psychological treatment is that people with bipolar disorder and other mental illnesses are more likely to be prescribed drugs before, or even instead of, psychological therapies. A total of 64.7 million antidepressant prescriptions – an all-time high – were dispensed in England in 2016, according to the most recent data from NHS Digital. That's 3.7 million more than in 2015, and represents a staggering 108.5% increase on the 31 million antidepressant prescriptions dispensed in 2006.

It's difficult to know if this means that some doctors are handing out drugs too freely, or if in fact more people are coming forward with mental health problems. Gillian Connor, Head of Policy and Development at the leading UK charity Rethink Mental Illness, says, 'The reasons for this increase in antidepressant prescriptions could include a greater awareness of mental illness and more willingness to seek help. However, with our overstretched and underfunded mental health services, too often antidepressants are the only treatment available.'

The result is that overmedication is a real risk for people with mental health conditions, including children. Research has shown an alarming increase in the amount of antidepressants prescribed for children in the UK and elsewhere. A 2016 report from the WHO revealed that the number of UK children prescribed antidepressants increased by more than 50% between 2005 and 2012, along with rises of 60% in Denmark, 49% in Germany, 26% in the US and 17% in the Netherlands.

More recent data from NHS England also shows that between April 2015 and March 2016, 64,765 under-18s, including 3,876 children aged seven to twelve and 315 aged six or younger, were given medication typically used to treat depression and anxiety.

Dr Sara Tai, Senior Lecturer in Clinical Psychology at the University of Manchester, sums up the situation like this: 'Our health service is heavily weighted towards psychiatry, rather than psychological interventions. It's the same in America. Of course drugs can help. But that shouldn't necessarily be considered as the first line of treatment. Whereas our whole system is pushed by diagnosis, particularly when you look at psychiatry, we should be treating the person not the condition. That's where medication really falls down – it treats the condition, the syndrome, the disorder, not the individual. Some of the people I work with learn to change their social factors or lifestyle and feel considerably better – no pill in the world is going to do that.'

That's not to say psychological intervention needs to be given instead of medication, but, as collective expert opinion generally agrees, alongside it.

We like the way John McManamy, a writer with bipolar disorder, puts it on his excellent website, www.mcmanweb.com (which is packed with up-to-the-minute research about the condition): 'Clearly two therapies (medication and psychotherapy) together represent one of those rare cases where one plus one equals three.'

In other words, when it comes to treating bipolar disorder, medication alone is useful, psychological therapy alone is useful, but medication *plus* therapy is the most powerful solution of all.

Q33. What drugs are used in the treatment of bipolar disorder?

Most people diagnosed with bipolar disorder are automatically given a prescription for medication to help stabilize mood. And, it seems, there are a million and one different drug combinations a psychiatrist can choose from, depending on a number of factors such as an individual's symptoms and previous mood patterns. The trouble is, a drug that works brilliantly for one person may not work for someone else, even if on the surface their symptoms appear to be similar. Or side effects caused by a medication may be terrible for one person and non-existent for another. Often a number of drugs need to be taken at the same time, and some drugs can interact with each other.

'There are a large number of medications used in the treatment of the phases of bipolar disorder and to help keep people well,' says Professor

Ian Jones, Professor of Psychiatry at Cardiff University and Director of the National Centre for Mental Health. 'One of the longest used medications, and still one with perhaps the best evidence for its effectiveness, is lithium, which has been used to treat bipolar for over 60 years. Lithium has allowed many people with bipolar to live a stable and productive life but probably is still underused – partly because it does have some potential long-term complications, partly because we have no way of predicting who will respond well to lithium and who won't. The trouble is, it can take a lot of trial and error to get an individual on the right medication or combination of drugs at the right dose for them and to know for sure what's being effective. One of the key goals of research I think is helping us predict which patients will respond to what drugs – in addition to developing new, more effective treatments with fewer side effects.'

Finding the right combination of medication can be challenging, as Professor Guy Goodwin, Senior Research Fellow at the University of Oxford, explains: 'The medicines primarily used to treat bipolar disorder have been studied under the controlled conditions of clinical trials. They have been shown to be effective at a particular dose in the majority of patients, and to produce negative effects (or not to work) in a minority of others. So when you prescribe any medicine to someone, all you know as a doctor is its average predictable effects. For the patient this seems like trial and error, which it is, but the advantage of the trials done to establish the drug mean that the odds of it working are quite favourable. Dosing is difficult because the human liver (and gut) is a wonderfully variable thing and the level of any drug in the blood varies ten-fold for any dose given by mouth. Indeed, the different ways a drug is metabolized in the body will contribute to different responses to the same dose. In an individual patient, it's wise to start with a low dose, go slowly, but build up to the highest well tolerated dose possible. That way you should always be giving enough, but not every doctor or patient seems to have the patience to follow that principle.'

Broadly speaking, there are four main types of medication for treating the symptoms of bipolar disorder:

- mood stabilizers (also sometimes called antimanics), which aim to treat both the highs and the lows
- antipsychotic drugs (also sometimes called neuroleptics), which are mainly used to bring mood down from the highs of hypo-mania, mania or psychosis
- antidepressant drugs to lift mood out of depressive mood swings
- sleeping pills and anti-anxiety drugs, such as benzodiazepines.

As Professor Goodwin indicates, potential benefits often vary between individuals and so do potential side effects. For a more detailed explanation of the uses and side effects of each drug group and its common types, the best advice is to refer directly to the drug manufacturers' leaflet or speak to a psychiatrist, a psychiatric pharmacist or your GP. Some mental health charities, such as Mind and Bipolar UK, also offer useful information about medication (go to www.mind.org.uk or www.bipolaruk.org).

The current NICE guideline for the treatment of bipolar disorder also contains detailed directions on the use of drug treatments for mania, hypomania and depression in people with bipolar. Go to www.nice.org.uk and search for 'bipolar'.

Mood stabilizing/antimanic drugs

Most people with bipolar are prescribed a mood stabilizer – commonly lithium, carbamazepine, sodium valproate or lamotrigine.

- Regular blood tests are recommended for people taking carbamazepine.
- Someone taking valproate needs to have regular liver function tests.

Lithium

Lithium is probably the most well-known and widely used of the mood stabilizing drugs in people with bipolar disorder. It can successfully treat mood swings without acting as a sedative, and has also been proved to reduce the risk of suicide.

- Lithium is a naturally occurring salt, so for anyone with a history of heart, thyroid, epilepsy or kidney problems should only be used after a careful specialist review of the risks and benefits.
- Family history may help decide if lithium can be prescribed – there's evidence that the response to lithium may be similar between family members, so if it works well for one family member with bipolar disorder, it may work well for another.
- Baseline and six-monthly renal (kidney) tests are recommended.
- Someone taking lithium should also have frequent and regular blood tests (usually every three months). Lithium levels must be monitored very closely because there is a very narrow range between beneficial and toxic levels.
- Levels of lithium in the blood can rise if someone becomes dehydrated.
- Lithium should only be used in early pregnancy after a careful specialist review of the risks and benefits.
- Anyone wanting to come off lithium should not do so suddenly (as the risk of relapse is very high) but gradually, in consultation with their doctor or psychiatrist.

Taking lithium? Take note ...

Before anyone starts taking lithium, they should have a blood test to monitor their thyroid function, followed by a thyroid function test every six months. This is because the drug can cause hypothyroidism – a condition where the thyroid gland doesn't produce enough of the hormone thyroxine, which controls the way the body uses energy. Symptoms of hypothyroidism can include slow body movements and speech, tiredness, weakness, poor concentration and memory problems. It can also increase the risk of depression, causing further complications for someone who already has bipolar disorder.

The risk of developing hypothyroidism when taking lithium is fairly high – one research study tracked a group of 713 people who took the drug over a 15-month period, and found that over 10% developed the condition. Women were at greater risk than men – 14% of the female participants developed hypothyroidism compared with only 4.5% of the men, and for women aged between 40 and 59 the figure was 20%.

Amanda's mum Irene's experience is typical of these results:

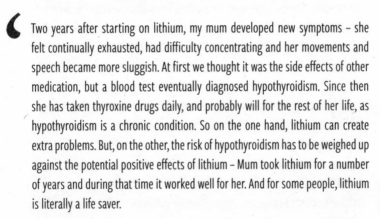

Two years after starting on lithium, my mum developed new symptoms – she felt continually exhausted, had difficulty concentrating and her movements and speech became more sluggish. At first we thought it was the side effects of other medication, but a blood test eventually diagnosed hypothyroidism. Since then she has taken thyroxine drugs daily, and probably will for the rest of her life, as hypothyroidism is a chronic condition. So on the one hand, lithium can create extra problems. But, on the other, the risk of hypothyroidism has to be weighed up against the potential positive effects of lithium – Mum took lithium for a number of years and during that time it worked well for her. And for some people, lithium is literally a life saver.

For more details about the link between bipolar disorder and the thyroid, see question 18, p. 48.

Antipsychotics/neuroleptics

- Antipsychotics are divided into two groups – older (or 'typical') antipsychotics such as haloperidol and chlorpromazine, and the newer generation of antipsychotics (more commonly known as 'atypical') such as olanzapine, quetiapine, risperidone and clozapine.
- Most atypicals have fewer side effects overall, and are usually the first choice, although the older antipsychotics are better for people who can't take or don't respond well to the newer drugs.

- Clozapine runs a 3% risk of causing a reduction in white blood cells, so weekly blood tests are usually recommended for the first 18 weeks of treatment and fortnightly after that.
- Both typicals and atypicals can encourage weight gain, with a risk of developing type 2 diabetes, though this is more common with the newer atypical drugs.
- A rare but potentially life-threatening side effect of neuroleptic/antipsychotic drugs is neuroleptic malignant syndrome, or NMS. Symptoms usually appear within two weeks of starting treatment and include high fever, sweating, muscular rigidity, unstable blood pressure and delirium.

Antidepressants

- Selective serotonin reuptake inhibitors (SSRIs) are the most commonly used type of antidepressant in the UK and are simple to take (usually as one daily dose).
- Risk of overdose from SSRIs is low.
- SSRIs should not be stopped abruptly, as there's a risk of relapse and unpleasant withdrawal symptoms.
- Concerns have been raised by some experts that SSRIs could increase the risk of suicide for anyone under the age of 18.
- Serotonin and noradrenaline reuptake inhibitors (SNRIs) were first developed in the early 1990s. They're very similar in action to SSRIs, but they act on the brain chemical noradrenaline as well as serotonin. They were designed to be more effective than SSRIs, but it seems that some people respond better to SSRIs, while others respond better to SNRIs.
- Tricyclic antidepressants (the oldest type of antidepressants, developed in the 1950s) and venlafaxine (an SNRI) may be effective for resistant depression.
- Monoamine oxidase inhibitors (MAOIs) work by making it harder for an enzyme (monoamine oxidase) that breaks down

noradrenaline and serotonin to do its job, causing these chemicals to stay active in the body for longer. Because they can have dangerous interactions with some kinds of food, they're only usually prescribed by specialists when none of the other types of antidepressants have worked.

- Caution is needed when prescribing antidepressants if treating someone with bipolar disorder, as sometimes these can trigger a switch into mania. To prevent this, mood stabilizers should be prescribed at the same time. See question 34, below, for more information.

Benzodiazepines/anti-anxiety drugs

- These drugs are usually only prescribed for anxiety and/or insomnia in the short term, as dependence can develop very quickly.
- Driving and operating machinery is not recommended, as the effects from taking a drug the night before can continue into the next day.
- Occasionally, these drugs can cause aggression.

Q34. *What does someone with bipolar disorder (or someone with a family history of bipolar disorder) need to know about antidepressants?*

Antidepressants treat the symptoms of depression. There are several different types of antidepressants, including SSRIs, SNRIs, tricyclics and MAOIs.

Most research on antidepressants has been done in people with unipolar depression (people who have never had a manic episode). Less research has been carried out on the use of antidepressants for people with bipolar disorder. What is known, however, is that taking antidepressants without a mood stabilizer may trigger mania and/or worsen the course of bipolar illness for some people. So it's extremely important that someone with bipolar disorder doesn't take antidepressants alone, but together with mood stabilizing medication. This also means that anyone with a family history of bipolar disorder going through a depressive episode is unwise to take antidepressants without a mood stabilizer. Why? Because of their genetic susceptibility, there's a chance their low mood could be 'bipolar in waiting' and that taking antidepressants could trigger a full-blown manic episode. Unbelievably, though, regardless of family history this is an all-too-common occurrence, as Amanda recalls:

> When Mum had her first breakdown, she was diagnosed with depression and given a course of antidepressants – even though she was treated in the very same psychiatric hospital where her brother Jim (Sarah's dad) had been sectioned with bipolar only a few years earlier. Her family history just wasn't considered, which seems an incredible oversight. Within weeks of starting on the antidepressants, her first manic episode struck, and knowing what we know now, the link seems so obvious. Would Mum have developed bipolar without the trigger of antidepressants? It's impossible to say. We'll never know. What we do know is that the manic switch she experienced after taking the antidepressants was fast, out of control and terrifying for her to experience and for us to witness.

Sarah – despite the fact that her father, sister and aunt have had diagnoses of bipolar disorder – was offered antidepressants in 2002.

> About a year after I'd had my second son, I found that I was completely physically and emotionally exhausted. I wasn't sleeping or eating properly. I cried a lot. My GP referred me to a psychiatrist who diagnosed postnatal depression and prescribed antidepressants. Luckily I didn't ever get the pills because the turning point came for me when I finally admitted to myself that I needed to ask for help. I got through my low patch with extra sleep, good food and lots of support from family and friends. I did keep the prescription for a while, though, in case my mood slipped down again. I didn't have a clue that taking antidepressants, with my family's medical history, could have triggered mania. Of course I'll never know

what would have happened, but I think it's shocking that I was given them without my genetic family tree entering into the equation.

The really important point here is that anyone who has a family member with bipolar disorder and who is seeing their GP because they're feeling depressed needs to emphasize their family background so that it can be taken into account if any medication is prescribed.

Q35. *What new drugs are in the pipeline for bipolar disorder?*

'Current medications for bipolar disorder reduce symptoms but often don't do a good enough job,' says Professor Allan Young, Director of the Centre for Affective Disorders at King's College London. 'The good news is that researchers are currently exploring a wide range of possible new treatments and I'm hopeful that by 2020 exciting new drugs will be available.' Ones to watch include:

Ketamine

Originally developed as an animal anaesthetic used by vets, several small clinical trials have shown that a single infusion of ketamine can work as a fast-acting antidepressant. Patients report an improvement in symptoms after two to four hours and the effect can last for between seven and 14 days.

Ketamine is typically delivered intravenously, though it can also be given via an inhaler or injected. Worryingly, Ketamine is sometimes abused as a 'club' drug known as 'K', 'Ket' or 'Special K' and has been linked to confusion, agitation, panic attacks and short- and long-term memory loss. Frequent use sometimes causes very serious bladder problems.

In a clinical setting, ketamine's promise as a rapidly acting antidepressant means many ketamine treatment clinics have opened (especially in the US) over the past several years. However, its clinical use is still highly cautioned; there are no current long-term safety data to support ketamine's repeated use in depression beyond a few weeks. It is hoped that larger, more rigorous clinical trials will be completed in the next few years.

Oxytocin

A natural hormone known for its role in childbirth and breastfeeding, oxytocin is now thought to be linked to social bonding and sexual fulfilment. Researchers at the University of Oslo in Norway have tested a new device for delivering the hormone oxytocin via the nose. Although there's still a poor understanding of how oxytocin reaches and affects the brain, early studies show it can help regulate social behaviour and improve mental health symptoms. Trials are ongoing.

Light therapy

According to a paper published in the *American Journal of Psychiatry* it seems that bright light therapy may lead to a significant improvement in the symptoms of bipolar depression. The timing of the light therapy appears to be key – researchers found that light therapy given between midday and 2.30pm was most effective.

Individuals increased their exposure to bright white light (7000 lux) from 15 minutes to 60 minutes a day. After six weeks, about 68% of those with a moderate severity of depressive symptoms were in remission compared to 22% of those who received placebo (red light) treatments. Interestingly, most of the improvement occurred during weeks four to six. As the study ended at six weeks, researchers speculate that an even higher number of participants would have improved if they'd continued with the treatment.

For more information about treating seasonal affective disorder (SAD) with light therapy, see question 41, p. 107.

Q36. *Does someone with bipolar disorder need to take medication for the rest of his or her life?*

Few people like the idea of taking medication, especially in the long term. It's a reminder of being ill, and the side effects may be unpleasant. When first diagnosed with bipolar disorder, Amanda's mum, Irene, did not want to take pills indefinitely, as Amanda explains:

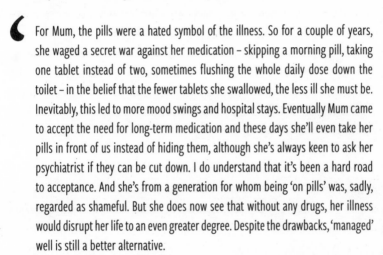

For Mum, the pills were a hated symbol of the illness. So for a couple of years, she waged a secret war against her medication – skipping a morning pill, taking one tablet instead of two, sometimes flushing the whole daily dose down the toilet – in the belief that the fewer tablets she swallowed, the less ill she must be. Inevitably, this led to more mood swings and hospital stays. Eventually Mum came to accept the need for long-term medication and these days she'll even take her pills in front of us instead of hiding them, although she's always keen to ask her psychiatrist if they can be cut down. I do understand that it's been a hard road to acceptance. And she's from a generation for whom being 'on pills' was, sadly, regarded as shameful. But she does now see that without any drugs, her illness would disrupt her life to an even greater degree. Despite the drawbacks, 'managed' well is still a better alternative.

The other problem can be that when the drugs are working and someone is feeling well, they can think, 'I'm feeling fine now – so that must mean I don't need these drugs any more!'

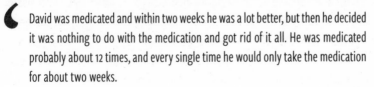

David was medicated and within two weeks he was a lot better, but then he decided it was nothing to do with the medication and got rid of it all. He was medicated probably about 12 times, and every single time he would only take the medication for about two weeks.

(PAULA)

The reality usually is, though, that feeling fine means that the drugs are controlling the symptoms, not that the illness has vanished. Also, if the drug treatment that's causing a patient to stay well is stopped suddenly, they are more likely to feel worse and suffer a relapse. A sudden break in medication can also trigger very unpleasant withdrawal side effects.

According to the Royal College of Psychiatrists, if you don't take or stop taking medication, the risk of having a manic episode in the next year depends on the number of manic episodes you have had in the past – the more manic episodes you've had, the more likely you are to have another one. For example, if you have had one or two manic episodes previously, your risk of having another one in the next year if you're not taking medication is 10% (10 in 100); if you've had three or four manic episodes previously your risk is 20% (20 in 100); and if you have had five or more manic episodes previously your risk is 40% (40 in 100). As you get older, the risk of having more episodes stays much the same. Even if you have been well for a long time, you still run the risk of having another episode.

The key to good mental health in the long term, then, is relapse prevention and acceptance. As someone with diabetes needs to accept that they have to take insulin every day for the rest of their life, someone with bipolar disorder is wise to do the same.

 I would say compliance is key, in terms of taking the drugs and following appointments, because I think mental health professionals listen better to you when you're compliant than when you're not, and I think you can play the game ... If you take the drugs and it doesn't work out, and they have the confidence that you are taking them, then I think you come from a position of power.

(NEIL)

That's not to suggest that people should just automatically agree to take drugs they're prescribed without question or discussion. In an ideal world, new medication (or changes to existing medication) needs to be agreed between the patient and their prescribing doctor or psychiatrist together. Useful points to discuss include:

- which symptoms need managing
- whether there's an alternative to taking the drug (e.g. psychological therapy)
- what benefits the new medication may provide
- the way the drug is taken (tablets? depot injection?)
- how often the drug needs to be taken
- if a drug can be prescribed as PRN (so it can be taken as and when needed)
- any possible side effects
- how new drugs may interact with other drugs already being taken
- how long the medication is being prescribed for
- when the drugs schedule will be reviewed again.

This means the patient can make an informed decision to accept (or refuse) treatment. It is worth bearing in mind, though, that someone who persistently refuses to take prescribed medication and becomes a risk to themselves or others could be sectioned into hospital (see question 55, p. 160) so that doctors can treat them against their will.

If someone with bipolar (or a member of their family) has a concern about any aspect of their medication, they should discuss it first with their doctor or psychiatrist, or seek the opinion of a psychiatric pharmacist.

Forgetting to take medication

Another potential problem is forgetting to take medication. In the best-case scenario, everyone follows the dispensing instructions to the letter and takes the right doses at the right times. But, of course, everyone's human and mistakes are made, particularly when someone is unwell. If medication has been forgotten, it's essential not to panic and/or not to take a double dose. Speak to a doctor or pharmacist as soon as possible about what action to take – it may depend on the type of drug being prescribed. Lithium in particular should *not* be taken as a double dose.

If forgetting to take medication happens regularly, the best thing is to be prepared – when a prescription is dispensed, ask a pharmacist for their advice on what to do if doses are missed. Practical measures can be taken to back this up. Why not try:

- pinning a medication chart up on the wall, with drugs labelled into daily doses
- linking a medication schedule with other routine daily tasks – making the first cup of tea of the morning, or cleaning teeth at bedtime, for example
- getting a plastic pill container with sections divided into days of the week and times of the day, so that it's easy to see what needs to be taken when.

Depot injections

If you've been taking an antipsychotic medication for a while so you know it works for you, you may be asked if you want to take it as a depot injection. This is a slow-release, slow-acting form of the same medication. It's injected by a healthcare professional into a large muscle (usually your buttock) between every week and every four weeks.

A depot injection might be a good option for you if:

- you don't like swallowing medication
- you find it hard to remember to take your medication every day.

Q37. *Will drugs encourage weight gain?*

There's plenty of evidence to show that some of the drugs prescribed for bipolar disorder do cause weight gain. Sarah's sister Rebecca has gone from a skinny UK size 10 to a size 16 since being diagnosed with bipolar disorder over 20 years ago – and she's not alone, although some doctors can be keen to play this down:

I've always done loads of sport, and yet I put on three stone in weight, which made all my self-confidence just fall away. I'm only 5 ft 4, and that's a huge amount to put on. And people don't look at you and say, 'Oh, you've got an illness and the drugs are making you fat,' people just think all those horrible things that are associated with weight – you know, like a slovenly attitude. You're just so bloated the whole time, and you see that they are judging you on that, and it becomes another issue in itself. And doctors won't acknowledge that drugs can cause weight gain either. They'll just say, 'It must be you,' or they'll sometimes talk about 'slight' weight gain. But that's just rubbish.

(TAMARA)

But according to Dr Ian Maidment, Senior Lecturer in Clinical Pharmacy at Aston University, honesty is the best policy: 'Some of the newer antipsychotics in particular do appear to cause weight gain. And the way I explain it is that they affect part of the brain which controls what we eat. And so these drugs make people think, "I want chocolate and I want it now." It's a real drive to eat more food, and it's really hard to over-ride. So weight gain may be a problem. The important thing for people is that they are aware of the side effects, so it's not unexpected. When I speak to people, I like to be totally honest and say, "This is what may happen – this is what the evidence suggests," because if I was on a drug, I would want to know exactly what the side effects may be.'

The obvious solution (eat less, exercise more) is easier said than done, but is possible, particularly if it's not too late for the 'prevention' rather than 'cure' approach. If it's too late for prevention, the NICE guideline for the treatment of bipolar states that if a patient gains weight when receiving drug treatment, mental healthcare professionals should:

1. Review the patient's medication
2. Consider:

   - giving dietary advice
   - advising regular aerobic exercise

- referring the patient to weight management programmes in mental health services
- referring the patient to a dietician.

Q38. *How can someone with bipolar self-manage their treatment?*

'Self-management' is not an alternative to drug or psychological treatments for bipolar disorder, but a way of gaining more control over the illness. Many of its underlying principles are similar to those used in psychological therapies, such as CBT (see question 31, p. 75). It's about using those times when you are well to prepare for those times when you're less well, such as looking for warning signs that you (from past experience) can identify as potential triggers for setting off episodes.

Sign up for an online self-management course

The mental health charity Bipolar UK has joined forces with the National Centre for Mental Health at Cardiff University and Healthcare Learning to create 'Beating Bipolar', a fantastic and completely free online programme designed to help you better understand and manage bipolar disorder. It includes videos of professionals and people with experience of bipolar disorder, and interactive exercises you might find helpful to manage the condition and its symptoms.

There are eight online modules covering key areas, such as the diagnosis and causes of bipolar disorder; the role of medication; relapse prevention and early intervention; psychological approaches to treatment; lifestyle; advice for family and carers; and bipolar disorder and women. There's also support via an online forum moderated by Bipolar UK. See www.beatingbipolar.org.

Learn to spot your own personal warning signs

Early warning signs are actions, thoughts and feelings that show you may be becoming unwell. For some, it is smoking lots of cigarettes or being more intensely absorbed in religious ideas – they are different for everyone. Spotting the early warning signs means that you can take action yourself, or seek help early on. This leaves more support, treatment and care options open to you and could prevent a crisis or a hospital admission.

You can learn to become aware of your warning signs by reflecting on the time before you became unwell in the past – did anything happen or did you feel or behave in certain ways that may have warned you that you were starting to become unwell?

Carers, friends and family often spend a lot of time with you, and their knowledge of you can also be a very helpful resource to use to keep well. They can spot subtle changes in your mood or behaviour and let you know if they are concerned for you. If carers, family and friends are aware of your early warning signs, they can provide you with feedback so that you can use relevant coping strategies and seek help if needed.

 My wife has been a tremendous help in spotting symptoms and nudging me and saying, 'Shouldn't you be calming down?' or 'Are you going to take something tonight?' And she's been very good at negotiating with the medical services when I've been out of it – she has a good relationship with them. She's very good at liaising with my CPN and my psychiatrist. She's very much involved.

(*KEITH*)

Keep a mood diary

Keeping a mood diary, or filling in a mood chart, can help you spot patterns and learn to know when to take action or get help. The Mood Scale and Mood Diary sections on Bipolar UK's website are both useful tools for understanding and managing moods – go to www.bipolaruk.org and search for 'mood scale' or 'mood diary' for more information.

I believe strongly in self-management courses. The self-management course I went on taught me how to manage bipolar, how to cope with things and also self-medication. So I take a particular drug if I feel high. If I'm not sleeping my eight hours, I take a sleeping tablet, just as a precaution, because I want to be in control all the time. If I had the chance to speak to someone who had just been diagnosed with bipolar, I would say acceptance is key, for your own benefit. It's almost like you have to go through stages, so first there's denial, and then you might get to acceptance, and then there's self-management of your condition and making sure that it disrupts your life in the least way possible. Learn as much about bipolar as you can. Education is an excellent means of defeating it.

(NEIL)

Q39. *What is electroconvulsive therapy?*

Electroconvulsive therapy (ECT) is a controversial treatment, to say the least. The phrase itself conjures up alarming images from the fifties and sixties of conscious and terrified patients tied to beds in dingy hospital rooms with live electrodes forcibly applied to their heads by doctors more intent on control (or even punishment) than effective treatment. Broken bones were not uncommon, as the electric currents could cause patients to thrash about, despite their restraints, and sometimes more than 100 ECT treatments could be administered to one person, causing severe memory loss and speech impairment.

Thankfully, the reality of modern ECT is rather different. Perhaps most importantly of all, a patient is treated in an operating theatre and is unconscious under a general anaesthetic. 'Paddles' containing electrodes are placed on the scalp, and instead of the steady stream of electricity that used to be given, modern ECT uses a high frequency electrical pulse, which stimulates the brain to induce an epileptic seizure, or 'fit'. It's not fully understood how or why inducing a seizure can help stabilize mood, but it's thought that it somehow boosts the chemicals used by nerve endings in the brain to communicate with each other.

Because the patient has usually been given a muscle relaxant too, there is no thrashing of limbs or broken bones – at most just a mild twitch shows when the electrical pulse is passing through the brain. The procedure lasts for under a minute and a course is typically between 6 and 12 treatments over a two-week period. Such is the 'respectability' of modern-day ECT that it's recommended by NICE in some circumstances for the treatment of bipolar. However, the NICE guideline firmly states that the treatment should only be used 'to achieve rapid and short-term improvement of severe symptoms after an adequate trial of other treatment options has proven ineffective in individuals with catatonia or a prolonged or severe manic episode'. ECT is far from being a routine treatment for most people with bipolar symptoms. And despite the changes in how it's administered in the twenty-first century, there are still divided opinions on its use and effectiveness. A survey by the UK charity Mind, which looked at 418 questionnaires from people who had previously received ECT treatment, reported that:

- 40% of respondents complained of permanent memory loss and 36% of difficulty in concentrating.
- 73% of respondents felt they had not been given any information about side effects.
- 43% of respondents felt the treatment was 'unhelpful, damaging or severely damaging'.
- 66% would not agree to ECT treatment in the future.

Other reported side effects from ECT include headaches, nausea, aching muscles and feeling confused and distressed for some hours afterwards. It's worth remembering, though, that the Mind survey was largely based on less recent experience – only one-third of the respondents in the survey had received ECT in the previous five years. And, as Mind itself acknowledges, ECT does work extremely well for some people, relieving their symptoms when all else has failed. There are many personal stories testifying that ECT can be extremely effective:

' Four lots of ECT treatment pulled me out of depression very quickly after only one week. There's a lot of misunderstanding around, but it really helped me. The only thing is that you get buzzy for two minutes when you come round. And the only memory loss I had was about what had happened in hospital – but that wasn't a bad thing. There were no headaches, no significant memory loss and no other effects at all. As far as I'm concerned, the whole experience of ECT is totally trivial ... Having ECT is no less disconcerting than having a filling. The actual thing itself is a non-event. Of course, years ago there were no anaesthetics or muscle relaxants as there are today – that's why there's so much misunderstanding surrounding the subject. But it's just not like that now. Forget the usual media rubbish. ECT definitely works on depression. My consultant psychiatrist told me that it's saved many lives. I think it's saved mine! '

(*RICHARD*)

It would seem that ECT provokes a black or white response – and that those for whom it works are fervent supporters. The bottom line for anyone being offered ECT (or for their family) is to ask for as much information as possible, so they can weigh up the risk of side effects against the potential benefits. Then they can make an informed choice based on their own individual circumstances. If someone decides that they don't want to receive ECT in the future, when they may not be able to make their wishes clearly known, the sensible step would be to declare this wish in a legal document called an 'advance decision' (see question 44, p. 112).

In the UK, the Mental Health Act 2007 introduced new safeguards for the use of ECT – the treatment may not be given to a patient who has the mental capacity to refuse consent (except in an emergency). ECT can only be given to a patient without mental capacity to give or refuse consent if this is not in conflict with an advance decision – i.e. if the patient has not specified beforehand that they don't want to receive this treatment.

The Act also states that a second opinion from another doctor has to be obtained before ECT treatment can be administered to patients under 18.

Q40. *What is repetitive transcranial magnetic stimulation?*

Repetitive transcranial magnetic stimulation (RTMS) is a relatively new therapy which uses pulses of magnetic energy to induce electrical currents in the brain. RTMS is currently being linked with a number of possible uses, including treatment for depression, hallucinations, anxiety disorders, migraine, epilepsy and tinnitus, and seems to have fewer side effects than ECT, as well as being less invasive.

In 2015, NICE stated that RTMS can be used without anaesthesia and can be done on an outpatient basis. An electromagnetic coil is held against the scalp to induce electric currents in the cerebral cortex, with repetitive pulses of electromagnetic energy delivered at various frequencies. Imaging may be used to help target specific areas of the brain. RTMS treatment is usually delivered in daily sessions lasting about 30 minutes, for between two and six weeks, and is considered for patients with depression who have not responded to antidepressants (as well as patients for whom antidepressants are not suitable).

The NICE guidance adds that evidence on RTMS for depression shows no major safety concerns, but notes that 'clinical response is variable' and that 'during the consent process, clinicians should, in particular, inform patients about the other treatment options available'.

Q41. *How can the symptoms of seasonal affective disorder be effectively treated?*

Light therapy can be a very effective treatment for season affective disorder (SAD) – around eight out of ten people with SAD find that sitting next to a light box for ten minutes every day during the darker winter months relieves symptoms in four to ten days. Most light boxes use special fluorescent bulbs rated at 10,000 lux. Some research shows that morning treatments work better, so place the box on the breakfast table or next to a computer for use at the start of the day. One study found that light exposure in the middle of the day may be more effective (see question 35, p. 96) so it may be worth experimenting to see what works for you.

A word of warning, though. Some research suggests that too much light can occasionally cause hypomania and mania, especially during the spring and summer months when more light is available naturally – so use a light box more sparingly when the typical SAD season is just beginning or about to end.

CBT or counselling may be helpful, and there is some evidence that the right diet can also make a positive difference. Dieticians recommend that people with SAD symptoms eat fruit, vegetables and nuts to raise energy levels and take vitamin B and D supplements to boost serotonin levels, which enhances mood. Also, taking exercise outside – even on a dull day – can help.

The SAD Lightbox Company is the longest established manufacturer in the UK to design and manufacture lightboxes specifically for SAD – visit www.sad.uk.com for more details.

Q42. *What is the best course of action if a child shows symptoms of bipolar disorder?*

As worrying as the situation might seem, don't jump to conclusions and start panicking if a child seems to be showing symptoms of bipolar disorder. Take things step by step.

Step 1: Prevent things getting worse

Regardless of the frequency and severity of symptoms, making positive lifestyle changes can help prevent the situation from deteriorating. These include encouraging him or her to:

- eat a healthy diet that's high in nutrients and low in sugar, artificial additives and junk food

- follow a good sleep pattern (going to bed and getting up at the same time; getting enough sleep; avoiding getting overtired)
- get plenty of exercise
- avoid stressful situations and family conflict
- feel good about themselves with plenty of praise
- get extra help to cope with the ups and downs of life, maybe from a child psychologist (contact the British Psychological Society via their website, www.bps.org.uk) or a play therapist (contact the UK Society for Play and Creative Arts Therapies – www.playtherapy.org.uk).

Step 2: Get a proper diagnosis

Because the symptoms are so many and varied, bipolar disorder is notoriously tricky to diagnose, and often goes undiagnosed or gets misdiagnosed. This is particularly true in children. It goes undiagnosed because children with bipolar are often written off as naughty, bad, defiant or difficult. And it gets misdiagnosed because bipolar behaviour overlaps with so many other childhood conditions, including attention deficit hyperactivity disorder (ADHD), depression, panic disorder and obsessive-compulsive disorder, to name but a few. In fact, research from Harvard Medical School found that up to 30% of children originally diagnosed with ADHD eventually receive a diagnosis of bipolar disorder.

Remember that there's an increased chance of bipolar disorder developing if it runs in the family (see question 20, p. 50) so a relative with a diagnosis should act as a warning light. Regardless of the genetic link, stress can also be a trigger, so any symptoms that appear or get worse after bereavement, trauma or parents' divorce should be noted.

Speak to the school nurse or the child's GP about any concerns, as they can refer the child to a psychologist or psychiatrist if necessary. An official diagnosis can then be made.

Step 3: Choose treatment wisely

Senior Lecturer in Clinical Psychology at the University of Manchester Dr Sara Tai says: 'Although our system is heavily weighted towards psychiatric treatments, psychological intervention should be considered first for children because we don't know what effect drugs will have on a developing brain. Psychological intervention can be highly successful if used at an early stage when problems first arise. The key is treating the individual child's behaviour, not the condition.'

If medication is considered as a last resort, it's worth bearing in mind the advice of co-author of *The Bipolar Child*, Demitri Papolos: 'We want to state clearly that, given the accumulating knowledge in the field of research and the reaction of the children in our study ... bipolar disorder should be ruled out before any of the stimulant drugs or antidepressants are prescribed.'

Why? Because giving children with bipolar stimulants or antidepressants can throw them into manic and psychotic states, causing violent, paranoid and suicidal tendencies.

'In coming years we are likely to develop better ways to define the mood problems of children,' says Dr Michael Miller, Senior Editor for Mental Health Publishing at Harvard Health Publications. In the meantime, some experts recommend prescribing mood stabilizers – often several drugs in combination – for children with a diagnosis of bipolar. In the UK, medication is much less likely to be prescribed.

For an extremely small minority of children and teenagers with bipolar, treatment in a psychiatric unit may be an option, either as an informal patient or (very rarely) under a section order. In the UK, the 2007 Mental Health Act introduced new safeguards for children in psychiatric hospital care, aimed at ensuring they're treated in an environment suitable to their age. This echoed a commitment made by the UK government in 2006 that no child under the age of 16 should be treated in an adult ward. Anyone whose child is being considered for hospital treatment should refer mental health professionals to this legislation and ask that an age-appropriate environment is provided.

Step 4: Work as a team

The NICE guideline for the treatment of bipolar states that when planning the care of children and adolescents with bipolar, parents and other loved ones should be involved in developing care plans so that they can give informed consent, support treatment goals and help ensure that suggested treatment is carried out. But the guideline also states that children and teenagers should be offered separate individual meetings as well as joint meetings with family members.

Step 5: Gather information

There are two brilliant books about bipolar disorder in childhood – *The Bipolar Child* by Demitri Papolos MD and Janice Papolos, and *Intense Minds: Through the Eyes of Young People with Bipolar Disorder* by Tracy Anglada. Both are available from www.amazon.co.uk. The first is a comprehensive yet easy-to-read round-up of the latest research into early-onset bipolar disorder. The second is a moving collection of first-person accounts describing what it's like to live with this condition as a child, plus a practical guide for parents on how they can help.

Q43. *Does treatment need to be different for older people who have bipolar disorder?*

The current NICE bipolar disorder guideline (CG185) directs that healthcare professionals should 'ensure that older people with bipolar disorder are offered the same range of treatments and services as younger people with bipolar disorder.'

However, some tailoring to age may also be necessary – the NICE guideline states that professionals offering medication to older people should take into account its potential impact on cognitive functioning and:

- consider using medication at lower doses
- take into account the increased risk of drug interactions
- ensure that any other medical conditions have been recognized and treated.

Martha Sajatovic, Professor of Psychiatry and Neurology at Case Western Reserve University School of Medicine, Cleveland, agrees that treatment should be tailored to the age group. For example, she says that lithium, the most extensively studied medication for bipolar disorder in the elderly and an effective mood stabilizer in older adults, should be prescribed at a dose reduced by one-third to a half of that given to younger patients and the dose should not exceed 900 mg/day.

For help in finding the right kind of care (such as care at home, sheltered accommodation or a nursing home) for someone with bipolar in later life or late-onset bipolar disorder, contact an independent care advisor such as Grace Consulting, a leading provider of independent care advice in the UK and Ireland. Visit www.graceconsulting.co.uk for more information.

Q44. *What is an 'advance decision'?*

The year 2007 saw the introduction in England and Wales of the Mental Capacity Act, which was drawn up by the Department of Health, 'to empower and protect people who may lack capacity to make some decisions for themselves, for example, people with dementia, learning disabilities, mental health problems, stroke or head injuries, who may lack capacity to make certain decisions'. The Act has five key principles:

- A presumption of capacity – every adult has the right to make his or her own decisions and must be assumed to have capacity to do so unless it is proved otherwise.
- Individuals are supported to make their own decisions – a person

must be given all practicable help before anyone treats them as not being able to make their own decisions.

- Unwise decisions – just because an individual makes what might be seen as an unwise decision, they should not be treated as lacking capacity to make that decision.
- Best interests – an act done or decision made under the Act for or on behalf of a person who lacks capacity must be done in their best interests.
- Least restrictive option – anything done for or on behalf of a person who lacks capacity should be the least restrictive of their basic rights and freedoms.

In line with these principles, the Mental Capacity Act recognizes the legal status of an 'advance decision' (also sometimes called a future directive, an advance directive or a living will), in which someone can state in advance, i.e. before illness or injury makes them unable to make their wishes known to health professionals, what treatment they *don't* want to receive if they become mentally incapacitated in the future.

Anyone aged 16 or older can make an advance decision. Although an advance decision can be given verbally, it's sensible to write it down, ideally with the name, address, date and signature of the person preparing the document, and with a sentence stating that they fully understand what they are doing and that they are legally competent to write their own advance decision. The particular circumstances and the treatment that a patient wants to refuse need to be mentioned specifically, so there's less room for doubt or misinterpretation later on. Giving reasons for the choices expressed in the advance directive also adds credibility.

It is a good idea for the document to be witnessed by a doctor (who can confirm that the person was fully capable of making decisions when the advance decision was written) or an advocate (someone, usually a volunteer, who supports someone with a mental health condition to communicate their needs – see question 46, p. 127). Copies need to be sent to the person's GP, any mental health professionals they are dealing with, and their family, ideally to their legally defined 'nearest relative' – see question 60, p. 172, for more details. It's important to review an advance decision regularly so that it always reflects current wishes.

It's worth noting that an advance decision has no legal status if the person who wrote it is later sectioned in a psychiatric hospital under the Mental Health Act, when treatment can be given without consent.

Rather confusingly, an 'advance statement' is where someone can say in advance what treatment they *do* want to have. An important difference between the two is that advance statements are not legally recognized by the Act, so these treatment preferences can be ignored by mental health professionals. Some people make both an advance decision and an advance statement.

Contact the Mind Legal Advice team on 0300 466 6463 or legal@mind.org.uk for help and advice on drawing up an advance decision, or an independent advocacy service may be able to help (see question 46, p. 127).

CHAPTER THREE

Support

Q45. *What professionals support someone with a bipolar diagnosis?*

There are literally thousands of dedicated individuals working in the mental health sector. In an ideal world, they are available to provide support whenever it's needed, although this very much depends on:

- the phase of the illness and the person's recent history. A 32-year-old man who's living with a partner, working and self-managing his moods and who hasn't been in hospital for four years is going to need less support than a 19-year-old who's living alone, unemployed, unstable and recently out of hospital, for example.
- the availability of support. In the UK, there is a chronic lack of funding for mental health services. At the time of writing this book's second edition, mental health problems account for 23% of the total impact of ill health in the UK, but only 13% of the NHS budget is allocated to mental health. And in two surveys carried out by the UK-based charity YoungMinds in

2018, only 6% of young people and 3% of parents agreed there is enough support for children and young people with mental health problems.

On a more positive note, a report by the Care Quality Commission (CQC) in 2014 concluded that, both in the NHS and the private sector, staff 'are genuinely mental health services' greatest asset'. So who makes up the team of mental healthcare professionals?

General practitioners (GPs)

A GP is a family doctor who sees patients with every ailment under the sun. In Europe, it's estimated that around one in three patients a GP sees has a clinically relevant mental disorder. The first health professional involved in the care of someone with bipolar disorder is often a GP.

Professor Richard Morriss, Professor of Psychiatry and Community Mental Health at Nottingham University, who has run courses for GPs on psychiatry, says that the GP's role is slowly changing: 'Not so long ago, bipolar disorder was completely off the map for GPs. They were taught that, on average, only 6 of the 2,000 patients on their list had bipolar disorder. But even if you take the most conservative estimate (of bipolar affecting only 1% of the population), that figure has got to be wrong, let alone if you take the broader view that around 5% of the population has it. So, generally, bipolar just wasn't really a priority for most GPs, who have so many other things to do. Also, there's no doubt that unless a GP makes a point of putting mental health at the top of his or her priority list, it's difficult to diagnose bipolar disorder in a ten-minute consultation. That's because, of course, a GP is rarely presented with the entire picture. However, there are signs that things are changing.'

Since the first NICE guideline on bipolar disorder was published in 2006, it has been more widely recognized in the healthcare system in general and this has filtered down to GP level. Also, the Department of Health has introduced a system where GP practices get extra money by earning QOF (Quality and Outcomes Framework) points. Most of these points are earned by monitoring their patients' weight, cholesterol, heart disease and smoking, but GPs can also be incentivized to monitor people taking lithium and to create a list of all patients with a serious mental health problem. Things like this help to put bipolar disorder on a GP's packed agenda.

A GP's role is crucial for several reasons:

- Everyone in the UK has the right to access a GP – when problems arise, they're likely to see a GP first.
- Even in a ten-minute consultation, a GP has a chance to run through what's called an 'index of suspicion', asking questions that can help to build up a picture of overall mental health. The index of suspicion for bipolarity should be high when the depression is episodic and/or there is a family history of bipolar illness or its counterparts, such as alcoholism, drug abuse, uncontrolled episodes of rage and/or violence, suicide attempts, postnatal depression, psychiatric hospitalizations for depression or psychotic states.
- A GP can refer a patient to other health professionals who can offer specialized help.
- Once a diagnosis is made, a GP can prescribe medication and alter dosages.
- If someone is taking lithium, the NICE guideline recommends that their GP provides a health check-up every year, reviews lithium levels every three to six months, takes a blood test to monitor thyroid and kidney function at least every 15 months and checks blood pressure annually.
- A GP is key in monitoring the physical health of someone with bipolar, as a diagnosis can increase the risk of other conditions, such as heart disease, obesity, diabetes and thyroid problems. In fact, the NICE guideline recommends that someone with a bipolar diagnosis has an annual physical examination to check

glucose levels, weight and waist measurement, smoking status, blood pressure and cholesterol (in people over 40). For more information about the impact of bipolar disorder on physical health, see question 17, p. 46.

There's no doubt that a GP or family doctor can be the cornerstone of support for someone with bipolar.

 I'm very lucky that I have a supportive GP. I had a blip four weeks ago. I got very depressed to the point where I was suicidal. My GP was fantastic and helped bring me back up very quickly with the right medication.

(*AMY*)

The community mental health team (CMHT)

If a GP is concerned about someone's mental health, they are likely to refer them to a CMHT, which is usually made up of between 8 and 16 people. The team is responsible for the well-being of people with mental health problems, not just when they're acutely ill but on an on-going basis. Even when someone with bipolar is well, they are entitled to continuing support. And rightly so: if someone has been in hospital in the previous 12 months, they have a 50:50 chance of an acute bipolar episode in the next 12 months. Today, thanks in part to the NICE bipolar guideline, much of the CMHT's work is about early intervention and preventing relapse.

The team usually includes a senior consultant psychiatrist, junior psychiatrists, a clinical psychologist, community psychiatric nurses, social workers, pharmacists, occupational therapists and support workers. They tend to work from day centres, outpatient departments and GP surgeries; sometimes they have a base in a clinic, or they see people at home. Someone with bipolar only usually meets the members of the team involved in their care, one or two at a time. Every so often there will probably be a 'review' meeting where the person with a diagnosis and the members of the team directly involved in his or her care review the situation.

Psychiatrists

Psychiatry is the study of mental disorders and their diagnosis, management and prevention. The most senior member of a CMHT is the consultant psychiatrist, who has the overall responsibility for the care and assessment of all patients and prescribes treatments. In the UK, qualifying as a psychiatrist usually takes five years of general medical training, plus two further years on a postgraduate foundation course, followed by up to six years of training in psychiatry. This is split into core and advanced training, and involves passing both parts of the MRCPsych examination. Junior psychiatrists, known as SHOs (senior house officers) or registrars, are still in training.

In the UK, a GP refers a patient to a psychiatrist via the NHS, or there's always the option to go private. Take care when choosing a psychiatrist privately – go by personal recommendation if possible or contact the Royal College of Psychiatrists (RCP), which is the main professional body for psychiatrists in the UK, for a list of practising psychiatrists in different areas. Always ensure that the psychiatrist is properly qualified and affiliated to the RCP. See Extra resources, p. 267, for contact details.

If medical insurance is used, there may be a list of approved psychiatrists offered by the insurance company – try to find out if any specialize in treating bipolar disorder.

In the USA, it's common to ask for a 'preferred-provider' list from an insurance company. Or there's a list of recommended professionals on the Depression and Bipolar Support Alliance website – see www.dbsalliance.org. Ensure he or she is 'board certified', which means they've passed a rigorous set of exams, indicating mastery in the specialty of psychiatry. To check the credentials of almost every licensed physician in the US, see the American Medical Association website at www.ama-assn.org.

Psychologists

Someone diagnosed with bipolar disorder may also see a clinical psychologist – either during a stay in hospital or as part of a general treatment plan. Clinical psychologists typically take a three-year degree course, followed by another three years at doctorate level and two to three years in between spent in on-the-job training. Psychologists use non-medical treatments with an emphasis on psychological therapies such as CBT and group therapy.

See question 32, p. 84, for more information about getting any kind of psychological therapy in the UK.

In the USA, a qualified psychologist can be found via the American Psychological Association at www.apa.org – go to the 'Psychology Help Center' in the menu bar and under 'Resources' you can type a zip code into the 'Find a psychologist' section.

Care co-ordinators

In most cases, one member of the team (often a psychiatric nurse or a support worker) is assigned the role of a care co-ordinator – their job is to get to know the person well and to ensure they're getting the help they need. The care co-ordinator is responsible for co-ordinating the care of the person to make sure all their mental health needs are met. They also need to make sure that someone with bipolar has a clear plan about how they're going to be supported to stay well – a personalized care plan.

Psychiatric nurse, previously known as a CPN or community psychiatric nurse

Psychiatric nurses support those with mental illnesses when they're not in hospital. Their role is to focus on what people can do, and the majority of their work is about prevention and self-help rather than just treatment and crisis management. They are trained to consider what needs to be in place to assist recovery.

This holistic, needs-based approach improves outcomes for people with mental illnesses in several ways:

- Psychiatric nurses can help someone with a bipolar diagnosis understand their prescribed medication – how and when to take it, potential side effects and the consequences of missing or stopping medication. If there is a problem, a good psychiatric nurse will pass on the information to the psychiatrist in his or her team and everyone will discuss a treatment change.

- One important area of a psychiatric nurse's work is risk management. Someone with bipolar can often be vulnerable and at risk of harmful behaviour and suicide. That should be central to a nurse's thinking, with regular risk assessments being made.

- Psychiatric nurses can listen while someone talks through their problems and can offer people with bipolar disorder increased support during significant events in their lives, such as losing a job or following the death of a close family member or friend. They can talk through financial problems, work dilemmas and parenting issues, helping someone deal with any problems as they arise and hopefully averting a crisis.

- Psychiatric nurses generally have more contact with people who are diagnosed with bipolar than any other professional group, so they are well placed to recognize the early warning signs that most people experience for several days or weeks before becoming seriously unwell. One of the most important roles of a psychiatric nurse is noticing these signs and helping to prevent relapse by getting help early.

- Psychiatric nurses are key in improving physical healthcare, which is important because people with bipolar disorder are more likely to be overweight, smoke heavily and be physically inactive. The NICE guideline recommends that nurses promote healthy living and arrange annual health checks.

- A psychiatric nurse's work now involves family members a lot more because it has been recognized that loved ones themselves need support. They are in a good position to offer that – in terms of practical advice and emotional support. In fact, a psychiatric nurse is the link between family and medical help in the chain of support.

- Some nurses have received extra training in particular problems and treatments, such as eating disorders or behavioural therapy – they are called nurse therapists.

The above list is the gold standard, with a psychiatric nurse maintaining daily contact when someone is acutely unwell, being available during unstable periods and seeing someone monthly during the maintenance stage. In reality, though, a psychiatric nurse's role, like the role of the CMHT in general, largely depends on the area of the country where they're based.

We speak regularly on the phone about how Irene and Rebecca are doing and know without a doubt that this inconsistency is true. Irene lives in the Midlands and has a brilliant CMHT that she or her husband Gordon can phone at any time, day or night. When she has a bipolar episode, members of the team respond immediately – sometimes within an hour or so of receiving the phone call, there will be at least two psychiatric nurses sitting on Irene's sofa, trying to help her through any difficulties. They'll keep visiting every day until they're happy she's stable, or if she doesn't respond to home treatment, they will support her through the hospitalization process. On the other hand, Rebecca, who lives in Kent, has a key worker who is completely overstretched. If she's on holiday, Rebecca, or her mum Rose, is told to phone in two weeks when the key worker is due back. Rose can spend all day phoning various numbers, desperate for support, and she still can't get through to anyone who can help. They've sometimes waited in all day for people to come, and then no one turns up. The contrast between the two standards of care is unbelievable. And others have had similar experiences.

 I couldn't get support for love nor money where I used to live. They only patch people up during a crisis and then they abandon you. It's such a postcode lottery. The mental health services are much better here in the Midlands. I had an assessment with a new consultant and now I see the same psychiatric nurse every single month. She got me on an anxiety management course. She's like a safety net. I know I can ring – for example, recently I had my antidepressant dosage reduced and I started feeling anxious. I phoned my psychiatric nurse and because she knows me, she suggested I go back to my GP and get the dose increased again. If I hadn't had that support I might have delayed going to my GP. It definitely helped that I could call her. And there's been a marked difference in my well-being. I'm less anxious and more confident. My nurse is really pleased with me.

(*RACHEL*)

My psychiatric nurse is good. She helps me 'manage' the condition and gives me tips on relaxing and how to deal with negative thoughts.

(*JUDE*)

I've got the number of my son Neil's nurse that I can ring if I see any danger signals. I haven't had to do it yet, but I could do. And I've got the nurse's email address too, but I've got to put it past Neil. I promised him I would speak to him first.

(*GILL*)

I get bugger all support. The community mental health team? Who? My nurse didn't actually contact me after I'd taken an overdose. She's so busy she's never available. I can understand why there's no help. It's the system not the people.

(*SHARRON*)

If it's impossible to get hold of a psychiatric nurse, the only alternative is to get help from other sources such as a GP or psychiatrist. But even if a psychiatric nurse is available, this doesn't guarantee optimum support. You can ask for a change of psychiatric nurse – although as yet this isn't an automatic right. Unfortunately, it's a case of pot-luck. The only consolation is that as the holistic approach becomes more widespread, the odds increase favourably year on year.

The Crisis Resolution and Home Treatment (CRHT) team

Most areas in the UK have a Crisis Resolution and Home Treatment (CRHT) team which is part of the wider CMHT. These teams are made up of a care co-ordinator, psychiatric nurses, social workers and support workers, and are meant to:

- be available 24 hours a day, seven days a week
- respond to a crisis within four hours (wherever possible)
- carry out assessments under the Mental Health Act to decide whether or not you need to go to hospital
- provide support and short-term help until another team is available or the help is no longer needed.

The theory behind a crisis team is that instead of someone who's acutely ill going straight to hospital, they're given medication and supported at home until the crisis has passed. The NICE bipolar guideline recommends crisis resolution and home treatment instead of hospital-based care because:

- hospital admissions are reduced
- the average length of stay in hospital, if needed, is shorter
- home care is usually more acceptable to people with mental illness than hospital-based care
- unwell people tend to stay in contact with health professionals
- clinical outcomes are marginally improved.

When a crisis strikes, someone who's being supported by a community mental health team should have a crisis number they can phone for immediate help – even during long weekends and holidays. When the system works, it's brilliant:

 When my partner went high and eventually ended up in hospital I don't know what I'd have done without the help of a crisis team. Tom had been drinking all day and, after an argument with his son where I thought he might become physically violent so I'd stepped in between them, he locked himself in the living room, which faced on to a main road. He was playing music very loudly and wouldn't come out. He was shouting. I couldn't communicate with him. I was frightened that he was going to hurt himself. He'd been cutting himself previously and punching things. I didn't know what he was going to do next. He felt dangerous, out of control. He was really aggressive. I felt like he really hated me. He had the phone and was ringing ex-girlfriends, shouting at me to leave him alone. At this point I knew I was out of my depth. I phoned the doctor, who said a member of the crisis team would come round in 40 minutes. I sat outside. But then I tried the door and the room was empty. I went outside. Some people on the street told me that he'd jumped out of the window – we're a storey up. They pointed towards the tube station. I ran up to the tube station in a blind panic. Tom was sitting there. He had pierced his nose and upper lip with a safety pin. He'd also tried to cut off a tattoo of an ex-girlfriend on his arm with a penknife. I said, 'I've called the crisis team, please come with me.' He wanted to get another drink from the off-licence so we had to go there first, but then he came back with me. They turned up in time. I've got nothing but praise for them... they were my salvation. When they arrived, Tom decided to put some pornography on. It was mortifying and embarrassing, but to be honest, it was pure relief that somebody was there to help me and they could see what he was really like, that this wasn't stable behaviour. He agreed to go into hospital.

(JO)

For Tom and Jo, and many others, support from the crisis team is there when they need it. But yet again, the level of service is inconsistent across the country. Part of the reason for this was highlighted in one study which found that provision of out-of-hours CRHT services varies widely across the UK – a small but significant percentage (12%) of areas had no crisis resolution teams providing an out-of-hours service at all, and 59% had no crisis accommodation available on a 24-hour basis.

This is illustrated by Sarah's sister Rebecca's experience:

Rebecca had been stable for about 18 months, but then started arguing a lot with her boyfriend, drinking more than usual. Mum and I knew she was heading for a high, and we tried to persuade her to go for help, but she wouldn't listen. One night, after a row with her boyfriend and drinking a lot, she phoned the crisis team saying that she was suicidal and asking for help. No one could come out to her and so eventually she took an overdose. The help just wasn't there when she needed it. **'**

So what can be done if a crisis team isn't available when needed? Frustratingly, not a lot. In a crisis situation, the only alternatives are to go straight to A&E or to phone for an ambulance. After receiving inadequate crisis support, it's worth writing a letter of complaint (see question 89, p. 249, for more information). Surely if enough people highlight the lack of emergency resources and crisis support, eventually the message will get through to the decision-makers and positive changes will happen.

Even when there is a crisis service, there's clearly a problem in getting the information to those who really need it. According to the same research, only 49% of people who use mental health services actually had the phone number of someone they could call out of hours in a crisis. That's a shocking statistic. It sounds so obvious – but mental health professionals must ensure that everyone who might need crisis support knows how to get it. Just providing the services is not enough.

Anyone with bipolar (who may need to call the CRHT team urgently if they experience a fast-moving mood swing) should ask the care co-ordinator for a crisis phone number to pin up next to the phone and store in their contacts list. They need to give it to their close friends and family too.

In the US, most areas – often at a county or district level – have crisis teams available to assess someone with a mental health condition in crisis quickly.

The changing role of teachers

Shocking research by University College London published in 2017 indicated that one in four girls and one in ten boys have depression by the time they're 14. And at least two children in every primary school class (based on an average class size of 27) are likely to have a diagnosable mental health condition. This rises to three to four students in every class at secondary school. Around six to eight more children in each primary school class will be struggling just below this 'unwell' threshold. It follows that some of them will go on to develop bipolar.

Yet with child and adolescent mental health services (CAMHS) seriously underfunded and overstretched in the UK, the NHS doesn't have the resources to support all these children. Instead, teachers increasingly have to play a crucial role in spotting at-risk pupils and intervening early to support them.

The National Association of Head Teachers recognizes the fundamental role mental health plays in children's success and says that poor mental health is a significant barrier to learning. That's why most schools provide a large number of activities to promote and support good mental health and emotional well-being.

For quality-assured information, advice and teaching resources, see www.mentallyhealthyschools.org.uk.

Q46. *What is an advocate?*

Most advocates are employed by a voluntary organization and work with people in and out of the hospital environment. They're trained to 'listen respectfully' to the needs and wishes of those with a mental health condition and to help get those needs and wishes listened to and taken seriously by mental healthcare professionals.

The UK charity Mind says that an advocate is there to support your choices and:

- listen to your views and concerns
- help you explore your options and rights (without pressuring you)
- provide information to help you make informed decisions
- help you contact relevant people, or contact them on your behalf
- accompany you and support you in meetings or appointments.

You can find out more about advocacy services in the UK at www.mind.org.uk – search for 'advocacy'.

In the US, NAMI (the National Alliance on Mental Illness) offers an advocacy service through its legal centre – find details at www.nami.org.

Q47. What role do family and friends play in the recovery of someone with a diagnosis of bipolar disorder?

It's reassuring to know that most health professionals acknowledge that loved ones can be key when it comes to supporting someone with a psychiatric disorder. One study, for instance, shows that those with bipolar disorder who return to high-conflict families have more manic and depressive episodes nine months after hospitalization than those who return to low-conflict families. Research also shows that individuals with bipolar disorder are much more likely to suffer a relapse if they live with families with high levels of expressed negative emotion, such as criticism, blame, sarcasm and emotional over-involvement with the person with bipolar. In other words, the more emotionally healthy and supportive the family environment, the better.

The NICE guideline for the treatment of bipolar states that families and friends have a very significant role to play in the management of the patient's condition. They can:

- help the person to recognize the onset of symptoms
- support their loved one through crises
- provide healthcare professionals with information about symptoms and behaviour that might help to reduce hospital admission in the long term.

Dr Sara Tai, Senior Lecturer in Clinical Psychology at the University of Manchester, says that if there's a foundation of trust, a family member or friend is in a much better position to monitor signs of relapse than healthcare professionals. 'Loved ones can help the person seek help before it's too late,' she says.

It does seem that some people with bipolar disorder find the support of their friends and family invaluable:

> Neil sometimes says to me, 'What would people that haven't got the support do, Mum?' My daughter and I watch him for warning signals if he's getting ill. If he says anything out of character, alarm bells start ringing, and I ask him when he's going to see his CPN. To someone whose adult child is going through bipolar, I'd say, 'Be there for them when they need you, but give them their independence. Help them, but also help them to lead a separate life.
>
> *(GILL)*

> I've been with my partner for five years and he's very supportive. He accepts me for who I am.
>
> *(SHARRON)*

> I was told by a CPN that my husband David wasn't getting more help because I lived at home with him and looked after him. The doctors have always said that David's family is his anchor. He worships the kids. We deal with his condition together.
>
> *(JACKIE)*

> My partner Jane has been so supportive through it all. She's my rock. She's there and rationalizes it out for me. It must be so hard for her, my swinging up and down. She can deal with it really well.
>
> *(DAVE)*

> My family has been very supportive. If I hadn't had that support from my family, I dread to think where I'd have ended up.
>
> *(LESLEY)*

> I have a great support system. There's my daughter's father who helps out. And I've got my mum and my cousin.
>
> *(REKA)*

' Being only 15, Vicki relies on me for pretty much everything. I'm very involved in her care. She asks things like, have I eaten enough? Is this right? Is that right? I want her to try and learn to manage herself as well as having my guidance. I'm trying to give her some independence so she can recognize things that might trigger her mood changes. '

(ALISON)

On the other hand, support from family and friends isn't always forthcoming:

' My parents didn't have a clue what was going on and how to deal with me as a teenager. My mum just thought teenage boys were different from girls as my older sister is fairly stable. My dad's very quiet. He didn't deal with it at all. '

(PAUL)

' My family mostly just ignore my illness. When I told my parents when I was first diagnosed, my mother said, 'I'm sure they've got tablets for that.' They're all in denial. '

(DEBBIE)

' My mum would come over and help out with the children when I wasn't well, but she only ever once came to visit me in hospital – it was just 'don't talk about it, it isn't happening.' So she'd come over and do housework and look after the children, but not talk about it. '

(SUE)

' My parents have never really accepted the fact that I'm ill. When I said I was coming off the medication and I seemed fine, they thought, 'Oh well, she's not on drugs, therefore she's not ill.' '

(TAMARA)

In *The Bipolar Disorder Survival Guide,* David J. Miklowitz says that family and friends are able to offer more support when they're better informed about the condition: 'The first step in dealing effectively with family members after an episode is to educate them about your disorder. It is important that they understand that at least a portion of your behaviour is biologically and chemically determined. Family members who know the basic facts will also be more supportive of your efforts to maintain consistency in your treatment.'

In an ideal world, family members would read up on the subject in books and on the internet. If that's not likely to happen, Miklowitz suggests giving out a short, absolute beginners' fact sheet on bipolar disorder – you can scan or photocopy the one opposite.

In the USA, the National Alliance on Mental Illness (NAMI) offers a 12-week course called 'Family to Family', which educates friends and loved ones about major mental illnesses and the available treatments. The course also works as a support group, encouraging friends and family to share how they feel about the illness. See www.nami.org for details.

Q48. *On a practical level, how can family and friends help someone with a diagnosis of bipolar disorder?*

There's no end to the practical ways someone can support a loved one with bipolar disorder. Sarah's mum Rose supports Rebecca in many ways:

❛ Rebecca doesn't drive so Mum is always taking her to appointments, picking up prescriptions and medication, driving her to the supermarket and to social events. Mum also does all her washing and cooks her dinners two or three times a week. They go swimming together in the evenings and clothes shopping at weekends. I honestly don't know what Rebecca would do without Mum. ❜

Much of the practical help revolves around helping someone to stick to regular eating and sleeping patterns, which tend to be disrupted during periods of depression and mania. Also, household tasks tend to be put on hold during periods of instability. A family member or friend can offer practical support by, for example:

WHAT IS BIPOLAR DISORDER?

Bipolar disorder causes extreme mood swings that go from high and energized (manic) to low and lethargic (depressed). These swings can last from a few days to a few months. The illness occurs in phases, but it is possible to remain well for long periods in between.

WHAT ARE THE SYMPTOMS?

Someone who's high may feel overly happy and excited or overly irritable and angry. They may also feel like they can do things that no one else can do (grandiosity). They may sleep less than usual, talk faster, spend lots of money and be easily distracted and impulsive.

Someone who's depressed may feel very sad, unmotivated, irritable and anxious. They may sleep too much, have little or no appetite, have trouble concentrating and making decisions, have low self-esteem and contemplate suicide.

WHAT CAUSES BIPOLAR DISORDER?

Bipolar disorder is probably caused by an imbalance in the brain's neurochemistry involving the ways that cells communicate with each other. There is sometimes a genetic link. Mood swings can also be affected by other factors such as stress, hormones, sleep patterns, alcohol and recreational drugs.

HOW IS BIPOLAR DISORDER TREATED?

Most people with bipolar are on mood stabilizing medication; some also take anti-depressants to control anxiety and antipsychotic drugs to prevent losing touch with reality. Some have therapy or attend support group meetings. Lifestyle factors, such as sleep, stress and diet, also play an important part in managing the symptoms.

HOW DOES BIPOLAR DISORDER AFFECT THE FAMILY?

Having bipolar disorder can affect someone's ability to relate to others, often causing conflict and misunderstandings. Family counselling or a family support group can help.

- picking up prescriptions and/or medication
- driving them to appointments
- updating a diary or calendar so important appointments aren't forgotten
- encouraging them to see their GP
- accompanying them to support group meetings
- going supermarket shopping with or for them
- making a hot drink
- cooking a favourite meal
- making meals for the freezer
- bringing them fruit or healthy snacks
- encouraging them to drink plenty of water
- running them a bath
- taking them out for a drive
- getting them a favourite film or boxset
- offering them a foot massage
- accompanying them on a walk
- helping them with housework
- washing and ironing clothes
- sorting out bills and household admin.

Another important practical way a family member or friend can support someone with a bipolar diagnosis is by planning ahead for a possible relapse. They can do this by:

- making a list of warning signs that indicate help is required
- keeping a list of numbers for an emergency (the crisis resolution and home treatment team, GP and psychiatrist)
- discussing what action they need to take when different scenarios unfold.

Q49. On an emotional level, how can family and friends help someone with a diagnosis of bipolar disorder?

Perhaps even more important than the practical details, someone with bipolar often needs extra support on an emotional level. Clinical psychologist Dr Sara Tai, Senior Lecturer in Clinical Psychology at the University of Manchester, says there are several ways you can support someone emotionally:

- Be non-judgemental and unconditional (remember that a person's behaviour can be understood as their attempt to control their perception of what is going on around them; many people have traumatic experiences, and in this context their behaviour is usually understandable).
- Be consistent.
- Try to help them establish some routine and to feel safe.
- Provide them with the space and opportunity to be heard and understood.
- Don't always give answers; sometimes listening is just as important.

Julie A. Fast, the author of *Loving Someone with Bipolar Disorder*, recommends devising a holistic treatment plan. She says: 'The most effective way to treat bipolar disorder is to have a holistic treatment plan ready and waiting when bipolar disorder symptoms start appearing. Medications are the backbone of treatment, but a treatment plan will teach you and your loved one to *respond* to what the illness says and does instead of *reacting* to the symptoms as though they come out of thin air. When you learn to memorize the specific symptoms individually, you will no longer have to wonder constantly, what is wrong? Instead you can look at your symptoms list and determine the exact problem your partner (or loved one) is facing and what you both need to do to stop it. It's often difficult to know how to help when they are ill. The solution is to write down what works and what doesn't, so that you can read the list as soon as you see the first signs of bipolar disorder. The symptom list becomes a tool you can both use to separate bipolar disorder from your relationship.'

Different things work for different people:

> My partner Jane walks in and can see that I've gone low and she'll say, 'Well, I'm not feeling low so I'm off to the gym.' That's great because when I'm feeling down I don't want to be pestered. Then when I'm ready, I'll come round. I definitely believe that reflective listening is one of the best tools a partner can have. It's a skill my partner has. It requires her to be silent even when the silence is uncomfortably long. She rephrases what I've said to show she understands and that she's been listening. It's a technique that works so well for us. If Jane uses that on me when I'm down, it works. All she needs to do is to be there and listen; she doesn't need to say much. In fact, it only works if she doesn't say much. That allows me to get right down to the problem, and I get to the trigger thought. At the end of the day, I need to work out that the way I'm feeling is probably me being irrational. But she can't tell me that, I have to work it out for myself. I always end up thinking, 'Yeah, she's right, I'm feeling better now.'
>
> *(DAVE)*

> Dave and I have been together for five and a half years and we talk a lot. The thing is, there's no textbook, and there aren't any hard and fast rules telling you how to deal with someone who has bipolar. Everyone's so different. I just think it's common sense to give people a little bit of space and let them work things through without feeling isolated. I try not to be too judgemental or to try to change him.
>
> *(JANE)*

> I have a really good friend, Elaine, who's on call to me 24/7. If I need her she's here. Four weeks ago when I was very depressed, I self-harmed and got quite upset. I had to have stitches. As soon as I'd done it, I phoned her. She took me to A&E and sat with me for six hours until my sister came home from work. She's done a lot of research on the internet. She's also got some books and watched the Stephen Fry documentaries. I feel like she really accepts me. Although she doesn't understand, she just accepts the way I am. She doesn't try to get her head around the way I'm

behaving; she just goes along with it. When she's here I can talk absolute rubbish until I'm all talked out. She just sits and drinks tea. She knows when to listen and when not to listen – I'm just getting things out of my system. Once it's all come out we just move on. She doesn't usually ask questions.

(AMY)

Q50. *If someone with a bipolar diagnosis feels suicidal or is self-harming, what is the best course of action?*

There are no two ways about it – statistics linking suicide, self-harm, mental illness and bipolar disorder are alarming:

- 90% of suicide victims have been reported to have a psychiatric disorder at the time of their death.
- The suicide rate for people with bipolar disorder averages at around 60 times higher than the international population rate of 0.015% annually.
- Approximately 17% of patients with Bipolar I and 24% of patients with Bipolar II attempt suicide during the course of their illness.
- The WHO estimates that for each death by suicide that occurs, 20 more non-fatal self-inflicted injuries are carried out.
- In the UK, 400 in 100,000 people self-harm, many of whom have a mental illness.

Amanda's mum Irene's first suicide attempt marked a new low in her struggle with bipolar:

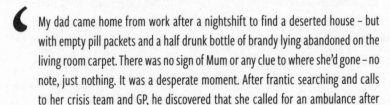

My dad came home from work after a nightshift to find a deserted house – but with empty pill packets and a half drunk bottle of brandy lying abandoned on the living room carpet. There was no sign of Mum or any clue to where she'd gone – no note, just nothing. It was a desperate moment. After frantic searching and calls to her crisis team and GP, he discovered that she called for an ambulance after swallowing the tablets and brandy, and by now was sedated in a hospital bed, after having her stomach pumped. So she was safe – but that day was still one of the bleakest our family ever faced. **"**

And the fear of Rebecca committing suicide never lifts for her sister Sarah or their mum Rose:

" Rebecca has taken several overdoses – usually a combination of paracetamol and her prescription drugs ... whatever medication is around. She also escaped out of hospital and deliberately threw herself in front of a car. It was a miracle that only her ankle was broken. These attempts have all taken place during times of extreme instability. Nothing can describe the fear and frustration my mum and I feel in the period leading up to an attempt. It's like you can see what's around the corner but you're powerless to stop it. Perhaps the worst time for us was during Rebecca's darkest depression when Mum found several towropes with a noose tied in them in the loft. Mum would throw one away and the next week she'd find another one. It got to the point where Mum dreaded going home for fear of what she might find. The worst thing was that there was absolutely nothing we could do to help because we couldn't connect with Rebecca at all. The shutters were down. If I saw Rebecca or spoke to her on the phone I'd wonder if it was the last time I was ever going to see or speak to her. Mum and I would talk on the phone every day about how anxious we felt. Our conversations never deviated from that one subject – who else could we share this extreme fear with? We did phone the psychiatrist and went to see her GP. They'd offer words of sympathy and change her medication, but nothing helped. Mum lost weight and looked terrible. We were literally worried sick, but all we could do was stand by helplessly, watching, waiting and hoping the fog of depression would lift ...

After a suicide attempt, Rebecca always looks so fragile, vulnerable and pale lying in a hospital bed. She says she's sorry and tells us how much she loves us, that she would never want to hurt us. We try to understand that she must be experiencing unimaginable emotional pain, but all we want to scream is, Why? Why?

Then you find yourselves questioning why you couldn't have helped to prevent her getting so low, why you couldn't have stopped it happening. That's when the guilt kicks in – like a physical wrenching pain in the stomach. How could this have happened – again? Why couldn't we have rescued somebody we love so very much?

Yet even during times of stability, when the risk of Rebecca attempting suicide is practically non-existent because she's feeling so well, Mum and I can't let go of the fear completely. It's like a constant companion, a feeling of dread gnawing away in the back of your mind.

Many people with bipolar disorder have suicidal tendencies during periods of instability:

At the worst point of my illness I tried to throw myself out of a top floor window and had six people trying to hang onto me.

(*RICHARD*)

In my late twenties and early thirties, I attempted suicide around 20 times, although it's true what they say – you want to switch off the pain rather than want to die. I currently get a mood stabilizer injected once a fortnight because I don't trust myself with the medication.

(*SHARRON*)

Vicki was first admitted to hospital because she took an aspirin overdose. Her medication wasn't working at all so her moods were changing really really fast. And she just didn't want to live. She also had a mixed state episode where she was trying to slit her wrists and also tried to throw herself out of the window. She won't say it to me, but she'll say it to the doctor: 'I do want to die.' I worry whether she's going to have a future. You have to be very strong. Nothing shocks me anymore.

(*ALISON*)

My daughter moved the cutlery because she was afraid of her dad killing himself. She took every knife, fork and spoon out of the drawer, put them in a plastic bag and hid them in her room. I don't quite know what she thought he was going to do with the spoons!

(JACKIE)

We suspect my mum's sister, my aunt, had Bipolar II. She committed suicide in hospital. She was very depressed and hanged herself. It's impossible to describe how absolutely devastated we were.

(JAYNE)

So what can a family member or friend do to help avoid the worst possible case scenario?

1. Let go of guilt

The first important thing to remember is that loving someone – however much – is not enough to rescue or save them. However hard it is to accept, if someone is determined to take their own life, they will. Nobody can be responsible for somebody else's life.

2. Know the risk factors

As well as mental illness, other factors are known to be associated with an increased risk of suicide, such as drug and alcohol misuse, unemployment, social isolation and family breakdown. Previous suicide attempts are also an indication of greater risk. Up to 20% of survivors try again within a year, and as a group they are 100 times more likely to go on to kill themselves than those who have never tried before. Many suicides take place during a depressive phase and/or after a recent negative life event.

Other factors can increase the risk of suicide:

- For people with bipolar, the risk of suicide is much higher during depressive and mixed episodes.
- Men are more at risk – in 2016, 75% of people in the UK who

took their own life were male. And suicide is the most common cause of death for men aged 20–49 years in England and Wales.

- Being single, divorced or widowed is a risk factor.
- The number of suicides by young people has increased and is now one of the main causes of death for this age group.
- Most people who self-harm (most commonly by cutting, burning, scratching or bruising) will not go on to commit suicide, although research shows that people who have self-harmed are 50–100 times more likely to commit suicide than the general population. If you are or your loved one is self-harming, there are some details below of organizations you or your family can turn to for help and support.
- Anyone with physical pain or illness is at greater risk of suicide.

3. Recognize the warning signs

The signs that depression might be leading to suicidal thoughts or intentions vary from person to person, but they may include some of the following:

- experiencing or expecting a personal loss or bereavement
- feelings of failure, hopelessness or worthlessness
- feeling and becoming withdrawn and isolated
- lack of self-care, such as poor personal hygiene or not eating properly
- building up supplies of medication or equipment which could be used in a suicide attempt
- suddenly making changes to wills, taking out life insurance or giving things away
- stopping medical routines, such as medications or special diets
- talking about suicide
- risk-taking behaviour.

4. Get help

Never ignore threats of suicide – on average, more than half of those who commit suicide tell their next of kin or a medical professional what they're planning to do before carrying it out.

So what's the best course of action in a crisis situation?

First, try to have an open discussion and encourage them to talk about their feelings. A loving gesture, such as a hug, can sometimes help. Next, try to persuade them to seek help or get help immediately on their behalf. And though the support available varies depending on the situation, whether or not a person is known to psychiatric services, and the area of the country they live in, help is always available in some form or other – a community mental health team, a psychiatrist, a GP, A&E or emergency services.

Whichever professional they see, encouraging the person to be open and honest about their feelings is useful. If they allow it, go with them to the appointment and, if they find it difficult to be honest, share as much information as possible.

Family and friends of those with bipolar disorder have had various experiences of support during suicidal crisis situations.

> For two weeks until a couple of days ago, Laura was having mixed states and constantly talking about killing herself. She stopped taking her medication altogether. I didn't know whether she was really going to do it or not. When I went home, I honestly didn't know what I was going to find. She had plugged the hairdryer into a socket in the kitchen and filled the kitchen sink with water. But then I found her asleep in bed. I phoned the mental health team and her GP for help, but they just said there's nothing they could do because she had to make the contact.
>
> (JUNE)

> I was feeling suicidal, so I rang a doctor who could fit me in. He spoke to the crisis team who were waiting for me when I got home and I've been under them

for two weeks. I'm back on medication and for the last 48 hours I've been feeling myself again.

(*DEBBIE*)

SAMARITANS

If other professional help isn't available or hasn't improved the situation, Samaritans is a UK charity that provides confidential emotional support 24 hours a day to any person who is suicidal or despairing. They won't judge or offer advice, but simply listen with an open mind and provide the time and space for someone to talk, think and find a way through their difficulties. Calls are charged at the local rate and are anonymous.

UK HELPLINE: 116 123

EMAIL: jo@samaritans.org

WEBSITE: www.samaritans.org

Other organizations set up to support those who feel suicidal

PAPYRUS

The national charity for the prevention of young suicide runs HOPELineUK, a confidential support and advice service for:

- young people under the age of 35 who may be having thoughts of suicide
- anyone concerned a young person may be having thoughts of suicide.

UK HELPLINE: 0800 068 41 41

EMAIL: pat@papyrus-uk.org

TEXT: 07786 209 697

WEBSITE: www.papyrus-uk.org

CALM – CAMPAIGN AGAINST LIVING MISERABLY

A UK-based organization, their aim is to reach young men before they become depressed and suicidal.

TEL: 0800 585 858

WEBSITE: www.thecalmzone.net

NATIONAL SUICIDE PREVENTION LIFELINE

In the USA, this helpline provides free and confidential support for people in distress and their loved ones 24/7.

TEL: 1-800-273-8255

WEBSITE: www.suicidepreventionlifeline.org

INTERNATIONAL ASSOCIATION FOR SUICIDE PREVENTION (IASP)

WEBSITE: www.iasp.info

Support if you're worried about self-harm

HARMLESS

User-led organization for people who self-harm, and their friends and families.

WEBSITE: www.harmless.org.uk

LIFESIGNS

User-led self-harm guidance and support network.

WEBSITE: www.lifesigns.org.uk

NATIONAL SELF HARM NETWORK (NSHN)

Closely monitored survivor-led forum for people who self-harm, and their friends and families.

WEBSITE: www.nshn.co.uk

SELFHARMUK

A pro-recovery charity committed to improving the lives of anyone impacted by self-harm.

WEBSITE: www.selfharm.co.uk

SELF-INJURY SUPPORT

Information and support for women and girls who self-harm, including a self-harm diary and local support groups.

TEL: 0808 800 8088 (helpline Mon–Fri 7–10pm)

WEBSITE: www.selfinjurysupport.org.uk

Q51. What is the best way for a loved one to cope during the really tough times?

It is an understatement to say that bipolar disorder can take a terrible toll on those who love and care for people with the condition. Someone who's in the grip of a mood swing is often unable to think rationally, which can mean it's impossible to persuade or reason with them. The unpredictability is inevitable. It's as though the loved one is temporarily gone and bipolar disorder has moved in. Partners and other family members can feel lonely, frustrated, guilty, stressed, exhausted, fearful, ashamed and confused in equal measure. Both the highs and lows of the illness can be devastating, as can the transition from a depressive to a manic phase.

Mania, excessive spending, infidelity, offensive/abusive/domineering behaviour and talking incoherently can cause distress to other family members and friends. It can be particularly upsetting when a person becomes manic for the first time, because their behaviour can seem out-of-character and inexplicable.

Depression takes a toll in a different way. The patient can seem 'cut off' from their loved ones, isolated in their own misery. Their loss of interest and any enthusiasm in life makes it hard to get on with the daily routine as normal.

According to the UK-based mental health charity Rethink Mental Illness, carers save the government an estimated £119 billion per year and, more importantly, drastically improve the lives and well-being outcomes for the people they care for. The charity reports that 46% of calls to their advice service (0121 522 7007) are from carers. Sarah's mum Rose gets physically exhausted when Rebecca is unwell:

> I'm always on edge when Rebecca is going through a bad patch. Either I'm with her – which is inevitably stressful – or I'm worrying about her, waiting for her to call so that I know she's OK. I don't sleep well. I can't relax. I get more and more exhausted until I wonder if I'll end up in a bed next to hers in the psychiatric ward. The trouble is, it's always about Rebecca, never about me. As much as I feel sorry for Rebecca because she's been through so much, I can't help wondering sometimes, 'What about me? What about me?' As a carer you give all the time. Most of the time I can cope with getting very little in return. But when I get exhausted and low, I can't. I think the trouble with bipolar thinking is that it makes the person very inward looking and very focused on their own needs. I suppose that must be a coping mechanism, but it's hard on the carers because their needs go completely unnoticed. I suppose I get some kind of relief when Rebecca goes into hospital because then somebody else is looking after her, but then I feel so guilty that I can't cope. Visiting Rebecca in hospital is emotionally exhausting. As you park the car, you just feel so apprehensive. What mood will Rebecca be in? Also, we never know what staff will be on duty. Will it be the friendly, relaxed nurses today or the less friendly ones who can't make eye contact? And what mood will the other patients be in? A couple of times, I've witnessed extremely aggressive behaviour. And though it's rare (most visits pass without incident) and I have compassion for anyone experiencing such extreme emotions, it can still be pretty frightening. Even though it's a relief to come home, I then always feel so desperately guilty leaving Rebecca behind.

And Amanda's dad Gordon has suffered ill effects on his health:

" Dad has always managed to keep reasonably well, even during the worst times of Mum's illness when he felt more emotionally exhausted than physically ill. But the last couple of years, as she moved towards more rapid mood cycling, really took their toll on his health. He started having panic attacks – his chest would suddenly feel very tight and painful, as if he had heavy weights pressing down on him, he couldn't breathe properly, his heart would pound, and he would feel too weak and dizzy to even stand up. Within the space of a few weeks, he suffered about a dozen panic attacks – one was so extreme he was rushed by ambulance to A&E. Thankfully the attacks ceased, but then his blood pressure shot up and has remained worryingly high, so he has to take tablets for that now. Dad and his GP are both certain that the stress of looking after my mum is the major reason behind all this. "

Many other loved ones have similar stories:

" I can't say it hasn't been a strain caring for David. In fact, the stress has brought on lupus. I've also got angina. The doctors say that both conditions are stress-related. "

(JACKIE)

" It's been incredibly stressful. I feel exhausted. I've always been a good problem solver and feel frustrated that I can't solve our family crisis. I feel like I'm cracking up and that I can't actually take care of myself. I'm not even going to be able to pay the mortgage next month because I'm in a constant state of stress. I can't look for work, but even if I did get a job, I'm just too stressed to work. I also feel incredibly guilty that I can't manage Laura's behaviour better. I can't imagine a future for us. I can only think half a day ahead at a time. Thinking further ahead than that is too overwhelming. "

(JUNE)

" The worry of my mum's bipolar has made me physically ill. I start off being sick. I get blinding headaches. I'm a civil servant and have to take a lot of time off work. "

(JAYNE)

It's also common for relationships to suffer. What can seem like the relent-less pattern of the illness can put relationships under considerable strain. Perhaps not surprisingly, divorce rates are around two to three times higher for individuals with bipolar than in the general population. This is a reflec-tion of the emotional damage the illness can do to long-term relationships.

> My relationship with my wife is suffering a bit. It must be a nightmare living with someone when you have no idea what their next move is going to be.
>
> *(PAUL)*

> Bipolar has impacted terribly on personal relationships. I change moods. I get angry really quickly. I get bored. I need to have excitement by causing trouble or having an argument, or causing friction. I like friction, because then I feel alive. I haven't held down a proper relationship for a long time.
>
> *(REKA)*

> My soul-mate turned into a monster when he was high. When he went into hospital, I felt like I'd failed and that I should have done more to help him. I also felt really sad and lonely and emotional and traumatized by what had happened. Bipolar disorder can be frustrating and confusing. But I knew I had to stay strong for the kids. I got valium from the doctor because I did feel as if I couldn't really cope.
>
> *(JO)*

> My diagnosis of bipolar has definitely affected my partner. She finds it hard to understand that some days I am very low. She found the manic side very distressing and until she understood it more, we were on the verge of splitting up.
>
> *(JUDE)*

> Bipolar has had a huge impact on my personal relationships. Up until I was 30, I was in four long-term relationships. I was classically either massively up or massively down, and it's very difficult for the person on the other side of it. And then in my thirties when I got clean, I just avoided relationships the best I could – for about eight years I didn't go near them. And then for the last year I've been in a stable

relationship. It's not been without its troubles, but she has an understanding of depression and bipolar from her family, which helps.

(ASHLEY)

It's not just partners who are affected, but mothers, fathers, brothers, sisters, sons, daughters and friends, too:

My relationship with my mum has been affected by her bipolar disorder. We probably drifted apart emotionally during my teens, and when she was high she just embarrassed me. In my twenties I used to get quite angry at her for getting so low and so high. She almost didn't seem like my mum, but some imposter. I wasn't sure who my mum really was. Now, when she is low my relationship with her is less tense and I feel close to her because she is so down. I feel sorry for her and I'm more patient. Alternatively, when she is high, I am never good enough. I can't do enough, I can't do anything quick enough or well enough and this disturbs me greatly. My mum's relationship with my children is also affected. She lets them get away with more when she is low. And when she is high she reprimands them for everything.

(INGRID)

I wish I had a normal mum. I see mothers and daughters in town and I feel so jealous. I can't let my mum look after my children. Even when she's on medication she wouldn't care for them properly because she's so preoccupied with herself. I can't trust my mum. It makes me feel sad. When she's taking her tablets they keep a lid on her symptoms, but when she stops completely she's as high as a kite within days. I feel terrified. When she's manic she gets aggressive towards me. I used to want to fix and rescue my mum. Now I've realized that there's nothing I can do to bring her down when she's high. I've taken a step back and I'm letting the professionals sort it out. I used to put my mum first. But now I've realized that I have to put myself first. Only then can I look after the kids, go to work and deal with my mum, in that order. Realizing that I have to be number one has helped a lot.

(JAYNE)

My relationship with my mum has been tricky. She is trying, but I go up and down so much. At the moment I've withdrawn a bit myself and feel like I could quite happily live without people around me. And when I was a teenager I didn't speak to my dad for four years. It was a nightmare – my mum, dad, sister and me all living together in such a horrible atmosphere.

(PAUL)

Julie A. Fast acknowledges that it's extremely difficult to have a healthy relationship when one partner is a caretaker and the other is a patient. Her advice? 'Answer this question honestly: What is my role in this relationship and how do I feel about it? If balance is to be found, you need to be happy with your caretaking role. If you're not happy with the role, you need to change it. Everyone gets tired eventually. You don't want to lose yourself.'

She recommends the following to create a more balanced relationship:

- Help the partner find independence so that the bipolar disorder doesn't end up defining the relationship.
- Establish clear and firm limits, adopting the view 'I do care and I will help, but I'm not devoting my whole life to rescuing'.
- Focus on prevention, looking to and planning for the future.

If you're a carer, there is support available:

- Find out about your rights at www.carers.org and talk to other carers on their forum.
- Join a local carers support group at www.rethink.org/services-groups.

Q52. *What support do mental health charities offer?*

There are a number of mental health charities all over the world which offer information and support for those with bipolar disorder. Many of these groups offer emotional support too, via helplines, local group meetings, social media and online communities.

Carers, partners and other family members who attend local self-help and support groups say they feel less negative about the illness, have fewer feelings of worry and guilt, and feel more positive about their relationship with the person with bipolar. Partners who attend groups also report a greater understanding of bipolar disorder and are more proactive about seeking out information. They report less disruption of family relationships as a result of their partner's illness and experience less worry about the future. They also put a high value on meeting other people who have shared the same experience.

As for social media, many people with bipolar disorder and their families find it helpful to join support groups and online communities on Facebook, Twitter and charity forums.

We particularly like Campfire – a hub for small online community groups, where you can connect with others going through similar life challenges. Co-founder Daniel Pourasghar, who has a diagnosis of bipolar, says: 'I'm building the product that I wish I had ten years ago when I was diagnosed with bipolar disorder. For most of my adult life, I kept this big secret due to shame and fear of judgement. I've always had a desire to connect with people that experience life in similar ways as I do; the problem was that due to the stigma around my disorder, I didn't know how to find them. Eventually, I did and it felt comforting to know that I'm not the only one.

'There's a certain kinship I feel when I meet another person with bipolar. It's like meeting someone from your hometown or someone who went to your school but a lot stronger. Talking to a peer is also always a unique learning opportunity for me. With Campfire, we're addressing exactly these needs by creating a space for people to connect around a common experience.'

You can join a group at www.campfire.care.

 It's good to share things with people who really understand what you're going through. Last week I put a post up asking about the funniest things you've done when you're manic. Loads of people replied with some brilliant stories. Instead of it being such a depressing subject, bipolar can also be a source of fun. People with bipolar really do some funny stuff. It's important to remember that and not only focus on all the negative stuff.

(PAUL)

Talking online has helped a lot. I'm not alone any more. I used to feel so lonely and worried, and wouldn't talk to people about it. It was such a taboo subject, and I felt ashamed and embarrassed. Now I can get advice from people who are going through the same thing. And to help other people is really great.

(JAYNE)

I find the online bipolar community really helpful. It's a support network. I can talk about total rubbish with people who really understand what I'm going through. The chat room is just as much for carers as it is for the people who are in the same boat as us. After all, David's the only bipolar in the village!

(JACKIE)

For a complete list of mental health charities (and other useful organizations) in the UK and beyond, see Extra resources, p. 267.

CHAPTER FOUR

Hospital Care

Q53. *What are psychiatric hospitals like?*

To the outside world, the reality of life inside psychiatric hospitals remains steeped in stigma and stereotype. The old joke about 'being carted off by the men in white coats' is still sometimes used, and in one study an overwhelming majority of the public admitted that they thought mental health units resemble the 1975 film, *One Flew Over The Cuckoo's Nest*, where treatments were essentially punishments administered by domineering doctors and nurses more interested in social control than psychiatric recovery.

Yet psychiatric hospitals have changed a great deal since the 1970s, and certainly since the days of the Victorian asylums. The wards are less obviously over-crowded and the duration of the average stay is much shorter. Patients get dressed in their own clothes, whereas years ago they would spend a hospital stay in pyjamas. But perhaps the biggest difference of all is that a lot more emphasis is now placed on an individual's human rights.

So what are today's psychiatric hospitals actually like?

Types of psychiatric units

There are four main types of psychiatric hospital care in the UK: acute admissions wards, intensive care wards, medium secure units and high security special hospitals.

Acute admissions wards have around 15 to 25 beds, with a staff ratio of five patients to one nurse. These wards can be part of a general hospital or in a separate psychiatric unit, and are usually the first stage of hospital care for a mentally ill person, especially if this is the first time they've been admitted. Assessment and first treatment steps will be carried out here, but these are short-term stay wards – some patients may only remain here for a few days and are able to return home, whereas others will then transfer to intensive care wards or medium secure wards (see below). Other people will be admitted straight to these two types of wards, bypassing the acute admission wards altogether if:

- they have been sectioned before admittance
- they have been in psychiatric hospital care before and, for example, have on their personal care plan that they should go straight to a medium secure ward
- they are showing signs of aggressive or potentially harmful behaviour to themselves or others.

Intensive care wards are usually small – the bed numbers vary across the UK (with sometimes as few as seven beds) – and often are part of a larger psychiatric unit or hospital. The wards are usually locked and cater for people who need short-term intervention and treatment, with a ratio of seven patients to three or four nurses, or three patients to two nurses.

Medium secure units (also called interim wards or units) are usually much larger wards with high levels of security, catering for patients needing longer-term care. Some of the large general hospitals in the UK have medium secure psychiatric units, and will take patients from a large geographic area. Medium secure units may take someone for whom a bed can't be found in a local psychiatric intensive care ward, and will also cater for people who have been sent from the criminal justice system for assessment. Despite the size of these wards, the staff ratios are almost as high as the intensive care wards, with one nurse for every two patients.

High security special hospitals (such as Broadmoor and Ashworth) cater for people with a mental illness detained under Home Office section as a result of criminal proceedings, as they have specific needs and security issues that are hard to meet in other psychiatric hospitals. On average, the patients are detained for five to seven years, although it can be longer in some cases.

Rules and regulations

Unlike other parts of a general hospital, many psychiatric units are locked to the outside world, so it's often necessary to ring a buzzer to be allowed in through the main door. Inside, psychiatric units have the power to set their own day-to-day rules and operational policies, which patients and visitors are expected to follow. Because it can be a struggle respecting patients' independence, whilst at the same time maintaining a safe environment for everyone, these rules can sometimes seem strict and unnecessary. Patients may have restricted kitchen access, so they're unable to make drinks for themselves or their visiting family, for example, and they may not be allowed to use china cups or sharp cutlery. Patients sometimes aren't allowed out into the garden area without being accompanied by a psychiatric nurse or a relative – and sometimes not even with a family member. Sarah has some painful memories of the impact the rules have had on her sister:

When Rebecca was in a psychiatric hospital for a year, there was a rule that the staff made tea on the hour. At the time, Rebecca wasn't allowed kitchen access for her own safety. Once, I turned up at five past three and Rebecca's request for a cup of tea for her visitor was denied. I could only stay until four o'clock, so

I didn't get a drink. I wasn't particularly bothered, but Rebecca kept on saying 'This is supposed to be my home, but I can't even give you a cup of tea.' Another thing that would frequently happen is that she would be waiting to be taken out on a planned trip at a certain time – either for a walk around the grounds or into town – and then it would turn out that there wasn't a psychiatric nurse available to take her after all. I understand why the rules are in place, but I think that the huge impact they have on someone's day-to-day life, and ultimately their sense of self, is often overlooked.

As with any other type of hospital environment, there are usually set meal times on a psychiatric ward throughout the day, and access to regular drinks. This is especially important as some medications produce a dry mouth side effect. Patients usually receive their medication after meals, as it's often better to take the drugs on a full stomach, and usually before bedtime too, as some patients may be medicated to help them settle at night. Sleep is an essential part of the recovery process, so patients are encouraged to go to bed earlier rather than later, although a ward doesn't usually have a 'set' bedtime or 'lights out'. Visiting hours are generally confined to afternoons and evenings, with a time between the two sessions when the ward is usually closed to visitors while patients eat their evening meal. But family members can usually come to a ward at other times by prior arrangement with the staff – for example, to meet with a psychiatrist.

Ian Hulatt, Mental Health Advisor to the Royal College of Nursing for 13 years, says that establishing stability and security through rules and routines is particularly important in a psychiatric ward, because the patients can be a potentially volatile mix of different conditions. And the situation is getting worse because of the shrinking number of beds. In 2013, according to the OECD (Organisation for Economic Co-operation and Development) the UK had 54 psychiatric beds per 100,000 population, compared to the international average of 68 beds per 100,000 population. And a report in the *British Medical Journal* in December 2017 found that mental health beds in the UK had been cut by 40% from 26,929 in 2007/8 to 18,730 in 2016/17. By comparison, general acute beds only fell by 17% during the same period.

'The number of psychiatric beds in the UK has fallen, which means the nature of in-patient work has radically changed over the last 10, 15 years because the concentration of very ill people is greater,' says Ian Hulatt. 'For people with bipolar, they may be hypomanic, very uninhibited, very irritable, full of energy and feeling on top of the world, and we're trying to medicate them and keep them on a locked ward, with other people around them who are very unwell too. It can be a very difficult environment.'

The hospital environment

In the UK, two Mental Health Acts (1983 and 2007) govern the care and treatment of patients with mental disorders, alongside a Code of Practice that not only provides guidance for professionals but also guides patients, their families and carers on their rights. The code was revised in 2015 to reflect changes in legislation, case law, policy and professional practice.

The full version of the code can be found on the government website www.gov.uk in the Publications section. Amongst other things, the Code of Practice recommends:

- giving each patient a defined personal space and a secure locker for the safekeeping of possessions
- ensuring access to open space
- organizing hospital wards to provide quiet rooms, recreation rooms, single sex areas and visitors' rooms
- providing all necessary help for patients with any type of disability.

Despite these guidelines, staying in a psychiatric hospital isn't always a good experience. The Care Quality Commission (previously known as the Healthcare Commission) is the independent regulator of health and adult social care in England, and their 2017 report, 'The state of care in mental health services 2014 to 2017', states: 'Our inspectors have found many examples of excellent care – but we also found too much poor care, and far too much variation in both quality and access across different services.'

My experience in hospital years ago was very short and very bad. The first morning I woke up, another patient in the bed opposite started getting a bit animated. He wasn't really doing much other than rocking backwards and forwards and making a bit of noise. The medical staff ran in, held him down, and forcibly injected him. I was shocked to see that.

(DAVE)

Amanda recalls some of her mum Irene's early stays at a hospital in Birmingham where the wards used to be divided into curtained cubicles:

Mum's peace and privacy were so easily disrupted. She would sometimes return to her cubicle to find another patient asleep on her bed, and this made her feel even more vulnerable – she felt that she had nowhere safe to go. During another stay, one woman became obsessed with Mum's shoes and kept sneaking into her cubicle to steal them. At night the ward was often very noisy, with other patients shouting or being disruptive, and even with medication Mum would still have disturbed sleep. None of this was very helpful to her recovery.

Nationally, mental healthcare and ward refurbishment (like many aspects of UK healthcare) is a postcode lottery, and some units are still badly in need of modernization. Indeed, the Care Quality Commission's report highlights that, as of May 2017, 36% of NHS core services and 34% of independent mental health core services were rated as 'requires improvement', with a further 4% of NHS and 5% of independent core services being rated as 'inadequate'. The report adds: 'On too many wards, the combination of a concentration of detained patients with very serious mental health conditions, old and unsuitable buildings, staff shortages and lack of basic training, make it more likely that patients and staff are at risk of suffering harm.'

However, the report does point to some positive signs: in May 2017, 68% of core services provided by NHS trusts and 72% of those provided by independent mental health locations were rated as 'good', whilst a further 6% of NHS and 3% of independent core services were rated as 'outstanding'. It is also encouraging to note that since the Care Quality Commission's inspection programme began, 16 of the 22 mental health NHS trusts initially rated as 'inadequate' or 'requires improvement' have improved their rating. The full report can be accessed in the Publications section of the Commission's website: www.cqc.org.uk.

So, slowly and steadily, it seems that psychiatric care and hospital environments are being improved, which can make a huge difference to the general atmosphere and recovery process. The hospital wards where Amanda's mum Irene is treated have undergone refurbishment, with single rooms now available, and so Irene's recent visits there have been more comfortable and peaceful.

> I do volunteer work in a new psychiatric ward, with facilities that are absolutely state of the art. Every room is fully fitted and kitted like a hotel room. It's made a hell of a difference. A consultant said to me that he couldn't believe we actually worked in those disgusting old wards, environments where it's impossible for anyone to get well. What you need is a nice fresh environment, with plenty of light – clean, tidy, modern surroundings. Everybody should have a private room, preferably with en-suite facilities. In the twenty-first century, why should you spend weeks or months in that ward system? Sharing a bathroom down corridors is medieval. It's also important to have easy access to the outside – a courtyard or garden – so you can get sunshine and fresh air outside.
>
> *(GEORGE)*

> In 1999 I was in an older-style ward that was part of the hospital, for 11 weeks. I just had a curtain pulled across a cubicle, so there was very little privacy and I was totally bored out of my brain. But my last stay in hospital was very different. They've built a new unit separate to the hospital where you get your own room.
>
> *(RACHEL)*

Private healthcare

For those who can afford it, paying for treatment in a private psychiatric hospital is another option. If medical insurance is being used, a referral will still be needed from a GP, who may know a suitable psychiatrist at a local private psychiatric unit (often because the psychiatrist works in local NHS hospitals too). Alternatively, a private hospital can be selected by the person with bipolar (or their family) but this needs careful thought – look beyond the smart décor and swimming pools. Ideally an independent hospital should be able to demonstrate that they have experience of treating bipolar disorder specifically – bipolar shouldn't just be lumped into their general treatment category of depression. Go by personal recommendation if possible and make sure that the hospital is recognized by a professional body such as the NHS Partners Network (www.nhspn.org).

 The NHS hospital eventually referred me to this voluntary counselling organization – and they wouldn't take me on. They said I was too complicated!! So in the end, my social worker said the best option I had was to go private and pay for my healthcare, which is what I did in the end, and I went to the Priory. It really helped – it was a very supportive environment, although I had to have two more stays there last year. The nursing staff were brilliant. I still see the psychiatrist from there every two weeks, and I see their psychologist in the week in between, for CBT. In terms of aftercare, there are different options you can take ... you can continue some of the group therapy, which I chose not to do because it was incredibly expensive. But I needed more individual therapy anyway. The only time I have anything to do with the NHS now is when my GP does my prescriptions and sick notes.

(LESLEY)

But be warned – the private hospital route may cut someone off from NHS post-hospital support:

Because my healthcare is now in the private sector, the NHS won't give me a psychiatric nurse or social worker.

(LESLEY)

Q54. What is an 'informal' patient in a psychiatric hospital?

Anyone who agrees to admit themselves to a psychiatric hospital voluntarily is known as an 'informal' or voluntary patient:

 I was relieved to be in hospital, to be honest, because I was really struggling to get the help that I needed. It was such a relief, and I think it was a relief for my family as well, that I was taken out of harm's way. I recognized that I needed to be there.

(*LESLEY*)

Many psychiatric patients are admitted informally and, in theory, are free to walk out of hospital at any time. But if the hospital staff believe they need to start applying for legal processes to detain an informal patient, the patient can be stopped from leaving hospital for a further 72 hours. This is known as a 'holding power', and is in place to allow a doctor to assess someone and decide if the application should be made. If a doctor isn't available, a psychiatric nurse can also exercise a holding power for up to six hours until a doctor can begin the assessment. So, although an informal patient is free to leave in theory, this isn't always the case in practice:

They treated me as a voluntary patient because I didn't try to escape, but I think I would have been sectioned if I had twigged what was going on and had wanted to leave. If I'd tried to leave, they would have stopped me. It's happened like that a couple of times ... staff say, 'You can't leave' and I'll say, 'Yes I can' and they'll say, 'Well, if you do, we'll section you.'

(*KEITH*)

Q55. What does it mean if somebody is sectioned?

In the UK, 'being sectioned' is an unofficial phrase which means compulsory admittance to a psychiatric hospital or ward. In other words, someone with a mental illness can be kept in hospital for assessment and treatment without their consent, if doctors feel their condition is serious enough and/or if they might pose a threat to themselves or other people. This is done through a legal process using different sections from the Mental Health Act (1983), which is where the term 'sectioning' comes from. And it's an extremely complicated process.

The decision to section someone has to be agreed by three people, usually two doctors and an approved mental health professional (AMHP) – a title introduced by the Mental Health Act of 2007 which replaced the previous title of 'approved social worker' or ASW. The role can be undertaken by professionals other than social workers, including psychiatric nurses, occupational therapists and psychologists as long as they have received appropriate training.

If both doctors agree that a person should be admitted into psychiatric care, the AMHP will then decide if a section application should be made – he or she has up to 14 days to consider if this is the right course of action or if there's any alternative to compulsory hospital detention.

Sectioning can seem like an alien, upsetting process to patients and their families, particularly if it's the first time it has happened.

 Being sectioned feels like you are completely taken away from any control over your life whatsoever. It's like a punishment. When you're in the mindset of being sectioned, there's hardly ever any reasoning left. You can only see that people are stopping you from doing something. There have been times when I've thought to myself, 'I wish someone would section me.' When I know life is getting out of control for me – when I've taken on too much work, I can't cope, but I can't give in and say no, I sometimes think, 'this is the time when I need to be sectioned to stop it getting any worse.' By the time you are sectioned, you've lost that power to reason. You can no longer look after yourself.

(*SHARRON*)

On top of this, if someone is forcibly resisting admittance and treatment – especially if they're as high as a kite with mania and can't see why they should go to hospital – the section order allows for physical intervention to be used. Sometimes, if the psychiatric professionals can't physically manage to admit a patient on their own, the police have to become involved in taking the patient to hospital. Sarah's mum Rose cites the first time her daughter Rebecca was sectioned as one of the worst moments of her life.

> Rebecca hadn't been to sleep all night and when I came home that lunchtime she was naked apart from a towel and preparing to go out. That was the point I knew something was really wrong and that I needed help. I phoned our GP. I'll never forget what he said: 'Oh God, not another mad person, I've already had one today.' Rebecca had absolutely no insight into her condition. She just kept saying, 'Mum, don't worry, please, I just feel happy.' But her behaviour became increasingly bizarre as she got further and further out of touch with reality. She was convinced she could do anything. We had to wait hours for the doctor to come, and then a psychiatrist. Then they had to find a social worker. And Rebecca was refusing to get into the ambulance so they called the police. There was me, my friend Eileen, two doctors, a social worker and two ambulance men in my living room, and two police cars with flashing lights outside. We eventually tricked Rebecca into getting in the ambulance at about 9pm by saying that her ex-boyfriend would be in there. I didn't want to lie, but it was the only way we could get her to safety. She's never forgiven me for that, even though it was several years ago.

For the families of someone who's been sectioned, the feelings are usually mixed – relief that they are safe after maybe days, weeks or even months of instability, coupled with fear, anger, despair, helplessness and uncertainty about the future. Guilt is also a common reaction after a relative is sectioned – guilt at feeling relieved, guilt that they're the healthy one left at home (survivors' guilt) and guilt that they weren't able to 'save' their loved one and stop them going into hospital in the first place.

Overwhelming guilt is the overriding feeling Sarah (and her mum) feel each time Rebecca is sectioned:

❛ Your instinct is to protect the ones you love; you feel responsible for their well-being. Handing them over to complete strangers because you can't cope makes you feel like such a failure. You feel guilty that you couldn't make them better and that you couldn't ride the storm without turning for help. You feel guilty that your life is carrying on while the one you love is locked up like a prisoner. ❜

Accepting that someone can be detained for hospital treatment against their will, in a supposedly 'free' society, can be difficult – the process appears more custodial than caring. But it may help to view the psychiatric ward as a 'safe' environment, rather than a 'locked' one.

Although it may feel as if a loved one must be the only person in the world going through this experience, it's becoming a more common occurrence. Official data from the NHS reported 63,622 involuntary detentions during 2015/16 – an alarming rise of almost 50% over a ten-year period (from 43,361 detentions in 2005/6).

In the US, involuntary hospitalization is the process of admitting some-one to a psychiatric hospital against his or her will. It can only happen for three reasons:

- If the person poses a danger to him- or herself.
- If the person is a danger to others.
- If the person can't care for him- or herself.

This is a simpler process in some states than in others, but all states require at least one physician (more often two) to evaluate the person first. The initial hospitalization lasts only for a few days; after that period, a court hearing is necessary to detain someone in hospital against their will. When it comes to involuntary medication, states vary widely in their procedures, but action typically requires at least one court hearing.

Q56. Are there different types of sectioning procedures?

The Mental Health Act (1983) contains different sections that are used to admit someone to psychiatric care, depending on the circumstances. Sections 2, 3 and 4 are the three most frequently used ones, and are explained briefly below:

Section 2

This can be used to detain a person with a mental disorder for up to 28 days. During this time, the patient will be assessed so that appropriate treatment can be recommended. At the end of this period, the section can't be renewed but doctors can make an application for further detention under section 3.

Section 3

Doctors will apply for a section 3 detention order if they believe that effective and appropriate treatment is only available in hospital and/or that the patient could be a danger to themselves or others if released. This detention can last for up to six months, and can be renewed (initially after another six months, then annually).

Section 4

In urgent cases, if there are enough reasons to apply for a section 2 but there isn't enough time to get more than one medical opinion, a person can be detained and assessed in hospital under section 4. This allows for a detention of only 72 hours, during which time the second medical opinion must be obtained in order to make a section 2 detention.

The type of section order used can influence where someone might be treated – in either an acute or an intensive care psychiatric ward, for example.

Mental Health Acts

In July 2007 the Mental Health Bill (which contained amendments to the 1983 Mental Health Act) was finally passed by the UK government and became the Mental Health Act 2007. Amongst other measures, the revised Act included:

- the scrapping of the definitions 'mental illness, mental impairment, severe mental impairment and psychopathic disorder' from the 1983 Mental Health Act and switching to a more generic definition of mental disorder as 'any disorder of mind or brain'
- changes to the criteria for ECT treatment (see question 39, p. 104)
- changes to nearest relative definitions (see question 60, p. 172)
- new advocacy rights for detained patients (see questions 46 and 58, pp. 127 and 166)
- the so-called 'treatability test' (where people should only be detained if treatment appropriate for their mental disorder is available)
- the creation of Community Treatment Orders for some post-discharge patients (see question 64, p. 179)
- new safeguards for children and young adults under 18 who are treated in hospital (see question 42, p. 108).

As we were writing this book's second edition in 2018, the Mental Health Act was undergoing an independent review, chaired by the former president of the Royal College of Psychiatrists Simon Wessely and due to report back to the UK government. Described as a 'first step towards a new Mental Health Act', it was announced that the review would examine the causes of the significant rise in involuntary detentions (sectioning), as well as investigate concerns about safeguards, such as tribunals and second opinions, and the use of Community Treatment Orders.

Q57. Can someone refuse to be sectioned?

No. Detention under the Mental Health Act is lawful, and once the correct section papers have been prepared, there are no legal grounds for resisting the section process. The best course of action for someone being sectioned is to keep communicating with the psychiatric professionals working on their case. This could mean asking questions about what's likely to happen next, or voicing any concerns about treatment. It might help to have a family member (see question 60, p. 172, on nearest relatives) or an advocate (see question 46, p. 127) present, although the professionals don't have to wait until an advocate is found before going ahead with the section process.

A patient can also ask to speak to a solicitor, although this won't prevent the section order being applied for or taking place.

Q58. What are a person's rights if they have been sectioned?

The rights of people who have been sectioned are protected by the 1983 and 2007 Mental Health Acts:

- Patients have the right to be told what's happening to them, to have their questions answered, and to have their views listened to, although the mental health professionals don't have to act on those views.
- The 2007 Mental Health Act states that all patients detained under section orders 2 and 3 should be told that advocacy services are available – an advocate can help a patient, for example, by going with them to meetings with a psychiatrist or asking for more information on their behalf. An advocate also has the right to meet with a patient in private, and see the patient's medical records if the patient is capable of giving consent for this. See question 46, p. 127, for sources of independent advocacy, or a hospital may have its own advocacy service – ask at reception.

- With the help of a solicitor, a detained patient can seek discharge by applying to the Mental Health Review Tribunal, an independent panel that decides if a patient should continue to be detained. There are separate tribunal panels for England, Scotland and Wales – see Extra resources, p. 267, for contact details. The Royal College of Psychiatrists has a useful guide on this subject – go to www.rcpsych.ac.uk and search for 'mental health tribunals'.
- It's a common belief that someone who's been sectioned loses their right to vote in local or general elections. This isn't true, but research shows that as few as 14% of eligible mental health inpatients cast votes in general elections, compared to 66% of the UK electorate as a whole. A hospital has a duty to clearly display key voting rights information to all patients and staff, including:

- when voters must be registered to vote
- how patients can register to vote (by providing their home address or the hospital address if it is regarded as their place of residence for long-term admissions)
- information on who is eligible to vote
- how patients can get support to register and vote
- different ways to cast a vote (e.g. a postal vote can be arranged).

Although this isn't specifically covered by the Mental Health Act, psychiatric patients should also be protected from sexual abuse and exploitation and the associated risks of sexually transmitted diseases and unwanted pregnancies. There isn't extensive research in this area, but a 2013 article in the *Journal of Psychiatric and Mental Health Nursing* reported on 'Sexual behaviours on acute inpatient psychiatric units,' a joint research project by King's College London, the South London and Maudsley NHS Foundation Trust, University College London and the University of York. The article notes a number of behaviours highlighted by the research:

'More than 1 in 10 patients engaged in some form of challenging sexual behaviour during the first 2 weeks of their admission. There were no differences in the rates of sexual behaviours between mixed and single gender wards, but men were more likely to touch another person sexually without their consent, or engage in masturbation in a public area. The purpose of the study was to assess the types and frequency of sexual behaviours displayed by patients during the first 2 weeks of admission to acute psychiatric units and what relationship these may have to other challenging patient behaviours. The method used was a survey of sexual behaviours, conflict and containment events carried out by 522 patients during the first 2 weeks of admission in 84 wards in 31 hospitals in the South East of England.'

This research throws up difficult questions – for example, if a person is unable to consent to treatment, can they consent to sexual activity? The key issue is of course that sexual harassment of patients by other patients (or staff) should not be tolerated. The hospital authorities must be told if there is evidence that someone is making unwanted sexual advances towards a patient, so that the rights of vulnerable people can be protected.

Q59. Who looks after patients in a psychiatric hospital?

Anyone diagnosed with bipolar disorder is assigned a named consultant psychiatrist (see question 45, p. 115) who is responsible for their treatment regardless of whether they are in or out of hospital. During a hospital stay, they are likely to see their consultant once a week for review meetings (sometimes called ward rounds). On a day-to-day basis, they're more likely to see a junior psychiatrist, known as an SHO (senior house officer) or registrar, who is still in training, and who usually defers to the consultant before making any major decisions. Further members of the hospital team may include psychologists (again, see question 45, p. 115, for more information) who also work with a patient in and out of hospital, and other professionals who tend to be more hospital-based – psychiatric nurses, psychiatric pharmacists and occupational therapists.

Psychiatric nurses

The front line staff in a psychiatric ward, with whom patients have the most daily contact, are the psychiatric nurses.

Every ward has a ward manager in charge, plus a deputy ward manager, and each patient has a 'named' nurse (also called a key worker) who is responsible for their care during their stay, with at least one other nurse who can step in when the named nurse is off-duty, so that there's a continuity of care. This role is particularly important, so that a patient feels there is a connection of trust between them and their named nurse – the Mental Health Act's Code of Practice reinforces this by asserting that all psychiatric hospitals should assist in 'developing a therapeutic relationship between each patient and key/nurse worker'.

UK nurses must now take three-year degree courses, which can include areas of specialization such as mental healthcare, or they can take degree courses specifically in mental health nursing. But there's much more to working in a psychiatric hospital than qualifications – for example, treating the person and remembering that they're much more than just a walking illness. Sarah has witnessed both insensitivity and kindness in her sister Rebecca's care, and says that the difference it makes to the recovery process can't be underestimated:

 I've seen Rebecca laughed at, ignored and shouted at by hospital staff in the past. Yet during one stay in hospital, a psychiatric nurse put her arm around Rebecca's shoulder and said, 'Rebecca is such a lovely girl. It's a pleasure having her in here.' It's no coincidence that Rebecca's recovery under such a lovely team was much quicker. And not only is it so much better for the person who's staying in the unit, but it's so reassuring for us, the family, to know she's liked and well cared for on an emotional level.

One of the most important roles carried out by psychiatric nurses is observation. Close one-to-one observation isn't unusual when a patient is first admitted, for a variety of reasons: a patient might be aggressive, agitated, elated, trying to take their clothes off, too depressed to eat, intent on doing themselves harm or even suicidal. Any psychiatric patient in any type of ward can be put under close observation – the decision to do this is usually made by a psychiatrist, and the patient (or their family) should be told if this is happening as well as the reasons for it. But psychiatric nurses are, in a sense, always observing the patients in their care – the Code of Practice directs them to look at a patient's 'general behaviour, movement, speech, expression of ideas, appearance, orientation, mood and attitude, interaction with others, and reaction to medication'.

Pharmacists

Psychiatric pharmacists work with psychiatrists to prescribe the right combination of medications. Qualifying as a pharmacist takes five years, which includes a master's degree and a one-year pre-registration course; on top of this, training as a psychiatric pharmacist takes at least two extra years. Psychiatric pharmacists may be accredited members of the College of Mental Health Pharmacy (go to www.cmhp.org.uk for more information) or the UK Psychiatric Pharmacy Group (whose website can be found at www.ukppg.org.uk).

Dr Ian Maidment, Senior Lecturer in Clinical Pharmacy at Aston University, describes the role of a psychiatric pharmacist in more detail: 'As a pharmacist based in two admission wards, I would go to every ward round, advise the doctors and all the nursing staff on prescribing, speak about medication to any patient who wanted to see me, on a one-to-one basis, also speak to families and carers if the patient was happy with that. I would also run a patient education group twice a week, where patients could ask me questions. This would involve educating the patients about their drugs, how to take them, and what side effects to look out for. I would really try to encourage patients to self-manage their own illness ... I also do a lot of education and training, not just of patients but also of nursing staff, doctors, social workers, support workers, etc., because they will all get asked about medication. We're also involved in developing drug protocols and providing written information on drugs.'

Sounds great, doesn't it? But, as with many aspects of mental healthcare, this service is not available in every psychiatric unit. If a patient and/or their relative have concerns over medication, it's worth asking a hospital staff member if the local health organization has a psychiatric pharmacy service, as well as speaking to their psychiatrist.

Occupational therapists

The Mental Health Act's Code of Practice states that hospitals should 'provide structured activities by professional staff', and many psychiatric units, particularly medium secure units where patients are more likely to stay for longer periods of time, employ occupational therapists as part of the psychiatric care team. The NHS Careers website defines occupational therapy (OT) as 'the assessment and treatment of physical and psychiatric conditions using specific, purposeful activity to prevent disability and pro-mote independent function in all aspects of daily life'. In simple terms, participating in OT activities, as well as helping to pass the time on a ward, can help a patient's recovery by giving them confidence and satisfaction in developing new life skills. Sarah noticed that during Rebecca's most recent hospital visit an aerobics instructor came in and held classes a couple of times a week, and that there's definitely more emphasis on creative pur-suits, such as art therapy. And others describe how therapeutic facilities have improved:

> There was lots to do ... occupational therapy was available Monday to Friday – arts, crafts, swimming, badminton. There was also a nurse-run women's group. That kind of thing is so important for a hospital environment. Keeping active is so much better than sitting around talking and watching videos, although I realize it must be hard to accommodate everyone. I found all these activities tremendously useful.
>
> (RACHEL)

Q60. *What is a 'nearest relative'?*

The Mental Health Act 1983 gives rights to the patient's 'nearest relative', who can act in the patient's interests. Section 26 of the Act lists the people who can be considered a patient's nearest relative in descending order – so, for example, if the patient has no spouse or partner, the Act will view an adult child as the next most likely candidate. The official order is:

- husband, wife or civil partner (including, since the Mental Health Act 2007, same sex partners)
- son or daughter
- father or mother
- brother or sister
- grandparent
- grandchild
- uncle or aunt
- nephew or niece.

If more than one person from a category qualifies – for example, if there are two adult children of a patient – then the oldest will be considered as the nearest relative. If a nearest relative can't be found according to the hierarchy described above, the courts can nominate a suitable alternative.

A patient can object to the nearest relative selected by making a court application that declares them as 'not a suitable person' – although the patient can't object on the grounds of simply wanting to choose someone else.

The nearest relative has a number of rights:

- They can apply for their loved one to be sectioned under sections 2 and 3 of the Mental Health Act 1983.
- The nearest relative can't stop a section 2 order application being made by an approved mental health professional (AMHP) – although the AMHP should try to keep them informed and listen to their views – but they can object to a section 3 application.

The AMHP can overrule this objection by applying to the courts to have the nearest relative removed from their position and for the role to be given to someone else.

- The nearest relative should be kept informed about the patient's care – if someone has been detained in hospital, they should be told why. They can't intervene or prevent treatment for a patient who has been sectioned, although they can discuss the treatment with staff or make a complaint. It's worth remembering, though, that under the Mental Health Act the patient can object to the nearest relative being told any of this information.

- The nearest relative also has the right to be told if and why a patient is being discharged and to be involved in planning the patient's post-discharge aftercare. Again, the patient can object to their involvement.

- Technically, the nearest relative has the right to discharge the patient from a psychiatric hospital, even if they're detained under section 2 or section 3 of the Mental Health Act. They must give the hospital 72 hours' notice of their intention. The patient's consultant psychiatrist can stop this process by issuing a barring certificate within the 72-hour notice period – and the nearest relative can be removed from their role if they try to discharge a patient 'without regard to patient or public welfare'.

Q61. *How can friends and family support a loved one in a psychiatric hospital?*

There are three main ways a friend or family member can help someone who's in a psychiatric unit – give them time, offer them practical help, and provide staff with useful information.

Time

Put simply, the most valuable way to support someone is by giving them time – helping them to still feel connected to their loved ones and to the world beyond the ward.

Sarah is convinced that the visits Rebecca receives from friends and family when she's in hospital make a world of difference to her recovery:

> Mum and I contact Rebecca every day when she's in hospital, as do her many friends. We phone a lot – just to connect and to see how she's feeling. And we visit as much as possible. I know Rebecca really looks forward to those visits. She's such a sociable person and even when she's really ill she misses friends and family so much. Her face lights up whenever I turn up – even if she knows I can only stay for half an hour because I've got to get back for the boys. I think she needs that contact with the outside world.

It's also helpful to the patient if a family member (who may also be their legal nearest relative – see question 60, p. 172) can be there at review meetings, when a patient's case is being discussed. Sarah's mum Rose goes to as many of Rebecca's review meetings as possible to keep up-to-date with the treatment changes and to support Rebecca emotionally. And Amanda's dad, Gordon, always goes to her mum Irene's review meetings, giving her invaluable support:

> My mum can become tongue tied when faced with a room of people, and not feel able to say what she wants. There have been times when she's been quite animated before a review meeting, discussing with my dad what she wants to say, but as soon as she walks in, she clams up, especially if there are faces around the table she doesn't recognize. So it's always really helpful for my dad to be there with her, as he communicates my mum's viewpoint on her behalf. For someone who's mentally ill, a meeting like this, even though it's being held in the patient's best interests, can be very stressful, and a family member can be a real support at these times – for example, voicing concerns about treatment if there have been side effects.

Family members can ensure a patient gets the best out of hospital care by helping make their feelings and wishes known, taking an active part in planning their future treatment and asking questions – for example, in a review meeting a relative can ask all health professionals present to identify themselves and state clearly what they do.

Practical help

Practical help is also important for someone in a psychiatric unit. Here are some suggestions as to what a newly admitted patient might need:

- comfortable clothing, preferably with a choice of layers for warmer or cooler weather
- nightwear, dressing gown and slippers
- personal toiletries
- family photos
- extra pillows or blankets
- books/magazines
- card games/puzzle books
- mobile phone, if allowed on the ward – if not, check if there's a pay phone, and make sure they have the right change, plus important phone numbers
- sweets/snacks/chewing gum, etc.
- notepad and pens.

Before handing anything over (especially anything potentially harmful, such as nail polish remover or nail scissors), ask for permission from a staff member. Expensive items such as iPads and radios may be allowed, depending on the type of ward and/or hospital policy, but check first if patients can store items in a secure place such as a personal locker.

Information

Remember that psychiatric staff may not have met the patient before they walk through the door, whereas their friends and family know them and their habits, behaviour and personal story better than anyone else. Make sure that staff are aware of any special requirements, like dietary/religious needs, language difficulties which might need the help of an interpreter, or just personal preferences. Any information can help staff to support the patient more effectively – Amanda's mum Irene, for example, used to cause staff concern about her eating habits:

 My mum doesn't have a large appetite, and usually only eats breakfast and dinner, with just fruit for lunch – but in the early days, when she was first admitted to the psychiatric unit, the staff weren't aware of this, and Mum didn't explain. So they kept insisting that she should eat lunch and pestering her to come to the dining room. Then they would write on her notes that she was 'refusing' to eat, as if this was unnatural behaviour, when of course it was perfectly normal for her! Once my dad had explained, they became more relaxed and stopped viewing it as a symptom of her illness or anything to be alarmed about.

It can be difficult for a relative to know who to speak to, but it's best to communicate with the nurse in charge or the patient's named nurse. If this isn't possible, writing down anything they think the team needs to know, with as much detail as possible, is useful. Most psychiatric teams usually then brief each other at the changeover of each shift.

Q62. *How can friends and family forge a good relationship with those who care for their loved one in a psychiatric hospital?*

For friends and family, it can be hard to come to terms with seeing their loved one in a psychiatric hospital and this can put a huge strain on the relationship between the professionals and the family. Ian Hulatt, Mental Health Advisor to the Royal College of Nursing for 13 years, puts it like this: 'Psychiatric staff engage in processes that people don't necessarily value or want, but we do so because we believe it's in the patient's best interests and we have the legal powers to do so. That brings with it some very real challenges because people want to leave, people don't want to take their medication, people don't think they are ill. Relatives might find that the work we do looks custodial ... and society is very confused about what mental health problems are about.'

He says that to establish a good relationship with psychiatric staff, it's important for relatives to try to understand why their loved one is being admitted to hospital and what the reasons are for their treatment: 'For families, what they need to do is see that nurses and psychiatrists are not there to spoil life for the individual, but they are there to support the individual and work with the family to keep the individual well. We need to have good lines of communication between family members and people caring for patients. We have to all work together.'

In an ideal world, there should be a two-way process, with hospital staff viewing family members as part of the healing process. Family members can be particularly helpful in spotting warning signs for mood swings, as they know the patient so much better than the staff, who, according to Ian Hulatt, increasingly recognize that the family is essential in maintaining the health of the patient: 'There's research that shows it's the family who notice signs of relapse long before medical staff or nursing staff. It's the family who know when someone is becoming unwell. We have to consider family members as partners in someone's care and all work together.'

Another way of forging a good family/staff relationship is if a relative asks a nurse: 'Is there anything I can do to help?' It might be persuading the patient to take their medication willingly, or even something as simple as brushing their hair or helping them to take a bath. Psychiatric staff will usually appreciate that kind of support – sometimes a family member can communicate better with a patient and get through to them when a nurse can't.

Q63. *Do psychiatric hospitals allow smoking?*

It is estimated that one in three people with a mental health illness in the UK smokes, compared to one in five in the general population. In 2008, psychiatric hospitals in the UK implemented an indoor smoking ban. And then in 2015, the ban was widened so that smoking was no longer allowed anywhere in the hospital grounds. Instead, when people who smoke are admitted onto a psychiatric ward they're supposed to be given nicotine replacement therapy (such as patches and inhalators) and offered stop-smoking support services. So what are the pros and cons of this smoking ban for psychiatric inpatients?

The pros

- Non-smoking fellow patients and staff no longer have to breathe in tobacco smoke inside or outside the hospital building.
- Research shows some adult smokers with mental health conditions – like other smokers – want to quit, can quit and benefit from proven smoking cessation treatments in hospitals.
- One study showed a reduction in physical assaults on staff in psychiatric hospitals after the introduction of smoke-free policies.
- Psychotic disorders are associated with high rates of cardiovascular diseases, so giving up smoking can improve physical health.
- Patients who smoke when they're taking certain antipsychotic drugs have an increased metabolism so do not process the drug as well as those who do not smoke.

The cons

- If someone is acutely unwell and taken into psychiatric hospital under section, they may not have the mental capacity to understand why they aren't allowed to smoke, which may cause them extreme distress.

- If inpatients aren't given adequate nicotine replacement therapy, they may experience acute nicotine withdrawal symptoms, such as cravings, irritability, restlessness, constipation and fatigue.
- If inpatients are given 'ward-leave' so they can get to a shop, or their visitors bring in cigarettes, it's challenging for staff to enforce a smoking ban.

> On one hospital visit when my sister Rebecca was sectioned, she took me into the ward's little courtyard garden. Someone had hidden a lighter in the flowerbed and there were several patients crouching behind a bush smoking in the rain. Considering there were plumes of smoke rising up, it's obvious the staff were turning a blind eye.
>
> (*SARAH*)

> Giving up smoking is the last thing on your mind when you're in a psychiatric unit, especially if you've been sectioned. If you're not in control and unable to reason, how on earth could you give up smoking? Reason goes out of the window.
>
> (*SHARRON*)

Q64. What happens when a psychiatric patient is well enough to leave hospital?

Before a patient leaves hospital, they are encouraged to think about how to recognize early warning signs of relapse and what the best course of action would be – i.e. which medication to use, who to call, and how to enlist the support of family and friends.

A discharge planning meeting should also be held between the hospital, the patient, local health and social services and a care co-ordinator – usually this is a key or support worker. The objective is to develop a post-discharge care plan for the patient, using the Care Programme Approach (CPA) – a national framework for the assessment and planning of patient care. The aim of the care plan is to support a patient's recovery from mental illness, so that they are at less risk of relapse and being readmitted to hospital (sometimes called 'revolving door' patients). Other areas can be included in the care plan, for example, housing issues, employment advice, or support for vulnerable patients with a history of drug and alcohol abuse. The UK mental health charity Rethink Mental Illness has detailed information on CPAs, as well as an excellent factsheet at www.rethink.org (search for 'CPA').

A discharged patient and their family can make the CPA work better for them by:

- asking for a written copy of the patient's care plan
- making sure they know their care co-ordinator's name, contact details and hours of availability, who to contact in their care co-ordinator's absence, and how to request a change of care co-ordinator if necessary
- asking for a care plan review at least every 12 months
- asking for written copies of any changes to the care plan after a review
- insisting that their views on medication are listened to during care plan meetings
- asking for help on other issues such as housing, employment, physical health and drugs/alcohol abuse.

Returning home after a section order

If a patient has been detained in hospital under a section order, they are likely to have 'staggered' home leave before the section order is lifted. So, for example, after a month's treatment, the psychiatric team might agree that a patient can have a day's leave, returning to hospital in the evening. If this goes well, then the patient might be allowed home leave for a weekend, then a week's leave. If all goes well and the patient is still making good progress outside the hospital environment, the section order will be formally lifted. This is typically what has happened with both Amanda's mum Irene and Sarah's sister Rebecca, each time they have been sectioned into hospital.

Community Treatment Orders

Controversially, the Mental Health Act 2007 introduced a form of supervised discharge for some patients when they leave hospital, known as Community Treatment Orders (CTOs). These orders have the power to force people (usually patients who were originally sectioned) to comply with treatment regimes after they've been discharged. Initially a CTO is issued for a six-month period, and can be renewed for another six months – after this the CTO is renewed annually. The legislation only affected England and Wales, although a form of the CTO was already used in Scotland (and in other countries including the USA, Australia and New Zealand).

Since then, concerns have been regularly raised by a number of sources, including UK mental health charities Mind, SANE and the Mental Health Alliance, that this legislation undermines a patient's rights. CTOs give mental health professionals the power to recall people to hospital if they believe patients are not following their prescribed treatment, and to enforce medical examinations.

At the time the legislation was issued, the UK government claimed that CTOs would only be used for a small number of patients, mostly with complex mental health issues who were likely to relapse and potentially cause harm to themselves and other people. However, the fact that CTOs have (at the time of writing) been earmarked for scrutiny in the 2018 Mental Health Act review is a sign that unease about them has not diminished – especially in light of the rocketing number of involuntary detentions.

Q65. What are the pros and cons of being treated in a psychiatric hospital?

It's an understatement to say that conditions in psychiatric hospitals can be far from perfect. Changes are being made, it's true, but not fast enough. Patients in NHS psychiatric hospitals still report not enough beds, overstretched staff, even a very small minority of staff who are (intentionally or not) less caring to a patient than they could be:

 To get so low, psychotic or manic that you need to go into hospital, to get so unwell that you need to be detained ... it's always going to be an unpleasant experience.

(RACHEL)

Added to this is the strain of being surrounded by other mentally ill people with their own challenging behaviour to deal with, feelings of grief, anger or even despair at being away from home, a loss of independence and a fear of being stigmatized in the future for having been a psychiatric patient. For many people, psychiatric hospital treatment is seen as the last resort, to be avoided at all costs, as Amanda recalls from the early days of her mum Irene's illness:

 In the beginning, for my parents and all our family, the thought of Mum being admitted to a psychiatric hospital was the worst possible thing that could happen to her. We didn't regard it as a place of healing but as a frightening unknown. We'd heard all the outdated 'mental asylum' stereotypes, so the hospital was a symbol of mentally being at absolute rock bottom. Yet in recent years, these feelings have become more complex. Understandably, Mum never wants to leave home. And none of us – least of all my parents – are happy that she and Dad are apart from each other. Usually she's admitted to hospital when she's in a mixed state, and is paranoid, depressed and agitated and refusing all treatment, so it's a distressing experience all round. But because she has stayed at the same psychiatric unit so many times, it has become familiar to her, just as she has become familiar to the psychiatrists, nurses and other staff, who now understand her better, and who usually care for her with great kindness and compassion. Within a few days of treatment, they are able to interrupt the circle of despair she's trapped in. Hospital treatment is not perfect by any means, but for Mum, her psychiatric unit has become a place of safety and healing – not the end of the line, but the beginning of her road back towards stability.

Admittance to hospital can give someone the breathing space to break a cycle of destructive behaviour (for example, if someone is self-harming) in a safe, low-stimulation environment, where they can be observed and cared for, where a normal daily routine can be re-established and where healing can take place without having to cope with the pressures of the outside world. Sarah's sister Rebecca doesn't sleep or eat properly for days when she's on a manic high, and can begin her recovery process only once she's safely cared for in the structured hospital environment. Or someone may have attempted suicide – they could still be dangerously depressed and require constant vigilance for their own safety, something their own (possibly exhausted) family may not be able to give.

A stay in a psychiatric hospital ward is a chance for someone with bipolar disorder who's become seriously unwell to find out what's happening to them, and why. They can begin to understand more about their condition, learn to recognize warning signs and develop ways of dealing with them. It's also an opportunity for their treatment and medication to be reviewed and stabilized, and for their future treatment to be planned – ideally with input from everyone involved in their care (them, their family and the appropriate team of mental health professionals).

CHAPTER FIVE

Lifestyle Choices

Q66. *Can a healthy lifestyle lower the chance of relapse for someone with bipolar disorder and reduce the risk of developing it in the first place?*

It's not rocket science... All the healthy-living rules apply. Research proves without a shadow of a doubt that making sensible lifestyle choices reduces both the chance of someone with a high genetic risk of bipolar developing full-blown symptoms and the risk of relapse for someone who already has a diagnosis. The ultimate health-promoting choices include:

- eating a balanced, nutrient-packed diet
- taking nutritional supplements
- not smoking
- drinking no more than two caffeine-loaded drinks in a day
- drinking only one or two alcoholic drinks in a day
- not taking recreational drugs
- exercising regularly
- avoiding too much stress
- getting plenty of relaxation
- getting seven to eight hours sleep a night.

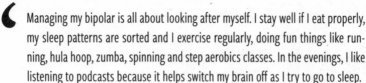

Managing my bipolar is all about looking after myself. I stay well if I eat properly, my sleep patterns are sorted and I exercise regularly, doing fun things like running, hula hoop, zumba, spinning and step aerobics classes. In the evenings, I like listening to podcasts because it helps switch my brain off as I try to go to sleep.

(MARISSA)

Q67. *What is the link between stress and mood swings?*

According to research published in *The Lancet* in 2016, more than 1.1 billion of the world's adults have high blood pressure.

When stressed, the body produces more of the so-called 'fight or flight' chemicals, adrenaline and noradrenaline, which prepare the body for an emergency. Blood pressure increases, the heart beats faster and stomach activity increases (often referred to as 'butterflies').

Because the body doesn't actually need these chemicals to fight or run away, they remain in the system and, over time, damage health and well-being. In the short term, stress can cause headaches, indigestion, nausea, aches and pains and palpitations. In the longer term, the risk of heart attack and stroke rockets through the roof. On an emotional level, chronic stress increases anxiety, fear, anger, frustration and depression. Stressed people can also become withdrawn, indecisive, inflexible, irritable, tearful or aggressive.

Many people with bipolar cite stress as one of their main triggers for a mood swing into mania or depression:

Stress and elation are huge triggers for me. For instance, when I pranged the car – I reversed out of a parking space and didn't see a concrete pillar – I was in an acute psychiatric unit within two weeks. The smallest things can tip me over the edge.

(SHARRON)

The stress of a car accident at 70mph on the motorway definitely tipped the balance. David was on his way home and I got a phone call. 'The car's smashed up, a wreck,' he said. When he got home he went to bed and pulled the covers over his head. After the accident his whole way changed. He was so depressed and bad-tempered. Before that he had never raised his voice. But then he started punching doors. Every door in the flat had a hole in it.

(JACKIE)

I remember my son's psychotherapist saying to me when he was first unwell that having a diagnosis of bipolar is often like having an allergy to stress. That was helpful because during his A level exams we noticed his stress levels going up and realized he needed plenty of support and to do lots of exercise (his antidote to stress).

(JUAN)

Yet it's not only negative stressful events that can set off a mood swing. Positive stressful events can be a trigger too. Sarah says that her wedding in 1996 was the event that sparked Rebecca's first real manic episode.

With hindsight, of course, we look back and recognize all the warning signs. At my hen party, Rebecca was full of non-stop energy – talking and laughing and dancing. At the wedding rehearsal, we were all quietly going through the order of service in the church when the main doors burst open and Rebecca actually cycled in. It was funny, and a bit embarrassing, although Rebecca wasn't in the slightest bit embarrassed. She just parked her bike in the back of the church and ran up the aisle, apologizing to the vicar for being late. On the morning of my wedding she was up first – probably at around 5am – and had done several jobs around the house, including setting up the breakfast table. I remember that all the cup handles and spoons were pointing in the same direction. Yet, at the time, we didn't pick up that anything was wrong. We were all excited and on a kind of wedding 'high'. It was only the next day when she got higher and higher that my mum realized anything was wrong.

Amanda also believes that her fortieth birthday party was a trigger for one of her mum's hospitalizations:

I threw a big party to celebrate my fortieth birthday, and invited hordes of friends and family, including Mum and Dad. The party was fantastic, and Mum seemed to be enjoying herself – laughing, chatting, dancing. It was such a great night. She was still in a positive mood when they drove home the next day, if a little tired, and I breathed a sigh of relief that the party hadn't affected her. How wrong I was. Her mood began to change almost as soon as they got back, and within hours she was lost in her usual mixed state of depression and agitation. Her psychiatric team initially tried to treat her at home, but a few days later she was back in hospital. Her psychiatrist said she might have experienced a mood swing anyway, but that the high emotion of the evening probably contributed to it. There's a lovely photo of her from the night of the party – she's arm in arm with me and my Dad, and she looks so happy – we all do. It's hard to believe that, less than a week after the picture was taken, she would be sectioned again.

Of course, it's virtually impossible to eliminate stress completely (from being caught in an unexpected rain shower to losing a loved one), but lifestyle choices play a huge role in nipping the stress reactions to those events in the bud. Here's how to tip the scales in favour of a less stressful life:

- Whenever possible, avoid people and situations which create problems.
- Include a form of relaxation, such as deep breathing or meditation, in your daily routine.
- Exercise every day.
- Eat a healthy diet.
- Restrict or stop smoking, drinking and recreational drug use.
- Take part in enjoyable activities.

Q68. *How can regular sleep patterns help to control symptoms of bipolar disorder?*

It's been said that sleep and mood are joined at the hip. That's true for anyone, but even more so for anyone with a diagnosis of mental illness. According to one study, 80% of psychiatric patients have sleep disorders, the severity of the insomnia matching up with the intensity of symptoms.

Sleep is a powerful regulator of brain chemistry and people with bipolar commonly sleep too much, not enough, not at all or not deeply enough.

Sleep and depression

There is a huge overlap between the symptoms of depression and sleepiness – social withdrawal, fatigue and difficulty concentrating. Research has linked persistent insomnia with the onset of a major depressive episode within one year.

Sleep and mania

According to the British Association for Psychopharmacology (www.bap. org.uk), sleep disturbance is perhaps the most common final pathway to mania. Even the loss of a single night's sleep can place someone with bipolar at severe risk of tipping into full-blown mania.

For many people with a bipolar diagnosis, good sleep plays a huge part in their mood and behaviour.

> I'm really sensitive to even one night without sleep. I try to reduce stress by chilling out as much as I can but I do find it really difficult. I'm a teacher and I sometimes work really late.
>
> *(JUDE)*

> If I'm not sleeping my eight hours I take a sleeping tablet, just as a precaution, because I want to be in control all the time.
>
> *(NEIL)*

Sarah notes that one of the most telling clues to Rebecca's moods is her sleep pattern:

> When Rebecca's mood is spiralling upwards, she goes to bed later and later and then stops sleeping altogether. When her mood is on the way down, she sleeps more and more until, on the very darkest days, she can hardly rouse herself out of bed.

And when Amanda's mum Irene is on the verge of a mixed state, her sleep pattern is always disrupted – at first she will start to wake up for periods during the night, but as the mood swing starts to escalate into agitation and paranoia, she becomes unable to sleep or rest at all.

A night of uninterrupted sleep tops up the body's energy tank enough to cope with the following day and helps ensure that hormones and neuro-transmitters in the brain can work efficiently. And though sleep problems are one of the main symptoms of bipolar disorder, it is possible to practice good habits to maximize the chances of a good night's rest.

> I do have a very strict sleep hygiene routine. I take my tablets 30 minutes before I go to bed. TV is banned in the bedroom. Now I just listen to relaxing music.
>
> *(DEBBIE)*

> I have a relaxation CD that bores me to sleep.
>
> *(CARL)*

Good sleep rules

- Try to go to bed at the same time every night and wake up at the same time every morning. This will 'train' the body to stick to a good routine.
- Get between seven and eight hours' sleep a night – that's the optimum amount, according to the world-renowned Sleep Research Centre in Loughborough, UK.
- Avoid shift-work as it prevents establishing a regular sleep pattern.
- Don't nap. In the same way as a snack blunts the appetite for food, a nap takes away the appetite for sleep.

- Avoid sleep-preventing caffeine and other stimulants, particularly after 4pm. See question 77, p. 216, for caffeine-free alternatives.
- Before bed, dim lights in the bedroom encourage your body to produce melatonin, the hormone that helps you sleep. The 'blue' light from electronic devices prevents melatonin production, which can disrupt your sleep. Stop using your phone, tablet, laptop or computer two hours before you go to sleep, charge your phone in another room and keep your bedroom screen-free.
- Do a soothing activity during the hour before bedtime. For instance, have a warm bath laced with calm-inducing lavender essential oil or listen to a relaxing classical music CD.
- Turn on an electric fan. Studies show that background 'white noise' can help induce sleep.
- Don't exercise in the evening. Research shows that, due to the production of the hormone adrenaline, physical activity increases mental alertness for four hours afterwards, which can lead to insomnia.
- Check medication. It usually helps stabilize and normalize sleep, but it can also cause side effects such as insomnia or excessive sleeping, so it's worth speaking to a doctor about its sleep-disrupting potential.
- Take medication. As a last resort during periods of poor sleep, a doctor can prescribe sleeping tablets or other medication to help re-establish a good routine.
- Have sex. The body releases a cocktail of hormones during sex, many of which trigger sleep.
- Be aware that long haul plane journeys across different time zones can disrupt the body clock and sleep patterns – there's some evidence that jetlag can be a trigger for mania.

Q69. *How does exercise affect bipolar symptoms?*

When it's a struggle to get out of bed to make a cup of tea or when the mind's racing so fast that the body has a job keeping up, it's unlikely that exercise is high up on the agenda. However, there's no getting away from the fact that physical activity is one of the best ways to keep the body strong and the mind calm. There's a whole catalogue of scientific studies to support the value of exercise for those with mental health problems. One even found that regular exercise is as effective as antidepressants for those with major depression. And a report by the Mental Health Foundation found that antidepressant use could be significantly reduced if GPs offered exercise on prescription to all patients with depression – that's because exercise triggers the release of endorphins (natural opiates that create a sense of well-being).

Yet exercise doesn't have to be sport-based to lift the spirits. Research at the University of Essex, UK, found that, after a country stroll, 71% of the participants reported reduced levels of depression and tension, and 90% reported a boost in self-esteem. In contrast, only 45% said they felt reduced levels of depression after walking in a shopping centre, and 22% said they actually felt more depressed.

On the other side of the bipolar coin, exercise can also help release excess energy:

 Exercise is the one thing that can get rid of a bipolar high. There's just no better buzz than exercise. It's so very relaxing for me. I force myself to do it even if I don't feel like it. I love going for an hour's walk when the weather is beautiful. I go running and to the gym a lot. I always think, if you look good you feel good. And I sleep so much better when I've exercised, although I never exercise any time after 6.30pm otherwise I can't get to sleep.

(DAVE)

And on a physical level, exercise helps to eliminate toxins, oxygenate every cell in the body and burn off calories, helping to shift any excess weight.

Government guidelines recommend adults do at least 150 minutes of moderate aerobic activity every week and strength exercises on two or more days a week that work all the major muscles (legs, hips, back, abdomen, chest, shoulders and arms). The best heart-pumpers? Walking, swimming, cycling, dancing, skating, running and aerobics (class or DVD).

Q70. *Can complementary therapies help control bipolar symptoms?*

Complementary medicine is just that: a treatment that *complements* mainstream medicine. It isn't intended to replace it, but to work alongside it. Research shows around a third of people across Europe and the US use complementary therapies.

Although some experts dismiss complementary therapies, saying that not enough evidence exists to prove they work, research carried out by the Mental Health Foundation shows that mental health service users want greater access to complementary therapies and that where these are provided, they are found to be well received and helpful. Many people with bipolar disorder find that including holistic therapy in a treatment plan can help to control symptoms and prolong periods of stability.

'For anyone with bipolar, stress management is absolutely vital. That's why holistic therapies can be helpful. Things like reflexology and acupuncture can activate the relaxation response, promoting better sleep and relieving anxiety in the body,' says Dr Arghya Sarkhel, a consultant psychiatrist who specializes in mindfulness. 'All I say to my patients is that these holistic therapies are never an alternative, but complementary – they work alongside medication and psychological and social support, never instead of them.'

Just make sure that any practitioner is registered with a professional association or regulatory body. So which therapies can help?

Acupuncture

A branch of Chinese medicine, acupuncture involves placing very fine needles into the skin at different points (called acupoints) in order to stimulate the flow of Qi (pronounced 'chee'), the body's energy. One study in America found that a group of seriously depressed women experienced a 43% reduction in their symptoms after a 16-week course of acupuncture, compared with a 22% reduction in symptoms for the placebo group.

COST: £35–£70 a session.

INFO: British Acupuncture Council at www.acupuncture.org.uk

Aromatherapy

A form of treatment using botanical essential oils, aromatherapy is now widely used in clinics and hospitals to reduce anxiety and promote relaxation. When inhaled, the scents work on the brain and nervous system through the stimulation of the olfactory nerves. In fact, work carried out at Yale University in America found that the scent of spice apple reduced blood pressure by an average of three to five points in healthy volunteers. Other essential oils known for their calming properties include bergamot, chamomile, clary sage, frankincense, geranium, grapefruit, jasmine, juniper, linden blossom, lavender, mandarin, marjoram, melissa, neroli, orange, palmarosa, rose, sandalwood, vetiver and ylang ylang. Simply add a few drops of one or more essential oils to a bath or burn in an aromatherapy burner. Only buy products with the words 'pure essential oil' on the label as this means they contain active botanical ingredients with healing properties. Cheaper imitations probably contain very little, if any, of the active ingredients.

COST: Essential oils vary enormously in price, but expect to pay at least £6 or £7 for 20ml. An hour-long consultation with a medical aromatherapist costs £30–£90 for an hour.

INFO: International Federation of Aromatherapists at www.ifaroma.org

Homeopathy

From the Greek word 'homoios' – meaning same – and 'pathos' – meaning suffering – homeopathy works on the idea that like will cure like. The remedies are taken in extremely dilute forms and no matter how many symptoms are experienced, only one remedy is taken, which is aimed at all of the symptoms. Although in 2010 a House of Commons Science and Technology Committee report on homeopathy said the principles on which homeopathy is based are 'scientifically implausible', several studies have reported positive results in the treatment of depressive disorders using homeopathy alongside conventional medication, including high levels of patient satisfaction.

COST: Between £30 and £175 for a consultation, plus sometimes there's also a small charge for the prescribed remedy.

INFO: Society of Homeopaths at www.homeopathy-soh.org

Massage

One of the oldest healing techniques, massage can be relaxing or stimulating, depending on which techniques are used, and can relieve tension and stress as well as combat general aches and pains. A study at the Touch Research Institute at Miami University's School of Medicine, Florida, USA shows that massage therapy plays an important role in the alleviation of stress and stress-induced illnesses.

COST: Around £30 to £60 for an hour-long treatment.

INFO: Massage Therapy UK at www.massagetherapy.co.uk

Reflexology

Based on the principle that certain points on the feet and hands (called reflex points) correspond to different parts of the body, reflexology is a treatment given by a trained practitioner who applies pressure to these specific points, helping to release tension and boost the body's own natural healing process. One report showed how reflexology alleviated the effects of extreme stress. Twenty patients being treated for 'neurasthenia' – a condition of extreme emotional stress – were given daily reflexology for a week at the hospital's department of physiotherapy. 40% of the patients experienced a complete cure, 35% were greatly improved, 15% were mildly improved and 10% reported no change.

COST: £30–£60 for an hour-long treatment.

INFO: Association of Reflexologists at www.aor.org.uk

Reiki

Reiki is a Japanese word meaning 'universal life force energy'. It is a non-invasive, hands-on therapy, which works to rebalance mind, body and spirit. Reiki practitioners are 'attuned' to open their own healing channels to allow the Reiki energy to pass through them so they can heal themselves and others. In one study published in the journal *Alternative Therapies in Health and Medicine*, participants who received weekly Reiki treatments for six weeks reported significant reductions in depression, hopelessness and stress.

Sarah, who learnt Reiki in 1998 and became a Reiki Master (which means she can teach Reiki) in 2006, has given Rebecca several healing treatments over the years.

> When Rebecca has been deeply depressed or agitated, it can be impossible to communicate or connect with her. During those times, I hold her hand or, if she agrees, place my hands on her head, shoulders or over her heart centre to give her Reiki. I have some really lovely memories, even in times of despair when she was seriously unwell in hospital, of the two of us sitting on a bench in the hospital garden, the energy flowing through me into her. We were connecting without words.

COST: An hour-long treatment costs between £10 and £50, although many Reiki practitioners are open to 'pay-what-you-can' donations.

INFO: UK Reiki Federation at www.reikifed.co.uk

Yoga

Yoga dates back to at least 3000 BC and fans say that practising the different poses – some simple, some complicated – helps keep the body stretched and supple and the mind calm and clear. There are many different forms of yoga – hatha and Iyengar are the forms most commonly taught in the West. A study published in the *Evidence-Based Complementary and Alternative Medicine* journal showed that after 20 classes of Iyengar yoga, patients with clinical depression had significant reductions of depression, anger, anxiety and neurotic symptoms.

COST: Classes usually last 60 to 90 minutes and cost £5 to £15.

INFO: British Wheel of Yoga at www.bwy.org.uk

In the UK, the British Complementary Medicine Association provides information on various therapies – visit their website at www.bcma.co.uk.

In the US, find a list of qualified practitioners trained in a range of complementary therapies at www.therapists.psychologytoday.com.

Q71. *How can meditation and mindfulness help control bipolar symptoms?*

A discipline rather than a therapy, meditation aims to achieve total relaxation of mind and body. Although there are many different forms of meditation, the underlying goal is to clear your mind. Once learnt, it can be practised anywhere – in the bath, in bed, on the bus – for an instant feeling of well-being and calm.

Meditation on the go...

With more than 1,000 to choose from, meditation apps you download on phones and tablets are a booming business. Industry leader 'Headspace' has over 500,000 subscribers, its own in-flight channel on some airlines and phone-booth-size relaxation 'pods' in airports.

Mindfulness

Mindfulness-based cognitive therapy (MBCT) has been recommended by NICE since 2004 as a way to prevent depression in people who've had three or more bouts of depression in the past. Mindfulness meditation involves sitting silently and paying attention to thoughts, sounds, the sensations of breathing or parts of the body, bringing your attention back whenever the mind starts to wander.

So how can mindfulness help someone with a diagnosis of bipolar? Research shows mindfulness meditation can help fight insomnia, improve sleep and sharpen focus. Studies have also shown mindfulness can spur the growth of areas of the brain linked with emotional regulation — if you have meditated regularly for five years or more.

'Acceptance that bipolar is a chronic illness can be quite difficult for some people, especially high-functioning people who can't accept their symptoms because they don't tie in with the way they view themselves,' says Dr Arghya Sarkhel, a consultant psychiatrist who specializes in mindfulness. 'Practising mindfulness can help someone accept their intense feelings and learn to live with the symptoms rather than wishing them away or expecting them to go away ... I find it helpful to imagine the mind as a sheet of metal and bipolar as a hammer that hits the metal when the going gets tough. If the metal is very fragile like a sheet of tin foil, the hammer will cause a big dent. If the metal is stronger like a sheet of steel, the hammer is unlikely to make such a big dent. Practising mindfulness helps to make the sheet of metal, the mind, stronger.'

What's the best way to learn mindfulness?

Mindfulness can be learnt in a group setting on a course, one-to-one, online, from self-help books and via apps and YouTube videos. If you're looking for a good read packed with practical exercises and a six-week DIY MBCT course, we can't recommend highly enough comedian and actor Ruby Wax's *A Mindfulness Guide for the Frazzled* (Penguin). She says: 'Mindfulness is the only thing I know to do that can dig me out of despair and give me even a few moments' break from my brain.'

> Eight years ago, I did a year-long course in mindfulness in a group of 15. I've learnt some really useful techniques to help slow down my thoughts. For example, I'll take three deep breaths when I'm washing up, take notice of what I'm eating for dinner or scan up and down my body when I'm on the bus. Mindfulness helps me live in the moment rather than think about the past or worry about the future. Now I'm much more aware of my feelings and accepting that I have to look after my mental health.
>
> *(HELEN)*

COST: Prices are variable, but expect to pay around £40 for a one-to-one session or £275 for an eight-week group course. YouTube videos and some apps are free. Other apps have a sign-up fee and/or monthly subscription fee.

INFO: Be Mindful has a list of mindfulness practitioners at www.bemindful.co.uk.

Q72. *What dietary changes can help control the symptoms of bipolar disorder?*

More and more evidence shows that diet has a huge impact on mood and behaviour and a lasting effect on mental health, yet a study in 2016 found that people with a diagnosis of bipolar disorder tend to have a poorer quality diet, high in sugar, fat and carbohydrates.

We are only just beginning to understand how the brain, as an organ, is influenced by the nutrients it derives from the foods we eat, and how our diets have an impact on our mental health. We know that the brain is made up in large part of essential fatty acids, water and other nutrients. We know that food affects how we feel, think and behave. In fact, we know that dietary interventions may hold the key to a number of the mental health challenges our society is facing.

In 2017, the Mental Health Foundation published a report, 'Food for Thought', with a number of recommendations, including that healthy diet advice should be given to everyone with a mental illness as an important cornerstone of treatment. Maybe one day soon it will be... In the meantime, more people than ever are coming round to the same conclusion – that food really does have a noticeable impact on mood.

> My diet plays a huge part in controlling my mood swings. I eat lots of organic soups, fresh vegetables, salads, meat, fish and lots of fruit; and because I have an intolerance to wheat, I shop from the gluten-free section in the supermarket. I do have treats, like the occasional scone. I'm never going to go back to the diet I used to have, because I feel so much better now I'm eating healthily.
>
> (*DAVE*)

> Caffeine is bad for me at any time. And sugar's not good either. There have been times when I have been on a low sugar diet and felt loads better.
>
> (*ASHLEY*)

Thinking about making dietary changes may sound daunting, but it's actually possible to tweak just a few simple things that can make a world of difference to mood and mental health.

Top 10 bipolar-busting diet changes

1. Eat more fish
2. Eat more fruit and vegetables
3. Eat lots of low-fat protein
4. Eat less processed food
5. Eat less sugar
6. Eat breakfast
7. Snack on nuts and seeds

8. Drink lots of water
9. Drink less coffee and tea
10. Cut down alcohol intake

Here's why these changes will help:

Eat more fish

Worldwide research clearly shows that the lower a country's overall fish intake, the higher the rates of depression, postnatal depression, SAD and bipolar disorder in its citizens. The reverse is also true – the more fish eaten, the fewer cases of mental health disorders.

Sadly the proof is all too obvious – people in the UK eat 59% less fish than they did in the 1940s, while the number of mental health disorders in the UK population continues to soar by the decade.

Why fish? 20% of the fat in our brain is made from the essential fatty acids omega-3 and omega-6. They are termed 'essential' as they can't be made within the body and must come from the diet. Each fatty acid performs vital functions in the structuring of brain cells (or neurons), ensuring that good communication is possible within the brain. Unequal intakes of omega-3 and omega-6 fats are linked to various problems, including depression, and concentration and memory problems. Yet most people consuming Western diets eat far too much omega-6 (found in a lot of processed foods) and not enough omega-3. Fish is loaded with omega-3, so getting three portions a week will help restore this important balance.

The best fishy dishes (in order of omega-3 content from most to least) are kippers, anchovies, mackerel, herrings, sprats, pilchards, salmon, sardines, tuna, trout, shrimps, crab, halibut, mussels, oysters, cod, scallops and lobster.

Eat more fruit and vegetables

A number of studies show that people with low intakes of certain vitamins and minerals are far more likely to be depressed than those with higher intakes. Nutrients in the research spotlight include folic acid (or folate), calcium, magnesium, iron, zinc and vitamins B1, B2, B6, B12 and C. Yet since the 1940s there has been a 34% decline in UK vegetable consumption, with the latest figures suggesting that only 13% of men and 15% of women eat at least five portions of fruit and vegetables a day.

Why fruit and vegetables? When there's a lack of nutrients, the body can't make neurotransmitters (chemicals that relay nerve impulses between brain and body), which can result in mood swings, depression and a range of psychiatric problems. Getting five portions of fresh (or frozen) fruit or vegetables a day will ensure good nutrient intake. All fruit and vegetables are loaded with vitamins and minerals, including: prunes, raisins, blueberries, blackberries, kale, spinach, raspberries, strawberries, Brussels sprouts, plums, alfalfa sprouts, broccoli, beetroot, oranges, red grapes, peppers, cherries, kiwi fruit, pink grapefruit, onion, corn on the cob and aubergine (eggplant).

Eat lots of low-fat protein

Research shows that a deficiency in certain amino acids, found in protein, can lead to feelings of depression, apathy, a lack of motivation and an ina-bility to relax. Protein is rich in amino acids, the brain's messengers, which the body needs to make neurotransmitters (as mentioned above, these are the chemicals that relay nerve impulses between brain and body). Different amino acids make different neurotransmitters. For example, the neurotrans-mitter serotonin, known as the 'happy chemical', is made from the amino acid tryptophan. Adrenalin and dopamine, the 'motivation chemicals', are made from phenylalanine. For a brain-healthy intake of amino acids, experts recommend getting at least one portion of meat, dairy, fish, eggs or tofu and two servings of beans, lentils, quinoa, seeds, nuts and wholegrains daily. Getting more protein can also help stop the carbohydrate cravings that many people with bipolar describe:

The trouble is, I eat too much when I'm down. I crave carbohydrates. I go through boxes and boxes of cornflakes and other cereals. I'm also trying to cut down on bread. I'm a couple of stone overweight.

(PAUL)

Eat less processed food

Processed foods damage the brain by releasing toxins or oxidants that harm healthy brain cells. They have been linked to an increased risk of mood disorders by interfering with the way the body processes nutrients, weakening the immune system and triggering hormonal imbalance. In general, a poor diet puts a huge strain on the liver, so it becomes sluggish and unable to detoxify the body effectively. This means more toxins find their way into the bloodstream, affecting the function of the brain, causing erratic mood changes, a general feeling of depression, a 'foggy' brain and the inability to concentrate or remember things. Common brain-drainers and mood-shifters include:

- 'Trans' fats – found in deep-fried food and food containing hydrogenated vegetable oils, these block absorption of mood-friendly essential omega fats.
- Chemicals, additives and preservatives – research shows that high levels are linked to mood disturbance.
- Simple carbohydrates (such as white bread and pastries) – these cause blood sugar imbalance which is linked to problems such as fatigue, irritability, dizziness, insomnia, excessive sweating and/or thirst, poor concentration and forgetfulness, depression and crying spells, digestive disturbances and blurred vision.
- The manmade sweetener aspartame (found in diet drinks and foods) may contribute to depression as well as other psychiatric problems, though more research is needed.

Eat less sugar

Sugar (often labelled glucose, fructose, dextrose, maltose, lactose or sucrose) and sugary foods, including honey, deplete the body of vitamins and minerals, and cause blood sugar levels to rise and fall rather than remain stable (an important factor in mood swings).

Eat breakfast

Research consistently shows that skipping breakfast leads to a noticeable effect on mood, memory and energy level. And a number of studies report that providing children with breakfast improves their daily and long-term academic performance. Experts recommend eating no later than one hour after waking up. Good breakfast options include porridge and berries, wholegrain cereal, or beans or egg on wholegrain toast.

Snack on nuts and seeds

Nuts and seeds are a great source of brain-protecting omega-3 fatty acids and there are a number of other vegetarian sources (listed in order of decreasing omega-3 content): flax seed oil, walnuts, pumpkin seeds, flax seeds, walnut oil, rapeseed (canola) oil, soya beans, green leafy vegetables (although they contain relatively less omega-3 than fish).

Drink lots of water

There is good research to show that dehydration seriously affects mood. Aim to drink 1.5 litres of water every day.

Drink less coffee and tea

Caffeine, found in coffee, tea and cola drinks, can affect mood. See question 77, p. 216, for more about the effect of caffeine on bipolar symptoms.

Cut down alcohol intake

Alcohol is one of the brain's worst enemies. See question 78, p. 219, for more about the effect of alcohol on bipolar symptoms.

For more useful information on how food can affect mood, visit www. foodforthebrain.org.

Q73. *What is the 'Mind Meal'?*

Launched by the UK mental health charity Mind, the Mind Meal is a simple-to-cook, three-course meal made up of the best mood-balancing foods around. It's bursting with vitamins and essential fats crucial for good mental health, yet doesn't contain any artificial added sugars or stimulants like coffee, which have all been linked to depression. There's also no wheat or milk, which can trigger food allergies and imbalances in the brain.

1. AVOCADO SALAD AND SEEDS

Ingredients

- 250g/8oz bag of mixed lettuce or 80g/4oz bag of watercress
- One avocado
- Handful of sunflower seeds
- Handful of pumpkin seeds

Method

- Place the mixed lettuce in a serving dish.
- Remove the skin and stone from the avocado. Cut into small pieces and add to the mixed lettuce.
- Sprinkle on the seeds.
- Serve plain or with olive oil or salad dressing.

2. WHEAT-FREE PASTA WITH PESTO AND OIL-RICH FISH

Ingredients

- 250g/9oz wheat-free pasta, such as corn and vegetable pasta shells
- 100g/4oz pesto sauce
- 170g/6oz tin of salmon (or herring, sardines or pilchards)

Method

- Cook the pasta in boiling water following the instructions on the packet.
- When the pasta is ready, add one tablespoon of pesto sauce per person and mix.
- Drain off the liquid from the fish, remove or crush any large bones, and flake with a fork. Add to the pasta and pesto and mix gently together.

3. FRUIT AND OATCAKES

Ingredients

- 2 bananas
- 2 apples
- 8 dried apricots
- 8 to 12 oatcakes
- 40g/2oz /½ cup (broken) walnuts

Method

- Peel the bananas and rinse the apples and dried apricots.
- Cut the fruit into small pieces, removing the apple core, and place together in a small saucepan.
- Add three tablespoons of water and simmer gently for ten minutes, or until the fruit is soft, adding more water if needed to prevent the mixture becoming too dry and sticking to the pan.

- Break and arrange the oatcakes in the bottom of individual bowls.
- When the fruit is soft, pour into individual bowls to cover the oatcakes. If the fruit mixture contains enough liquid, the juices will soak into and soften the oatcakes.
- Serve with a sprinkling of broken walnuts.

Q74. *Can nutritional supplements minimize the symptoms of bipolar disorder?*

Nutritionist Patrick Holford, author of the best-selling book *Optimum Nutrition for the Mind,* is convinced that taking supplements can dramatically reduce symptoms for people with depression and bipolar disorder. 'In one study at the University of Calgary in Canada, 11 adults with bipolar were given 36 vitamins and trace minerals in addition to their prescribed medication,' he says. 'Over the next six months, on average, they halved their need for the medications and every patient experienced a 55–66% reduction in symptoms.'

And the greatest news of all is that it only takes three simple changes to achieve all these fantastic benefits:

Top 3 bipolar-busting supplements

1. Take a good-quality multivitamin daily and/or supplements to ensure intake of the following: calcium, folic acid, iron, magnesium, manganese, vitamins B1, B3, B5, B6, B12 and C and zinc.
2. Take a good-quality omega-3 supplement daily.
3. Sprinkle a tablespoon of lecithin granules over breakfast cereal every day.

Here's why making these changes and loading up on the extra nutrients can help:

Calcium

A lack of calcium affects the central nervous system, and causes nervousness, apprehension, irritability and numbness.

FOOD SOURCES: low-fat dairy produce, leafy green vegetables, almonds, Brazil nuts, sesame seeds, tofu, dried fruit, wholegrain cereal.

IDEAL DAILY INTAKE: 800mg

Folic acid (or folate)

Research consistently shows that a lack of folic acid increases the risk of depression, and in one study at King's College Hospital Psychiatry Department in London, a third of 123 patients were found to have low levels of folic acid.

FOOD SOURCES: leafy green vegetables, broccoli, melon, asparagus, beetroot, brewer's yeast (Marmite/Vegemite), wholegrains.

IDEAL DAILY INTAKE: 100mcg

Iron

Low levels of iron have been linked to fatigue, poor concentration, depression, weakness, lack of appetite and headaches.

FOOD SOURCES: red meat, wholegrain cereals, leafy green vegetables, pulses such as kidney beans and lentils, dried fruits.

IDEAL DAILY INTAKE: 14mg

Magnesium

A deficiency in magnesium can cause anxiety, irritability and hypersensitivity to noise and has been linked to an increased risk of depression and confusion, anxiety, agitation and hallucinations. One study of nine people with rapid cycling bipolar symptoms found that half of them were stabilized by magnesium supplementation, and intravenous magnesium sulphate has been used with some success for calming manic patients.

FOOD SOURCES: leafy green vegetables, soya products such as tofu and soya milk, seeds, nuts, wholegrains, bananas, dried apricots, avocados.

IDEAL DAILY INTAKE: 200mg

Manganese

This metal plays a role in amino-acid formation, so a deficiency may contribute to depression that stems from low levels of certain neurotransmitters.

FOOD SOURCES: nuts, wholegrains, dried fruit, pineapple, green leafy vegetables, oats, brown rice.

IDEAL DAILY INTAKE: 3mg

Vitamin B1 (thiamine)

The brain uses this vitamin to help convert glucose, or blood sugar, into fuel, and without it the brain quickly runs out of energy, leading to fatigue, depression, irritability, anxiety and thoughts of suicide.

FOOD SOURCES: red meat, peas, spinach, wholemeal bread, nuts, bran flakes, soya beans.

IDEAL DAILY INTAKE: 25mg as part of a B vitamin complex to ensure maximum absorption

Vitamin B3 (niacin)

A lack of vitamin B3 is linked to agitation, anxiety and mental 'fog'. Pellagra, a condition that leads to psychosis and dementia among other symptoms, is caused by vitamin B3 deficiency.

FOOD SOURCES: red meat, poultry, fish, peas, peanuts, soya beans, kidney beans, wholegrains.

IDEAL DAILY INTAKE: 25mg as part of a B vitamin complex to ensure maximum absorption

Vitamin B5 (pantothenic acid)

Symptoms of deficiency are fatigue, chronic stress and depression. Vitamin B5 is also needed for good hormone function.

> **FOOD SOURCES**: sweet potatoes, avocados, mushrooms, yoghurt, red meat, fish, lentils, broad beans, haricot beans.

> **IDEAL DAILY INTAKE**: 25mg as part of a B vitamin complex to ensure maximum absorption

Vitamin B6

A lack of B6 means the body is unable to make serotonin (the 'happy chemical') so efficiently, which could potentially lead to depression.

> **FOOD SOURCES**: wholegrains, brown rice, soya products, bananas, strawberries, oats, broccoli, asparagus, fish, chicken, watermelon.

> **IDEAL DAILY INTAKE**: 25mg as part of a B vitamin complex to ensure maximum absorption

Vitamin B12

Without vitamin B12, neither the senses nor the brain can work properly and it has been shown to be vital for a healthy nervous system.

> **FOOD SOURCES**: brewer's yeast (Marmite/Vegemite), fish, meat, poultry, eggs, low-fat dairy products.

> **IDEAL DAILY INTAKE**: 10mcg

Vitamin C

Low levels of vitamin C are associated with an increased risk of depression. One study found that about a third of psychiatric patients had blood vitamin C levels that were below the threshold that has been associated with behavioural problems.

> **FOOD SOURCES**: papaya, broccoli, spinach, strawberries, kiwis, oranges, peppers, pineapple.

> **IDEAL DAILY INTAKE**: 1,000mg

Zinc

Someone with bipolar disorder has a high probability of lacking in the mineral zinc, which has been linked to apathy, lack of appetite and lethargy. When zinc is low, copper levels in the body can increase to toxic levels, resulting in paranoia and fearfulness.

> **FOOD SOURCES**: chicken, fish, shellfish, low-fat dairy products, peanuts, legumes.
>
> **IDEAL DAILY INTAKE**: 10mg

Essential fatty acids

Two papers published in the *British Journal of Psychiatry* show that, put simply, taking 2g of omega-3 essential fatty acids daily can help decrease depression, suicidal behaviour and stress. Dr Andrew Stoll and his team at Harvard Medical School also found that patients with a bipolar diagnosis who took omega-3 fats had much longer periods without any symptoms than another group who were taking an olive oil placebo. It seems the fats slow down the electrical activity in the brain.

> **FOOD SOURCES**: oily fish, nuts, seeds, nut and seed oils, soya beans, leafy green vegetables.
>
> **IDEAL DAILY INTAKE**: a fish oil concentrate that contains between 1.5 and 4g of the active ingredient EPA (eicosapentaenoic acid).

❛ What have really helped to control the lows are the fish oil supplements I take. From my research on the internet, I found out that there are a lot of grades of fish oil, starting from the old fashioned cod liver oil right up to Rolls Royce fish oil – high grade EPA concentrates. I've been taking PuraEPA capsules for five years. They didn't seem to make much of a difference at first, but then I read somewhere that it's not a miracle cure. It takes a minimum of three months for the oil to be fully absorbed. You have to be patient. Also, trans fats in the diet can put the brakes on the absorption process so I tried to cut them out. Now I take six capsules a day;

two in the morning and four at lunch-time. The body can't absorb a large amount of oil in one go, so I split them up.

(DAVE)

Choline (in the form of lecithin)

A nutrient similar to the B vitamins, choline has shown some promise in small trials in the US with people who have rapid cycling bipolar disorder. It's thought that choline accelerates the synthesis and release of the neurotransmitter acetylcholine, which is involved in many nerve and brain functions.

FOOD SOURCES: eggs, beef, cauliflower, tofu, almonds, peanuts.

IDEAL DAILY INTAKE: 500–800mg daily. Nutritionist Patrick Holford recommends adding a tablespoon of lecithin granules (the body absorbs choline more easily in the form of lecithin) to breakfast cereal every morning.

The best way to ensure a good intake of these nutrients is by eating a healthy diet. It's also perfectly safe to take a good-quality multivitamin and minerals supplement and a good-quality omega-3 supplement (in the doses recommended above) without consulting a professional, even when taking prescribed medication. Both are widely available from health food stores.

The future

Although more clinical trials are needed to back up current knowledge, it's thought that taking extra amino acids in supplement form can help bump up the supplies of neurotransmitters in the brain (a lack of which is linked to depression). It's claimed that taking various doses of some nutrients, such as amino acids L-tyrosine, L-phenylalanine, L-tryptophan, L-theanine, TMG, GABA or SAMe, can improve symptoms of mental health conditions, but these should only be supplemented under the guidance of a professional. To find a qualified nutritionist in the UK, contact the Association for Nutrition at www.associationfornutrition.org. In the US, visit www.eatright.org.

Q75. *Can herbal remedies help control bipolar symptoms?*

It's important to stress that herbal remedies are not necessarily safe to take alongside prescription medication. That's because the interactions between herbs and medicines may not have been fully researched yet. And some herbs may not be suitable to take if you have bipolar, regardless of whether you're taking medication or not.

For example, St John's wort (Hypericum perforatum) – perhaps the best-known and best-researched herbal remedy to help lift low mood – is licensed in Germany and other European countries as a treatment for mild to moderate depression, anxiety and sleep disorders, and has been shown in clinical trials to boost the production of serotonin (the brain's 'happy' chemical). A daily dose of 900mg of the standardized extract (which means the amount of active ingredient is guaranteed) is as effective in counteracting mild depression as some prescription antidepressants. Reported side effects include stomach complaints, oversensitivity to sunlight and fatigue. And, because of potential adverse interactions, St John's wort should not be taken at the same time as other antidepressants or with some medications, including indinavir (used to treat HIV), the contraceptive pill, theophylline, warfarin, digoxin, reserpine, cyclosporine and loperamide. Perhaps more importantly for those with a diagnosis of bipolar disorder, in spite of its great antidepressant effect, there have been a few cases of St John's wort inducing mania.

There's a small (yet growing) body of research and lots of anecdotal evidence to show that other herbal remedies – including kava kava (which is currently banned in the UK), valerian, magnolia rhodiola, ginkgo biloba and black cohosh – can help control bipolar symptoms. The best advice for anyone with anything more serious than mild depression or the slightest indication of a family history of mania? Always seek professional help before taking any new herbal supplement.

To find a qualified herbal practitioner in the UK, contact the National Institute of Medical Herbalists at www.nimh.org.uk.

In the US, a list of qualified herbalists is available via the American Herbalists Guild at www.americanherbalistsguild.com.

Q76. *How does nicotine affect bipolar symptoms?*

In the grand scheme of things, giving up smoking is hardly likely to be high up on the list of priorities when someone's experiencing a manic episode or down in the depths of depression.

> I started smoking when I was 13 – the year after, I can pinpoint when my behaviour started to change and when my bipolar symptoms kicked in. I've had lots of periods when I've not smoked. In fact, I don't smoke at all when I'm manic. I'm too busy doing everything and anything to find time to smoke. When I'm stable, I don't really smoke a lot – probably five or six a day, usually in the afternoon with a cup of tea. But when I'm low, I smoke constantly. I've always got a cigarette on the go. That's because when I'm depressed I become a thinker. I don't smoke in the house. I go in the garden and sit on the doorstep. It's amazing how long I can make a cigarette last when I'm depressed. I use it as time for thinking and dwelling. Smoking is a comfort thing when I'm depressed.
>
> (*AMY*)

However hard it is, quitting during a period of stability is definitely worth thinking about. As well as the huge expense, a single puff of a cigarette contains a trillion cell-damaging oxidants, which immediately travel into the brain. The chance of getting cancer goes up and the risk of foetal abnormalities in pregnancy increases. Smokers also take in high levels of the heavy metal cadmium, the gradual accumulation of which depletes the depression-fighting nutrients zinc and vitamin C. Cadmium has also been linked to disturbed mental performance and increased aggression. One study by Dr Corvin of St James's Hospital in Dublin found that smoking doubled the incidence of psychotic symptoms among patients with bipolar.

Passive smoking also has significant risks. According to research in the *Journal of the American Medical Association*, just 30 minutes in a smoky environment can damage your heart by reducing its ability to pump blood.

So what's the best way to give up?

- Studies show that using Nicotine Replacement Therapy (NRT) – patches, gum, lozenges or tabs – doubles the likelihood of success. And did you know that you're up to four times more likely to quit successfully with the help of a stop smoking service? Find a local one at www.nhs.uk/smokefree or call the Smokefree National Helpline on 0300 123 1044.

- Since e-cigarettes were first sold in China in 2004, millions of people all over the world have used them to help them quit smoking. E-cigarettes are battery-operated devices that allow you to inhale nicotine in a vapour rather than smoke. And though most experts agree vaping is less harmful than smoking cigarettes because they don't burn tobacco or two of the most damaging chemicals in tobacco (tar and carbon monoxide), this doesn't mean they're harmless. While Public Health England is calling for e-cigarettes to be available on prescription, some experts say not enough research has been done yet to know for sure what effects the chemicals in e-cigarettes have on health in the long term.

- Allen Carr, the late give-up guru and celeb favourite with the likes of Richard Branson and Ruby Wax, has clinics all over the world that claim a 90% success rate. See www.allencarr.com for details of his 'Easyway Method'.

- In an article published in *New Scientist* magazine, it was reported that 'hypnosis is the most effective way of giving up smoking, according to the largest-ever scientific comparison of ways of breaking the habit'. And in a study conducted at the Scott and White Memorial Hospital in Texas, smokers were given eight sessions of hypnotherapy over two months and told to quit smoking one week after beginning the course of treatment. By the end of treatment 40% had given up. At a follow-up 12 weeks later, 60% had quit.

  Find a practitioner at www.nationalhypnotherapysociety.org.

- Research published in the international medical journal *Addiction* shows that moderate exercise, such as walking, greatly reduces nicotine withdrawal symptoms. The theory is that exercise boosts the body's levels of the hormone dopamine, which enhances mood and reduces the need for nicotine.
- In the US, the Foundation for a Smoke-Free America runs campaigns and offers support and advice to anyone trying to quit. See www.anti-smoking.org.

' I started smoking in a mental hospital when I was first ill at the age of 18. I'd used marijuana quite a lot before then, but in hospital there was a bloke who smoked and I thought, well, I'm allowed to smoke in here so I will. I smoked 20 or more Marlboro a day for 20 years and didn't quit until I was 38. The reason I stopped was because my wife nagged me. By that time we had kids, and she was pulling out that card. Quitting smoking was part willpower, part Nicorette gum and part nagging by my wife. It was pretty hard, especially the first time. I would quit and then start again. I'd try and hide it from my wife, but eventually it was easier to stop, especially as I was working in a non-smoking office at the time and I used to have to sneak off to the toilets. I haven't had a cigarette at all for six years now. Health-wise, I feel so much better. I can exercise without running out of breath. '

(*CARL*)

A word of warning ...

Zyban – a nicotine-free quit-smoking prescription drug – contains the same active ingredient as the antidepressant Wellbutrin. It works by boosting the levels of several chemical messengers in the brain, which leads to a reduction in nicotine withdrawal symptoms and a weakening of the urge to smoke. More than a third of the people who take Zyban at the same time as participating in a support programme are able to quit smoking for at least one month. However, Dr Ian Maidment, Senior Lecturer in Clinical Pharmacy at Aston University, says: 'Zyban contains Bupropion (also marketed as an antidepressant). Like all antidepressants, it can cause mania in bipolar, induce seizures and cause problems in children and adolescents. According to the British National Formulary volume 74 (a standard prescribing reference book), Zyban is contra-indicated in bipolar, so should be avoided in a patient with bipolar.'

Q77. *How does caffeine affect bipolar symptoms?*

Tea, coffee, chocolate, cola and energy drinks contain caffeine, a stimulant that takes over and eventually replaces the natural processes in the brain for increasing alertness and motivation.

 I constantly drink tea. I feel like it kick starts my brain, especially if I've done nothing for a while. I have set times that I drink it – 7:30am, 11am, 2pm, 4pm, 7pm and 9pm. I *have* to have it at those times. The first one of the day is particularly important as I can't move or see properly until I've had it. It's almost an extension of my medication – in fact, I take my meds with it!

(*AMY*)

Coffee contains between 30 and 150mg of caffeine, depending on its strength. Tea contains between 20 and 100mg. A can of Coke contains 46mg. In the UK, consumption of energy drinks soared 185% between 2006 and 2015, and is still growing. These drinks usually contain loads of caffeine – for example, a can of Red Bull contains 80mg, while Monster has 160mg. Chocolate contains small amounts of caffeine. It's also worth mentioning that some over-the-counter medicines (such as pain relief, flu remedies, appetite control pills and fatigue-fighters such as Pro Plus) can also contain significant amounts of caffeine.

The trouble with caffeine is that it can lead to the over-stimulation of the nervous system, increased anxiety levels and insomnia. And even if it doesn't actually prevent sleep, studies show that an intake of as little as 250mg caffeine per day can reduce the amount of time spent in deep sleep.

But the irony is that, according to research at Bristol University, drinking coffee doesn't make coffee drinkers feel any more alert and energized than non-coffee drinkers. In other words, drinking coffee simply relieves the symptoms of withdrawal from coffee.

And the assumption is that, although they carried out their research on coffee, the caffeine in tea, cola, energy drinks and chocolate will have the same effect in the body, particularly as they contain other chemicals that have also been linked to sleep disturbance. For instance, chocolate contains the stimulant theobromine, whose action is similar to caffeine's. Coffee contains theophylline, a chemical stimulant known to disturb normal sleep patterns. Tea is loaded with tannin that prevents the body from absorbing certain mood stabilizing nutrients, such as the B vitamins. Soft drinks and chocolate are laden with sugar. Energy drinks can contain other stimulants, such as guarana, taurine and ginseng, of which the long-term health effects are unknown. Even more worrying is the emerging evidence that energy drinks can be linked to kidney damage, poor mental health and risk-seeking behaviour. And a review of them by the WHO describes a number of potential health risks – especially when they're combined with alcohol – including panic attacks, nausea and vomiting, tremors, chest pain and a racing pulse.

The good news is that it's not necessary to cut out caffeine altogether. Two caffeine-loaded drinks a day can feature in a healthy diet, but any more can significantly affect mood. It's also worth thinking about what time of day caffeine is consumed. Because of its sleep-disturbing potential, caffeine is better as a morning pick-me-up than as an evening drink or snack, particularly during periods of mania and/or insomnia.

> I tend to avoid stimulating food and drink in the evening ... I won't have a coffee after seven o'clock, or anything very sugary.
>
> *(KEITH)*

> I've given up caffeine. I no longer drink Diet Coke and only have one cup of tea in the morning. I then drink decaffeinated tea throughout the day. Now I wake up more easily and sleep better, which means I'm less tired for the rest of the day.

Sometimes it's hard at college when others are having coffee in between lectures, but I'm never tempted because my concentration levels are so much better and I'm doing better at college.

(*RACHEL*)

Remember that it is best to cut down caffeine intake gradually to avoid headaches and other withdrawal symptoms, such as fatigue and irritability. If problems do occur, increase water intake and they will eventually disappear.

So what are the alternatives to coffee, a cup of tea, a can of Coke or a bar of chocolate?

Caffeine-free hot drinks

- herbal teas – chamomile is good for inducing calm and sleep, peppermint is good for indigestion, lemongrass is refreshing
- roasted herbal roots, such as barley, chicory and dandelion
- grain coffee – Rombouts and Wilson's Heritage are popular choices.

Caffeine-free cold drinks

- water
- fresh fruit juices (not those made from sugar-laden concentrate or dilute-with-water squashes that are loaded with additives and sugar or saccharine)
- milk.

Caffeine-free chocolate

- carob, a plant extract available from health food stores

Another healthier way to enjoy chocolate is by switching to 70% cocoa dark chocolate as it's lower in saturated fat, additives and sugar than its milk chocolate counterpart.

Q78. *How does alcohol affect bipolar symptoms?*

So-called dual diagnosis (where a condition such as bipolar disorder is accompanied by another clinical condition such as an addiction to alcohol) is common and the WHO says that sufficient evidence now exists to assume that alcohol plays a contributing role in the development of depression. In fact, substance abuse is seen in more than half of people with bipolar disorder, and alcohol is top of the abused substances list.

 It's really hard to avoid alcohol, but it is a trigger. If I have one drink, well, I'll probably have six or seven. But it doesn't seem to make me drunk; it just makes me more hyper.

(TAMARA)

Drinking may be a habit and/or a way to shut out the world, but there's no getting away from the fact that alcohol is the brain's worst enemy. It's thought that alcohol uses up and depletes the neurotransmitters that the brain needs to ward off anxiety and depression naturally. It also dissolves brain-friendly omega-3 fatty acids within brain cells and prevents the brain from being able to use them. Too much alcohol can interfere with the liver's normal functioning (the liver is the organ that metabolizes alcohol), trigger blood sugar imbalances (alcoholic drinks contain a lot of sugar) and cause deficiencies in a number of vitamins linked to good mental health.

Alcohol is especially harmful for those with bipolar because it depresses the central nervous system, which leads to less inhibited behaviour and impulse control. It reveals or magnifies underlying feelings, which is why many drinkers become angry, aggressive, anxious or low (worsening the symptoms of depression). Research also shows it interferes with good-quality sleep by significantly reducing the time spent in slow-wave (deep) sleep. This can lead to a constant feeling of fatigue, demotivation and depression.

Even more worryingly, alcohol can prevent antidepressants from working properly, interact in dangerous ways with certain medication, including lithium and tranquillizers, and increase the likelihood of suicidal thoughts. The statistics are sobering: 60% of suicides in Britain are alcohol related, and alcohol-related deaths have almost doubled since the 1990s.

> Tom was worrying he was starting to get high again, but the medication wasn't working. He started drinking a lot of alcohol – eight cans of cider in one go. And as he gradually got worse, he didn't ever seem to get drunk. He started ringing old girlfriends. He started self-harming, cutting himself. He would also bring random people home he'd met drinking on the streets. The day he eventually ended up in hospital he had been drinking all day.

(JO)

Government guidelines recommend not drinking more than 14 units of alcohol a week for both men and women – that's six glasses of wine (175ml) or six pints of lager or five pints of cider. The guidelines also suggest spreading your alcohol consumption over three or more days rather than binge drinking, and having several alcohol-free days each week.

If alcohol dependence isn't an issue, cut down to one or two drinks daily (and ideally have two booze-free days a week) or stop drinking altogether. If alcohol dependence is a problem, talk to your doctor, who may prescribe a certain type of medication (benzodiazepines) to help minimize withdrawal symptoms from alcohol, which include the 'shakes', sweating, headaches, nausea, stomach pains, poor appetite, insomnia, anxiety, low mood, mood swings and, in some rare cases, even hallucinations, paranoia, disorientation, psychosis, severe memory problems and epileptic fits. For this reason, anyone with a bipolar diagnosis and an alcohol dependency should never go 'cold turkey' – give up alcohol suddenly – but seek medical help first. See www.drinkaware.co.uk.

Some people find it helpful to contact Alcoholics Anonymous (AA).

Founded in 1935, AA has more than two million members in 150 countries and is well known for the high success rate of its Twelve Step Programme and the support provided at weekly meetings. The basic premise of AA is to get well and sober. Don't pick up the first drink; acknowledge and accept one's powerlessness over alcohol; try to live a day at a time; accept that there is a greater power, whatever or whoever that power might be. AA suggests a code word for new members to remain sober – HALT: try to be never Hungry, Angry, Lonely or Tired.

For information about AA in the UK, see www.alcoholics-anonymous. org.uk. You can find a local AA group anywhere in the world at www.aa.org.

' My bipolar was masked by self-medicating with alcohol over the years. I am an alcoholic. From the age of 21, I probably drank daily. I drank lager, bitter and whisky, and sometimes would drink all day. On a Sunday, I would make a fry-up with a can at my side. Then I'd take a nap at lunchtime. I kidded myself that alcohol was keeping me on an even keel and that it prevented me from getting too high and helped me to sleep. I never got really drunk. In my mind, the drinking was justified because I was using it to make me a better person and feel better. But it got to be too much. When I left my job as a motorcycle mechanic and became a house-husband, I would drink all day and was lying to my wife about my drinking and hiding it. I would promise to stop, but couldn't. I began to withdraw into myself rather than communicate with my wife. I was really short-tempered and not a very nice person. Our marriage was falling apart. She was so fed up with me that she was sleeping in a different room and we were talking about separate living arrangements. That made me really sad, and suddenly I realized how serious the situation had become and that I was going to lose everything.

AA was the only way I found I could stop. The reason I went was to try to save my marriage. It was my last chance, basically. They say you have to go to any lengths to stop the drinking and I was willing to do what they said. It's hard to describe the compulsion. Even though you tell yourself you're not going to do it, you do. I started by going to three meetings a week and I still do now. I haven't had a drink for two years and seven months. My life is much better for having left that vice behind me. I'm more clear-headed. I feel much more on top of my whole personality and find it much easier to let go of things. I'm no longer so compulsive, obsessive or perfectionist. My marriage has never been better.

(CARL)

Q79. Can over-the-counter medications be harmful for someone with bipolar disorder?

Not all medicines bought from a pharmacy without a prescription (over-the-counter, or OTC medicines) are safe for somebody with bipolar. It's always worth checking with a pharmacist or psychiatrist that prescription and OTC medication can be taken together. OTC medicines to note include:

Pain relief, such as ibuprofen and aspirin

'You should avoid taking ibuprofen (found in pain relief such as Nurofen) at the same time as lithium because it can affect the way lithium is passed out of the kidneys and increase lithium levels in the blood by about 20%, potentially causing toxicity. Aspirin should also be avoided, although paracetamol is thought to be safe,' says Dr Ian Maidment, Senior Lecturer in Clinical Pharmacy at Aston University.

Decongestants

'Decongestants based on ephedrine that you take for blocked sinuses or a cold, found in medicines like Sudafed, could potentially cause mania and make a person with bipolar a bit speedy,' says Ian. 'Ideally someone with bipolar should talk to a pharmacist before taking a decongestant.'

Cough medicines

'The problem is that codeine-based cough suppressants, such as pholcodine, could induce euphoria; again anyone with bipolar needs to discuss what they're planning to take with their pharmacist,' Ian advises.

Q80. *Can prescription drugs taken for conditions other than bipolar disorder influence recovery?*

'Numerous prescription drugs can affect symptoms of depression or mania,' says Dr Ian Maidment, Senior Lecturer in Clinical Pharmacy at Aston University. Although a GP or psychiatrist writing out a new prescription should advise about any possible interactions between different medications, it can't harm to know the following facts:

- Antidepressants and corticosteroids (usually prescribed to treat inflammatory skin disorders), such as prednisolone, can trigger mania.
- Research published in the *World Journal of Psychiatry* in 2015 reports a link between the active ingredient in the drug Roaccutane, prescribed for severe acne, and production of serotonin in the brain, leading to an increased risk of depression and suicide.
- Beta-blockers (usually prescribed to lower blood pressure) and some anti-convulsants (for epilepsy), such as topiramate, can cause depression.
- Lariam (mefloquine) – the prophylactic anti-malarial medication – can trigger psychiatric disorders in some people.
- People who have been prescribed the appetite suppressant drug Rimonabant (marketed as Acomplia) are 40% more likely to become depressed than those who take a placebo drug, according to Danish research.

Q81. *How do recreational drugs affect those with a bipolar diagnosis?*

Regardless of mental health, the misuse or abuse of or dependence on any recreational (or 'street') drug can seriously damage well-being and lead to a number of problems, including psychotic symptoms, relapse of psychotic illness or a need for the dosage of medication to be adjusted. Whatever the reason for taking drugs – to numb painful memories, pump up mood or hide feelings of shyness or inadequacy – the 'benefits' are short-lived, while the negatives are huge.

According to research carried out by the Mental Health Foundation in 2014, half of people with drug dependence are receiving mental health treatment and adults with drug dependence are twice as likely as the general population to be using psychological therapy. In short, the use of recreational drugs can only delay diagnosis of the real problem or make an existing problem a hundred times worse. So what effects do the most common recreational drugs have?

Cannabis (pot, skunk, weed)

Some people claim that cannabis can ease pain associated with various conditions, such as cancer, multiple sclerosis and AIDS. Usually mixed with tobacco and smoked in a joint or inhaled through a hand-held apparatus commonly known as a 'bong', occasionally it is baked into cakes or brownies and eaten. Cannabis has a disorienting effect that can be pleasurable (users can feel relaxed and giggly) or horrible (symptoms of depression, psychosis, paranoia and anxiety are common).

Worryingly, the newer strains of cannabis and marijuana now available, sometimes known as skunk, are much more powerful and likely to cause symptoms and addiction – mental health hospital admissions in England due to cannabis have risen by 85% since the late 1990s. And according to research from the Institute of Psychiatry, Psychology & Neuroscience at King's College London, the risk of psychosis is three times higher for potent 'skunk-like' cannabis users and five times higher for those who use it every day.

An increasing body of research suggests long-term use of cannabis can contribute to various mental health problems and the inability to live a happy life.

> My youngest son developed bipolar symptoms in his late teens. We didn't recognize the symptoms as bipolar at first as his presented themselves differently to mine ... he started doing a lot of cannabis which we didn't know about at first and started self-harming which is not something that I've ever done. So the symptoms kind of appeared in a different guise for him – it was only later that we realized it was all part of a grand picture. I do think the cannabis could have been a trigger ... we found out too late that he was going out every night and getting stoned with his mates. And it's much stronger stuff now.
>
> (*KEITH*)

> I put a lot of energy into just trying to get to a level where I felt how I imagined everybody else would feel. But I didn't feel right – my moods were all over the place. I had to devote my time just to feeling OK. Alcohol and drugs gave me temporary relief, and I experimented until I found the right sort of level ... it was mainly weed and I did a fair amount of acid. But weed was mainly the drug. I wanted something to bring me down – I hated drugs that took me up. I had so much hyper energy, so I did anything to bring me down. For a while it was alcohol, but that sort of faded out and I basically became a classic stoned pot-head, just chain smoked dope all day long. If I didn't have it, I was hyper agitated and anxious ... it was like living in an electric shock. That's one of the sadnesses and regrets about my teenage years and my twenties. I put a hell of a lot of energy into going nowhere, and I think a lot of people with bipolar probably feel the same.
>
> (*ASHLEY*)

Cocaine (charlie, coke)

Extracted from the leaves of the coca plant in South America, cocaine usually comes in powder form that a user snorts up the nose through a straw or rolled-up banknote. The effects – increased confidence and energy, and a higher body temperature, pulse rate and blood pressure – last around 30 minutes. Crack cocaine (a powder blend of cocaine, baking soda and water) is usually smoked and has a similar but more concentrated and shorter effect to cocaine. Both are highly addictive and can lead to serious mental health

problems ranging from mild depression to the extremes of cocaine psychosis, in which the user has symptoms similar to schizophrenia. Heavy regular
use can cause restlessness, confusion, paranoia and feelings of desperation.

Ecstasy (E)

This is a man-made drug sold as a tiny pill, often taken in dance clubs. Its
effects last for anywhere between an hour and six hours, with an initial
adrenaline rush followed by calm energy. The user will find colours, music
and emotions more intense and an increased feeling of empathy for others. It
also affects body temperature – government statistics show that 20 people a
year die from taking ecstasy, usually as a result of hypothermia, dehydration
or over-hydration caused by drinking too much water. The next day, low
mood, aching bones and fatigue are common. In the long term, there's an
increased risk of memory loss, depression and anxiety.

Heroin (smack, gear)

Derived from the poppy plant, a small dose of heroin – usually in liquid
form injected into the arm – gives an instant high. A bigger dose can cause
drowsiness, unconsciousness or even instant death. It suppresses pain, but
also affects concentration and increases feelings of anxiety and fear. It is
highly addictive. Long-term use means more is needed for the user to feel
normal, and horrendous withdrawal symptoms last for at least three days:
hot and cold sweats, aching, vomiting, sneezing and spasms. Long-term
use usually causes financial problems and even criminal activity to fund the
drug – a heroin habit can cost thousands of pounds a year – and can lead
to a total breakdown of normal life.

LSD (acid)

A powerful hallucinogenic drug, LSD comes from a fungus found growing on
rye and other wild grasses. A 'trip' lasts for up to 12 hours, altering perception,

movement and time. Trips can be enjoyable or disturbing, and there's no way to stop one once it's started. Users often experience fear, paranoia and disorientation. And long after the drug has been taken, flashbacks can occur without warning. LSD can make symptoms of depression and anxiety worse in the long term, and a bad trip can trigger bipolar:

 My first manic episode happened when I was 18 following an LSD trip – it was a flashback sort of thing, and I wound up sectioned for 14 days. I got out and they put the whole thing down to the drug taking. I wasn't diagnosed with manic depression until five years later when I was 23.

(*CARL*)

Speed (whizz, uppers)

One of the most impure drugs in circulation, speed is often mixed with talcum powder or bicarbonate of soda and sold in the form of a powder that's sniffed up the nose. Its effect is described as 'an adrenaline rush that lasts for several hours' linked to a faster heart rate and quickened breathing. Users feel increased energy and confidence and appetite is suppressed. The next day, the user often wakes up feeling lethargic, hungry and deeply depressed (known as the 'speed blues'). Anyone with a bipolar diagnosis is likely to find that taking speed greatly exaggerates mood swings.

'Legal highs' (spice, GHB, black mamba)

In 2016, the Psychoactive Substances Act came into effect in the UK, making so-called 'legal highs' illegal. These contain one or more chemical substances which mimic the effects of traditional illegal drugs, such as cocaine and cannabis, and are often stronger, cheaper and potentially just as dangerous. 'Legal highs' have been linked to thousands of hospital admissions, and were the cause of 204 deaths in the UK in 2015 alone.

Three ways to get help

- The Talk to Frank service provides information about drugs and advice for drug users, parents and carers. Find support near you at www.talktofrank.com or call the helpline: 0300 123 66 00.
- Adfam is a UK-based charity working to improve life for families affected by drugs and alcohol. Find a local support group or get more info at www.adfam.org.uk.
- Founded in 1953, Narcotics Anonymous uses the 12 steps as the backbone of its recovery programme. In the UK, see www.ukna.org. To find a support group anywhere in the world, see www.na.org.

CHAPTER SIX

Living with Bipolar

Q82. *Is there still a stigma around bipolar disorder?*

There's no getting away from the fact that mental illness can still be a source of shame and stigma – defined as 'a sign of disgrace or discredit, which sets a person apart from others'.

Sir Graham Thornicroft, a professor at King's College London and one of the world's leading researchers in psychiatry, says: 'In all my years as a psychiatrist, I've listened to patients tell me that the discrimination is as bad as the mental illness they are experiencing. Discrimination blights the lives of many people with mental illness, making marriage, childcare, work and a normal social life very difficult.' Feelings of shame, blame, secrecy, isolation and social exclusion are common.

Research also shows that stigma can prevent people seeking help for mental health problems. 'The profound reluctance to be "a mental health patient" means people will put off seeing a doctor for months, years, or even at all,' says Professor Thornicroft. 'This in turn delays their recovery.'

Stigma has an even stronger effect on certain groups of people – young people, men, people from minority ethnic groups, those in the military and health professionals – and is even more likely to stop them seeking help.

Amanda's mum still finds it very difficult to talk about her condition:

> When my mum was first diagnosed with bipolar, and indeed for years afterwards, she was deeply ashamed of her condition. No one could talk about it in her presence – it was the proverbial 'elephant in the room'. Things have changed, and we can cautiously refer to her being ill, but even now the phrase we all have to use in her presence is that she 'isn't very well' – I've never once heard her use the terms 'manic depression', 'bipolar disorder' or 'mood swing'. She detests those words, because she feels there is such a stigma attached to them.

Many others have had similar experiences.

> My dad's illness was kept very secret and it wasn't actually until I had my diagnosis in my late 30s that I found out about his. When we were younger, every time he went into hospital we were told he'd had a heart attack. He must have had the most heart attacks of anyone I'd ever heard of! Even after I was diagnosed, my family would not talk about it. It was just, you know, you don't talk about it, it isn't happening.
>
> *(SUE)*

> Though bipolar is definitely not a big secret in our immediate family, it is outside the family. David's mum says, 'He's got nerve trouble.' There is still a stigma attached to mental illness. People say 'he's a nutter' or 'he's a fruitcake'. Because they can't see it, they don't think anything's wrong. That infuriates me. You need to get to know the person behind the illness. There are some lovely people with mental illness who are just struggling to get through each day. It's upsetting to see them blamed for not being perfect. You can't imagine how hurtful comments can be.
>
> *(JACKIE)*

> At first my diagnosis was like a big pile of dirty washing in the cupboard, a big secret. Only my ex-husband knew, but I didn't confide in anyone else. When I met my current partner I didn't tell him the truth about my illness, but I finally told him a few weeks ago. He had thought I just suffer from depression, but since I told him about the bipolar, he's been amazing and so supportive. He says he'll do anything

that he can do. He talks to the team. We speak to each other all day long. I'd like to think it is possible to get rid of the stigma.

(DEBBIE)

My father is a 'manic depressive', although I didn't know anything was wrong until I was 25. He was an actor. He was always cheery and putting on a brave face. He would always whistle and sing, but I knew that there was a lot more going on under the surface. His real feelings were always hidden but his children sensed what was really going on even from a young age.

(CARL)

I have a brother who's three years younger than me, and I think it's been really hard for him. I suppose it's like anyone having an illness in the family, but there was quite a lot of shame there because I don't think he felt he could talk to anyone about it.

(TAMARA)

Telling someone I have bipolar is always interesting. It took me a while to tell my family. If anything, I've found it easier to tell strangers. When I'm getting to know someone, I slip it into the conversation. Guys I'm dating tend to be perfectly fine about it. I believe we should all be talking more about mental health. Bipolar doesn't define me, it is part of who I am. And there should be no shame in that.

(MARISSA)

So is it better to keep a diagnosis quiet or to shout it from the rooftops? We're still a way off from a world where mental health is seen and treated with the same priority and attitude as physical health. We haven't yet arrived at the point where there's no shame, no stigma, no blame, no guilt, no ignorance. But we think we're definitely moving in the right direction.

The stigma of mental illness is shrinking all the time. Thanks to high-profile people such as Stephen Fry, Russell Brand, Demi Lovato and many others who have 'come out' of the mental illness closet, more and more people have heard of and are less afraid of the words 'bipolar' and 'manic depression'.

Several surveys indicate that stigma and prejudice against people with mental health problems are reduced when the general public is better informed. Since the public awareness campaign Time to Change began in 2007 to raise awareness of stigma and its effects, surveys show that:

- fewer people fear those with mental health problems
- there's greater support for integrating people with mental illness into the community
- there are higher levels of tolerance.

Plus research published in 2016 by the Institute of Psychiatry, Psychology & Neuroscience at King's College London showed that people with mental health problems in England were facing 7% less discrimination from family, 15% less discrimination from friends and a 10% reduction in discrimination when dating. Encouragingly, there had also been a 6% increase in people with mental health problems saying they experience no discrimination at all.

INFO: www.time-to-change.org.uk

Bipolar UK has received widespread coverage over their 'I am/I have' campaign, helping to promote the idea that those with a mental health condition are so much more than their diagnosis.

INFO: www.bipolaruk.org

Another high-profile anti-stigma campaign in the UK, Heads Together, spearheaded by the Duke and Duchess of Cambridge and Prince Harry, has been getting people talking about their mental health. William, Kate and Harry got the ball rolling by opening up about their personal struggles. And various A-list celebrities are on board to help spread the charity's message. On their website's homepage they state: 'Too often, people feel afraid to admit that they are struggling with their mental health. This fear of prejudice and judgement stops people from getting help and can destroy families and end lives. Heads Together wants to help people feel much more comfortable with their everyday mental well-being and have the practical tools to support their friends and family.'

INFO: www.headstogether.org.uk

In the US, actor Glenn Close has set up a non-profit organization, Bring Change 2 Mind, to raise awareness and work against the stigma that often surrounds mental health. On their website there's a brilliant 'conversation tool' with a library of videos showing how to talk to anyone about mental health.

INFO: www.bringchange2mind.org

Other people in the public eye have also been waging war against stigma.

Actor, comedian and author Ruby Wax has talked openly about her own experiences of depression in her books and during her one-woman show. She says: 'It's so common, it could be anyone. The trouble is, nobody wants to talk about it. And that makes everything worse. We need to take the stigma out of mental illness. People shouldn't be ashamed of it.' Ruby manages her depression using a combination of mindfulness, therapy and medication and is optimistic about the future: 'It used to be the "C" word – cancer – that people wouldn't discuss. Now it's the "M" word. I hope pretty soon it'll be okay for everyone to talk openly about their mental health without fear of being treated differently.'

James Wade, professional darts player and Bipolar UK patron, says: 'My job has a very macho, sporting environment and when I was first hospitalized, I came out to find some people acting very differently towards me. My experience with bipolar has been very up and down, like I'm on the fastest rollercoaster but there's no getting off! Now I'm on the right path with good support, therapy and medication. I'm now very open about my condition and happy to talk about it to others to dispel the stigma and preconceptions about bipolar. As well as being a professional darts player, I also work on cars, which are my passion, and enjoy fishing! I'm also a husband to Samantha who's been there with me through the toughest times. I have bipolar but I am also a darts player, a mechanic, a fisherman and a husband.'

We think the late Carrie Fisher, who was diagnosed with bipolar at the age of 24, sums it up perfectly: 'One of the things that baffles me (and there are quite a few) is how there can be so much lingering stigma with regards to mental illness, specifically bipolar disorder. In my opinion, living with manic depression takes a tremendous amount of balls.'

So how can individuals help turn the tide of stigma? The only way shame and stigma can be erased forever is for those with mental illness and their families – one by one – to be honest and open about their condition. That doesn't necessarily mean going into intimate details about the highs, lows and mixed states in between. Saying, 'I have bipolar,' or 'He's been diagnosed with bipolar disorder,' is enough. Every time those words are spoken it's a nail in the coffin for ignorance, shame, prejudice and stigma.

And if questions that feel uncomfortable are asked, they can be answered with a simple, 'I don't want to talk about that now, although I might another time.' Someone with bipolar has nothing to feel awkward, embarrassed or ashamed about; just as someone with cancer has nothing to feel awkward, embarrassed or ashamed about.

 I've compared bipolar to having diabetes. That's a chemical imbalance in your body; bipolar is just a chemical imbalance in your head.

(ALISON)

As a daughter, sister and niece of people with bipolar disorder from two generations, Sarah has completely changed her attitude over the years:

 I remember not wanting any of my friends to know about my dad's illness. I just so desperately wanted him to be 'normal'. We bumped into a school friend when we were out for a walk once – I must have been about ten – and I was so mortified that dad was stepping side to side because of the medication he was on. Maybe it's just that all children are embarrassed by their parents, maybe I've just grown up or maybe times have changed, but I never feel embarrassed by Rebecca or her illness. For a start, the medication she takes doesn't make her physically agitated in the same way so there's not the same obvious outward sign. And even if there was, I see the person, not the condition. If anything, I feel proud of her, not ashamed.

Q83. *What is the best way to explain to a child that their parent has been diagnosed with bipolar disorder?*

Telling a child that their mum or dad has been diagnosed with bipolar disorder will never be easy, but Clare Armstrong, an NHS Operations Manager, who's carried out research into the impact of a parent's mental illness on a child, recommends this step-by-step approach:

1. Be honest and open

There is no point in trying to hide the truth from children in order to protect them. Even really young children pick up on moods, behaviour and atmosphere, and seem to have a sixth sense about what's going on. Hiding or diluting the truth will just make them worry more. The best approach is to use age-appropriate language and to be totally honest. So, for an eight-year-old, saying something like, 'Daddy's not feeling very well. He's got bipolar disorder. It's an illness that means he can get too excited or feel very very sad. But he still loves you' is enough. Children don't need complex explanations – it's about the here and now, and how it affects them and their world. An older teenager might need a more detailed explanation, such as, 'Your dad has bipolar disorder which is an imbalance in the brain's neurochemistry involving the ways that cells communicate with each other.' Whatever their age, the next crucial step is to allow them to ask questions in their own time.

2. Listen

When a parent is unwell, they can be hostile, abusive, violent, socially offensive or embarrassing, self-destructive and generally disrupt the daily routine. Once a diagnosis is made, it's important for a child to have the opportunity to be able to share any painful past experiences with someone who will listen. All that some children need is a significant adult in their life to talk to, such as a teacher, grandparent or aunt. If the child's behaviour is worrying for more than a couple of weeks (if they cry excessively, or become aggressive or withdrawn, for example) seek help from the GP who can refer them to a specialist CAMHS (child and adolescent mental health service) if necessary. It's also worth keeping the school informed about what's happening so teachers can be supportive.

3. Point out that it's not their fault

Children have a tendency to think that everything's their fault, feel guilty and blame themselves. One of the most important things to say is, 'This is not your fault, it's an illness. Mum still loves you.'

4. Explain what's happening when a parent is in hospital

No matter what their age, most children experience huge separation anxiety when a parent goes into hospital, worrying about their condition, wondering how long they're going to be in for and fearing that they're going to die. Children need to be kept up-to-date with what's happening to prevent them from inventing their own worst-case scenario. Explain that hospital is a place where doctors and nurses can help Mum or Dad get better and that they will come home. And keep lines of communication open with regular phone calls and visits, whenever possible.

 At the age of eight it was upsetting to see my mum crying so much. I very often became upset myself when I saw her and felt that perhaps I was doing something wrong. I felt helpless that I couldn't make her feel better or happy – I cried myself to sleep a lot. So it had quite a depressing effect on me when I was very young. During my teenage years, I think I was so used to it I almost blanked it out – there was nothing I could do to make her feel better so I stopped trying.

(INGRID)

I've never hidden it. Because I grew up with it being hidden, I didn't want to do that. We've always talked about it. And my children are quite supportive, although they're a bit embarrassed about some of the things I've done. My youngest son, who's 16, does the cooking and basically takes over when I'm not well. My oldest son, who's 19, is supportive and talks to his friends about my bipolar.

(SUE)

I only told my children about my bipolar diagnosis recently. It was such a relief to tell them. My 18-year-old son has been amazing – round every day since to see if I'm OK. I suppose my daughter, who is 16, has been a bit flaky. She asked if I'm schizophrenic. I explained to her that I just have wonky neurotransmitters. She'll come round. I'm really proud of them.

(DEBBIE)

Q84. *Is a person with a bipolar diagnosis legally obliged to inform their employer?*

The stigma of mental illness has long been an issue in the workplace.

Years ago you didn't really want to have the word 'depression' on your medical records because there was such a stigma about having depression, and you didn't mention it in jobs or anything like that because you wouldn't get a job if you admitted to having depression.

(SUE)

> When I was first diagnosed with bipolar at the age of 22, years ago, the psychiatrist said, 'We think you've got bipolar disorder, but we don't want to diagnose you as such. You've just got your degree and are at the start of your career, but you'll never get a job if you've got bipolar on your medical records.'
>
> *(LESLEY)*

Under the Equality Act, made law in the UK in 2010, it is illegal to discriminate directly or indirectly against people with mental health problems in the workplace, and employers have a duty to make reasonable adjustments to their premises or working practices to help job applicants and employees. The law is supposed to counteract the discrimination disabled people face in their employment, yet:

- Mental ill-health is the leading cause of sickness absence in the UK, costing an average of £1,035 per employee per year.
- 95% of employees calling in sick with stress gave a different reason.
- 48% said they would not talk to their employer about their mental health.

> I work for an insurance company as a recoveries handler. It's not a stressful job, but I can't cope with it at the moment. My colleagues were supportive for the first couple of weeks, but it's a small team, and they have to cover my work. If they don't like it I shall leave and find another job because I have to put my well-being first. I'm sure they'd be more supportive if I told them I had cancer and support me all the way to the end of the treatment. Nobody realizes what a huge impact bipolar has on your life.
>
> *(DEBBIE)*

> Last year, around the time I was diagnosed, I had been manic and suspended from work on medical grounds. My work colleagues had seen me high and witnessed some terrible behaviour. Some who were friends are not so close anymore. They just changed with me. This has been the hardest thing for me to deal with, the

social side. I no longer get invited out with the gang and people have stopped texting me.

(JUDE)

Perhaps not surprisingly, a report by the Mental Health Foundation found that two in three people don't disclose details of their mental health problem on job application forms and 55% hide their diagnosis from colleagues.

When I was originally diagnosed, I did all I could to try to hide my problems from work. In the end I was self-managing the symptoms and becoming more and more ill. I thought that if I told work they'd think I was a freak.

(JUDE)

While I was manager of a business centre, I took an overdose and told the company I was working for that I had a really bad ear infection. They found out the truth because I had to send in a sick certificate and the name of the hospital was a psychiatric unit and the truth was written on the certificate anyway.

(SHARRON)

Legally, this area is extremely complicated. In theory, there's usually no obligation to tell an employer about any medical condition, including a bipolar diagnosis, although there are some instances (defined as 'being in the public interest') where an employer has a right to ask about previous mental health and the employee has an obligation to answer honestly – teaching or working with children, for example. Also, there's an argument for being honest with an employer from the outset, because if the illness is later mentioned as, for example, an excuse for poor performance, the employer is less obliged to be supportive than if it were mentioned in the first place.

So what can you do?

- Bipolar UK runs a Workplace Training service. Employers and employees can download employment support guides via their website at www.bipolaruk.org.

- Time to Change is encouraging employers to sign a pledge to support employees with mental health problems, raise awareness and reduce stigma and prejudice in the workplace. See www.time-to-change.org.uk.
- The Mind website Mental Health at Work is a brilliant round-up of resources, toolkits and case studies to help support good mental health in the workplace. See mentalhealthatwork.org.uk.
- The American Psychiatric Association Foundation runs a centre for workplace mental health and well-being. Find details at www.workplacementalhealth.org.

Telling employers about a mental illness isn't necessarily a bad thing. A survey shows that within the workplace over half of those who had been open reported that they 'always' or 'often' had support when they needed it, with a further one in five 'sometimes' getting support.

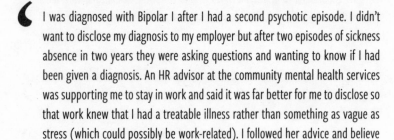

I was diagnosed with Bipolar I after I had a second psychotic episode. I didn't want to disclose my diagnosis to my employer but after two episodes of sickness absence in two years they were asking questions and wanting to know if I had been given a diagnosis. An HR advisor at the community mental health services was supporting me to stay in work and said it was far better for me to disclose so that work knew that I had a treatable illness rather than something as vague as stress (which could possibly be work-related). I followed her advice and believe it was the right decision.

Sometimes it's hard because I feel as though I am under extra scrutiny but I know that my colleagues are just looking out for me so that they can help nip another episode in the bud. Six months after I returned to work, I still have weekly supervision meetings with my manager and termly review meetings with HR to discuss my progress at work.

It's difficult knowing that my colleagues all know about my diagnosis although they generally don't treat me any differently. I would eventually like to try and get an extra day of work each week but want to wait until I've been stable for three years. The most important thing is being able to maintain my current role and staying well.

(*AMANDA B*)

" Since I got seriously ill, my boss has been amazing. "

(JUDE)

" I told my employer that I have bipolar disorder after I'd been cleaning for her for two years. Sometimes I clean her house from top to bottom in two hours. Other times I call in sick. Now she's willing to take the rough with the smooth. "

(SHARRON)

" When I became ill the first time in this job, I knew that I had to be honest, otherwise relapses would keep recurring. I'd been working for my line manager for about a year when I told her what to look out for if I was high and if I was low – for example, a lack of eye contact and not finishing sentences – so I think I've been as upfront as I could be about it. I believe very strongly that honesty is truly the best policy. The relationship between my line manager and me was good, and her reaction was good. Her husband is a trained psychologist and so I know she talked to him. I have always treated having bipolar as if it's the same as a broken leg. I do feel very proud of the way I have handled things and in return I have been treated excellently. Occupational health has been exceptional and done their level best to get me back to work. It was definitely the right thing to do. Even though I am not returning to work in my old position, I have no regrets. "

(NEIL)

" I'm very open with people about having bipolar. I'll tell anyone who wants to listen to me! If I go back to work now, I would tell my employers. I'm quite proud to be bipolar. It has a special link to being gifted. "

(REKA)

" I have absolutely no issue telling people that I have bipolar. I'm really open with my personal training clients. There's no stigma whatsoever as far as I'm concerned. "

(DAVE)

Q85. *What is the most sensible way for a woman with bipolar disorder to approach pregnancy?*

Most healthcare professionals are supportive if a woman with bipolar wants to have a baby. There are some risks associated with all the hormone changes – previously the focus was on the mother's mental well-being after the birth, but it is now more widely recognized that mood fluctuations can be triggered by hormonal changes during pregnancy as well as in the months after giving birth. This shift of focus is recognized in the DSM-5 – previous editions referred to 'postpartum onset' whereas the current edition uses the term 'peripartum onset'.

But the good news is there are a lot of things a woman can do before, during and after pregnancy to stack the odds in favour of her staying well.

Pre-conception

As for all women, taking folic acid before and during pregnancy can help reduce the risk of neural tube defects. Current official UK advice is that women should take 400 micrograms of folic acid each day from before pregnancy up to 12 weeks.

Pregnancy

Most women with bipolar disorder will need to take some medication during pregnancy to stay well, as depressive symptoms and episodes can occur during pregnancy. Certain medications are safer for the foetus than others – this depends on each individual and needs to be discussed with a healthcare professional, ideally before conception. Some women find it helpful to have a pre-birth planning meeting at around 32 weeks of pregnancy to write a care plan with their partner, family and healthcare team.

As well as medication, other options to help pregnant women stay stable include psychotherapy, ECT, light therapy and omega-3 fish oils.

After the birth

Studies show that about half of women with bipolar disorder stay well after having a baby and about half become unwell. Of those who become unwell, approximately 25% experience postnatal depression and 25% experience postpartum psychosis, also known as 'puerperal psychosis' or PP.

The risk of PP is even higher if a woman has:

- had PP before

or

- a mother or sister who has had PP.

Common symptoms include feeling 'high', confused and paranoid, hearing or feeling things that aren't really there and experiencing odd thoughts or beliefs that are unlikely to be true. Most commonly PP begins in the first few days or weeks after birth.

So what can a new mother do?

- Try to reduce other stressful things going on in your life.
- Try to get as much sleep and rest as you can in late pregnancy and after the birth.
- Ask your partner or family to take on some of the night time feeds if possible.

If any symptoms do emerge, the key is to spot and treat them as soon as possible.

You can find more information and get support from:

- Action on Postpartum Psychosis, the national charity for women and families affected by PP: www.app-network.org.
- Maternal Mental Health Alliance, a coalition of UK organizations that support women during pregnancy and in the year after giving birth: www.maternalmentalhealthalliance.org.

Q86. *What is the most sensible way for someone with bipolar disorder to approach university life?*

Deciding where to apply

Anyone who's deciding which universities to apply for is likely to take into account the courses, the locations and average grade offers. If you have a diagnosis of bipolar, you might also want to consider:

- the university's well-being/student satisfaction rankings – every year *Times Higher Education* runs a 'Student Experience Survey' to rank things like 'campus environment', 'student union', 'sport', 'social facilities' and 'sense of community'
- which well-being support services are available – have a look at individual services online or drop into Student Services if you're visiting on an Open Day.

Deciding what to say on your UCAS form

Everyone who applies for one of the 380 universities or colleges across the UK has to fill out an online UCAS (Universities and Colleges Admissions Service) form. You can find this at www.ucas.com.

Alongside all the questions about where you live, your GCSE results and predicted A level grades, there's a disability/special needs section where you're asked whether or not you have a mental health condition. If you tick the box, your course provider is legally required to make reasonable adjustments that take account of your needs.

You can also decide whether or not to mention your diagnosis in your personal statement – to explain why you've had time off school or college or to explain lower than predicted grades, for example.

My son's teacher advised him not to mention his diagnosis of bipolar in his UCAS personal statement, but my son felt strongly that he wanted to say in one sentence why he'd had to retake a year of college. His mother and I supported his decision, but we were a bit fearful that the universities might discriminate. He got four offers from all four universities he applied to in the end, so our fears were unwarranted. I feel proud of him for having the courage to ignore that teacher's advice and relieved that having bipolar hasn't stopped him moving forward in life.

(*JUAN*)

Getting ready for university

The summer before university is a brilliant time to develop some good lifelong habits to help you stay well with bipolar – like remembering to take your medication and going for annual physical check-ups without your parents reminding you, for example.

So that you know where to find support if you need it, why not spend some time finding out which well-being services are available? Depending on the university you're going to, there may be:

- a well-being officer at the Students' Union
- mental health advisors
- a free counselling service
- a university health centre with a GP service
- drop-in clinics
- student-run helplines
- well-being groups
- relaxation/stress-relieving activities, such as mindfulness sessions.

And don't forget your personal tutor and hall tutor/manager (if you're living in a hall of residence) are usually your first points of contact for any academic, personal or health-related problems.

When you get to university ...

1. SET REMINDERS TO TAKE YOUR MEDICATION:

- Download an app on your phone.
- Put your medication where you'll see it – next to your hairbrush on your bedside table, or next to your box of cereal on the kitchen worktop, for example.
- If you're likely to get back late after a night out, plan in advance how you'll remember to take your medication. Could you leave a note on your pillow? Or ask a friend to remind you?
- If you're worried about remembering to take your medication while you're away, why not talk to your psychiatrist about switching from daily tablets to monthly 'depot' injections? See question 36, p. 100, for more details.

2. REGISTER WITH A NEW GP

This may be at the university health centre, if there is one, or in your new local area. Your university should help you sign up with a new GP, or find your nearest GP practice via NHS Choices at www.nhs.uk/service-search. It doesn't take long and your medical records will be transferred, so your new GP will be able to read all about your condition, current prescription and medical and family history.

3. TELL YOUR NEW FRIENDS/HOUSEMATES

You don't need to call an intense house meeting or anything, but when the time feels right tell your new housemates you have bipolar. You could explain what they should do or who they should call if they spot any symptoms. If you feel embarrassed about telling them, remember that a survey carried out in 2017 found that one in eight university students experiences a mental health condition. You are not alone!

4. GET ORGANIZED WITH YOUR PRESCRIPTIONS

As soon as you turn 19 you need to pay for prescriptions. If you need more than one prescription a month, it might be cheaper to get a Pre-Payment Certificate. Some students are also eligible for the NHS Low Income Scheme – ask your GP or university welfare team about the 'NHS HC1 claim form'.

You can get lots more helpful info from:

- Student Minds, the UK's student mental health charity, at www.studentminds.org.uk.
- The University Mental Health Advisers Network, a network of mental health specialists working in higher education, at www.umhan.com.
- The Mix, a brilliant helpline (0808 808 4994) and website (www.themix.org.uk) set up to support people aged 16–25.

Q87. *How can someone with bipolar manage their money?*

A report published by the Money and Mental Health Policy Institute in 2016 found that 93% of people with a mental health diagnosis spend more when they're unwell, while 88% revealed they were at least two months behind in paying bills. High-spending problem areas include online gaming, subscriptions, premium rate phone lines and too-easy access to loans with huge interest rates.

Martin Lewis, founder of MoneySavingExpert.com, who has teamed up with UK mental health charity Mind to help people struggling with mental health and debt, says, 'The relationship between money and mental health is toxic. Every day I hear from people who struggle to control their spending in periods of poor mental health ... We've already looked at mechanisms for self-restricting access to future credit. Now we're adding potential spending controls too such as a 24-hour window to review high-cost purchases, setting daily spending limits, or being able to involve a trusted friend in managing your finances.'

If you're in debt

- Download a free 'Mental Health & Debt 2017' leaflet via www.moneysavingexpert.com/credit-cards/mental-health-guide.
- Ask about the government's 'Breathing Space' scheme which gives people in problem debt a six-week window without fees or charges and during which they won't be pursued by creditors if they seek debt advice at www.moneyandmentalhealth.org.
- Find out what welfare benefits, charitable grants and support services you might be entitled to at www.turn2us.org.uk.
- Get free advice about your finances and budget at www.moneyadviceservice.org.uk/en.

Q88. *What is a 'lasting power of attorney'?*

A lasting power of attorney (LPA) is a legal document that lets you appoint one or more people (known as 'attorneys') to help you make decisions or to make decisions on your behalf. There are two types of LPA:

- health and welfare
- property and financial affairs.

You can choose to make one type of LPA or both. An LPA can only be used when you're unable to make your own decisions because you've lost 'mental capacity'. It can cover decisions about things like:

- what treatment you have
- where you live
- managing your finances.

Your attorney needs to be aged 18 or over. They could be:

- a relative
- a friend
- a professional – for example, a solicitor
- your husband, wife or partner.

You must appoint someone who has the mental capacity to make their own decisions. Your attorney doesn't need to live in the UK or be a British citizen. When choosing an attorney, think about:

- how well they look after their own affairs – for example, their finances
- how well you know them
- if you trust them to make decisions in your best interests
- how happy they will be to make decisions for you.

The process of appointing an LPA depends on where you live in the UK. Find out more at www.gov.uk/power-of-attorney.

Q89. *What is the best way to make a complaint about any aspects of care?*

In general

ENGLAND

If you want to make a complaint about a mental health service, either contact the service provider or the local clinical commissioning group (CCG). There's a round-up of your rights and the best courses of action at www.nhs.uk – type 'how to make a complaint' in the search box.

The Patient Advice and Liaison Service (PALS) offers confidential advice, support and information on health-related matters. You can find officers from PALS in your local hospital or call 111 for details of your nearest PALS.

WALES

Contact the Board of Welsh Community Health Councils at www.wales.nhs.uk or call 02920 235 558.

SCOTLAND

The Scottish Public Services Ombudsman says they are a 'one-stop-shop' for individuals making complaints about organizations providing public services in Scotland – find them at www.spso.org.uk.

NORTHERN IRELAND

There's useful information about making a complaint about your NHS care at www.nidirect.gov.uk.

In hospital

If a patient, or a member of their family, is unhappy about any aspect of the care and treatment they've received in hospital, the first step is to talk to a member of staff or a ward manager. If your concerns haven't been addressed, the next step is to go through official channels. All trusts have a formal complaint system. Leaflets are available with details of the official procedure.

The hospital may have its own advocacy service, which is an independent support and information service. They may be able to help with a complaint – ask the ward manager or at reception for details (see question 46, p. 127).

If you wish to complain about the use of the Mental Health Act in relation to someone detained in hospital, contact the Care Quality Commission (CQC), which is an independent public body responsible for healthcare standards, at www.cqc.org.uk.

Complaints can also be made to your local Member of Parliament – see www.parliament.uk/get-involved/contact-your-mp/ or send an email at www.writetothem.com.

Complaints about private treatment

Many private hospitals belong to the NHS Partners Network, the primary representative body for independent sector healthcare providers (see www.nhspn.org), but generally there's no standard complaints procedure in the private healthcare industry. As with making a complaint about NHS hospital treatment, the first step is to raise concerns with staff and then ask to see a copy of their complaints procedure.

If this route isn't satisfactory, ask for independent advice on pursuing a private complaint from the Patients' Association, an organization which represents the interests of patients. Or contact the CQC, which can also offer advice on complaining about private treatment. See Extra resources, p. 267, for contact details of these organizations.

If the treatment has been paid for by private health insurance, contact the insurance company for advice on making a complaint.

Gross professional misconduct

For very serious allegations about a mental healthcare professional working in either the NHS or the private sector, complain to their relevant professional body (see Extra resources, p. 267, for contact details of relevant professional organizations). It's thankfully a rare occurrence, but someone who commits a very serious offence may need to be struck off their professional register.

Q90. *Where can somebody with a bipolar diagnosis get insurance?*

Life and travel insurance can be expensive for somebody with a diagnosis of bipolar disorder. It's not unheard of for people with bipolar to pay premiums that are 2,000% higher than people who don't have or don't declare a mental health diagnosis. Each quote depends on individual circumstances and questions will be asked such as: 'How recently were you hospitalized or sectioned? Are you currently well and taking medication? Are you travelling alone?'

Bipolar UK works with two insurance companies that are able to offer specialized insurance for people with a diagnosis of bipolar:

- Active Minds Insurance Services – contact them on 01274 518 393 or at www.activemindinsuranceservices.co.uk
- Free Spirit Travel Insurance – contact them on 0800 170 7704 or at www.freespirittravelinsurance.com.

Q91. *Is it ever unsafe for someone with a bipolar diagnosis to drive?*

The Driver and Vehicle Licensing Agency (DVLA) doesn't need to be notified about very minor short-lived illness or about anxiety or depression that doesn't cause significant memory or concentration problems, agitation, behavioural disturbance or suicidal thoughts.

However, the Drivers Medical Group, part of the DVLA, does need to be informed if a medical condition has got worse since a licence was issued or if a new medical condition, including bipolar disorder, is diagnosed. Failure to do so is a criminal offence and is punishable by a fine of up to £1,000 at the time of writing. The driver's licence and car insurance also become invalid. Call the DVLA on 0300 790 6801.

There are three reasons why driving can become unsafe for someone with a bipolar diagnosis:

1. During a manic period, impulsive and reckless behaviour can lead to speeding and dangerous driving decisions, such as overtaking or pulling out when it's not safe. The risk of an accident is far greater and someone who is manic should never drive.

2. Depression can impair concentration and reflexes, slowing response times and resulting in erratic driving. A driver who feels so low he or she doesn't care whether they live or die may make unsafe driving decisions and should never drive.

3. Some bipolar medication can cause side effects that mean it's unwise to drive. For example, benzodiazepines are commonly found in the blood of those involved in accidents. A psychiatrist or GP will explain the potential side effects of each prescription.

> I can't even drive at the moment because of the antipsychotic (what I call the 'stop the voices' drug) medication that I've been taking for three months. It makes me dizzy and uncoordinated.
>
> *(DEBBIE)*

But this certainly doesn't mean that a person with a bipolar diagnosis can never drive again. Each individual case is different, but the rule of thumb is that re-licensing will be considered when the person has remained well and stable for at least three months, is compliant with treatment, is free from adverse effects of medication which would impair driving, and is subject to a favourable specialist report.

Q92. *What well-known people have/had bipolar disorder?*

Although most people who are faced with a diagnosis of bipolar disorder aren't of course famous, more and more people in the public eye are stepping forward to talk about their experiences. And other famous people have been given a posthumous diagnosis based on various aspects of their behaviour. Here's a round-up of some of them:

Paul Abbott (born 1960)

Screenwriter Paul Abbott (best known for the TV dramas *Shameless, Clocking Off* and *No Offence*) was first admitted to a psychiatric ward at the age of 15 following a suicide attempt. In an interview on Radio 4's *Desert Island Discs,* he talked openly about his bipolar diagnosis. 'As bipolar, suicide is a constant presence in your life. It's not that you actually feel suicidal, but you don't stop thinking about it. It crosses your mind every day. I was plagued by it for a long time. Except that the love for my family and children is so powerful and so much greater than anything that could make me damage them in that way. They were my immunity [...] I think it forced me to write – the extremity of my mood swings became really rapidly productive. I can't not write. I write every day.'

Adam Ant (born 1954)

Singer Adam Ant (real name Stuart Goddard) made a TV documentary in 2003 entitled *The Madness of Prince Charming,* charting his career and his struggle with bipolar disorder. He says, 'When I was sectioned for six months, it was one of the worst experiences of my life, not being able to go out and have freedom. Having experienced it, it's almost inexplicably awful.'

Ludwig van Beethoven (1770–1827)

Beethoven spent most of his life alternating between periods of brilliance (playing the piano, and composing sonatas and concertos) and periods of utter despair and alcohol addiction. A friend describes what he was like during a busy period: 'He ... tore open the pianoforte ... and began to improvise marvellously ... The hours went by, but Beethoven improvised on. Supper, which he had purported to eat with us, was served, but ... he would not permit himself to be disturbed.' Many experts speculate that Beethoven had bipolar disorder.

Russell Brand (born 1975)

Comedian and actor Russell Brand began abusing drugs and alcohol in his teens. He became clean in 2002 and talks candidly about his diagnoses of ADHD and bipolar in interviews and during his stand-up show. In 2017, he wrote a book about the things that helped him on his road to recovery: *Recovery – Freedom from our Addictions*.

Frank Bruno (born 1961)

World champion boxer Frank Bruno was sectioned for 28 days in a psychiatric hospital and diagnosed with bipolar disorder in 2003 following his marriage break-up. He describes his behaviour in the run-up to his breakdown: 'I got confused and snappy and impatient. I couldn't, couldn't, couldn't function. Losing my wife, seeing my kids less regularly, not eating properly, staying up late, living by myself, getting uptight, wound up, over stupid little things [...] It's like a kettle. I wish I could put a hole in my head and let the steam out.' In 2017, he wrote a deeply personal book about his experiences: *Let Me Be Frank*.

Lord Byron (1788–1824)

Known for his eccentric behaviour and charm, Lord Byron was one of the most celebrated English poets of the nineteenth century. Fellow poet and friend Shelley wrote that he was 'an exceedingly interesting person, but as mad as the wind'. Experts who have studied his life say it's almost certain he had bipolar disorder.

Mariah Carey (born 1970)

In 2018, Mariah Carey told a US magazine that she has bipolar disorder. One of the most successful singers in the world with 18 number one hits, she says when she was first hospitalized and diagnosed in 2001, she didn't want to believe it. 'Until recently I lived in denial and isolation and in constant fear someone would expose me. It was too heavy a burden to carry and I simply couldn't do that anymore. I sought and received treatment, I put positive people around me and I got back to doing what I love – writing songs and making music. I'm actually taking medication that seems to be pretty good. It's not making me feel too tired or sluggish or anything like that. Finding the proper balance is what is most important.

'I'm just in a really good place right now, where I'm comfortable discussing my struggles with Bipolar II disorder. I'm hopeful we can get to a place where the stigma is lifted from people going through anything alone. It can be incredibly isolating. It does not have to define you and I refuse to allow it to define me or control me.'

Patricia Cornwell (born 1956)

Crime fiction writer Patricia Cornwell has spoken of the depression she experienced during her late teens and describes herself as being wired differently. 'It's not unusual for great artistic people to have bipolar disorder. My wiring's not perfect. The diagnosis goes back and forth, but I'm pretty sure that I am. I take a mood stabilizer.'

Kurt Cobain (1967–1994)

Lead singer, guitarist and songwriter of the Seattle-based rock band Nirvana, Cobain was diagnosed with attention deficit disorder as a child, then later with bipolar disorder. Troubled by insomnia and an unidentified stomach complaint, Cobain self-medicated with drugs and committed suicide at the age of 27.

Carrie Fisher (1957–2016)

Actress Carrie Fisher, best known for her role as Princess Leia in the *Star Wars* films, was diagnosed with bipolar disorder at the age of 24 and often spoke about her experiences: 'I was on drugs for years, and I don't think you can accurately diagnose bipolar disorder when someone is actively drug addicted or alcoholic. I didn't accept the diagnosis fully until I had a psychotic break in 1997. Now I'm fine. I'm on seven medications, and I take medication three times a day. This constantly puts me in touch with the illness I have. I'm never quite allowed to be free of that for a day. It's like being a diabetic.'

Stephen Fry (born 1957)

Actor, comedian and writer Stephen Fry has talked often and with much courage about the highs and lows of his diagnosis of bipolar disorder. In a two-part documentary for the BBC, *The Secret Life of the Manic Depressive*, he talks of the downside of the condition: 'I may have looked happy. Inside I was hopelessly depressed. I'm actually kind of sobbing and kind of tearing at the walls inside my own brain while my mouth is, you know, wittering away in some amusing fashion,' as well as the upside: 'I love my condition too. It's infuriating, I know, but I do get a huge buzz out of the manic side. I rely on it to give my life a sense of adventure, and I think most of the good about me has developed as a result of my mood swings. It's tormented me all my life with the deepest of depressions while giving me the energy and creativity that perhaps has made my career.'

Vivien Leigh (1913–1967)

Two-time Oscar-winning actress Vivien Leigh was affected by bipolar disorder for most of her adult life. According to one of his biographers, her second husband, Laurence Olivier, came to recognize the symptoms of an impending episode – 'several days of hyperactivity followed by a period of depression and an explosive breakdown, after which Leigh would have no memory of the event, but would be acutely embarrassed and remorseful.'

Demi Lovato (born 1992)

A Grammy-nominated singer, songwriter and actor, Demi Lovato was diagnosed with bipolar disorder at the age of 22 after years of struggling with substance abuse and an eating disorder. On social media, she has a combined following of more than 145 million.

Demi says: 'Getting a diagnosis was kind of a relief. It helped me start to make sense of the harmful things I was doing to cope with what I was experiencing. Now I had no choice but to move forward and learn how to live with it, so I worked with my healthcare professional and tried different treatment plans until I found what works for me.

'Living well with bipolar disorder is possible, but it takes patience, it takes work and it is an ongoing process. The reality is that you're not a car that goes into a shop and gets fixed right away. Everyone's process and treatment plan may be different. I am so grateful for my life today and I want to protect it. It isn't always easy to take positive steps each day, but I know I have to in order to stay healthy. If you are struggling today with a mental health condition, you may not be able to see it as clearly right away but please don't give up – things can get better. You are worthy of more and there are people who can help. Asking for help is a sign of strength.'

In 2017, Demi was named by Global Citizen as the organization's official ambassador for mental health. In July 2018, she was admitted to hospital following a suspected drug overdose.

Sinead O'Connor (born 1966)

Ever since she was 23, Irish singer Sinead O'Connor says she had thoughts of suicide. 'I began to have this quiet little voice every now and then – although "voice" is the wrong way to put it. It's your own thoughts just gone completely skew-whiff: "Look at that tree, you might hang yourself on it". But after my son Shane was born I was really ill, and I was really worried because I was close to actually doing it. So when he was about five months old, I took myself to hospital.' She was diagnosed with bipolar disorder, which O'Connor describes as like having a gaping hole in the centre of her being. She took the drugs she'd been prescribed and says, 'Within half an hour, it was like cement going over the hole.'

Graeme Obree (born 1965)

Scottish world champion cyclist Graeme Obree candidly describes how he coped with his diagnosis of bipolar disorder and the dark depressions that he's experienced all his life in his autobiography *The Flying Scotsman*. In the film of the same name, Graeme is played by actor Jonny Lee Miller.

Obree says, 'I have suffered depression at various times in my career, and there were times when I wanted to give up riding altogether. But it was only after I retired from international cycling that the illness really took hold. I drank to cope with the effects of depression. I've since been diagnosed as manic depressive, but fortunately doctors have been able to help me with drugs. I used to need cycling to cope with my illness; but with the help of my family, and with counselling, I've begun to overcome the personal issues that caused the depression. Through therapy, I have learned to handle my emotions better, be in touch with what I am and what I feel.'

Sylvia Plath (1932–1963)

American poet and author Sylvia Plath wrote in her journal, 'It is as if my life were magically run by two electric currents: joyous and positive and despairing negative ... ' She committed suicide at the age of 30 by putting her head in an oven and turning on the gas. She has been given a posthumous diagnosis of bipolar disorder.

Vincent van Gogh (1853–1890)

The Dutch artist Vincent van Gogh produced more than 2,000 works, including around 900 paintings and 1,100 drawings and sketches, during the last ten years of his life. Most of his best-known works were produced in the final two years of his life, during which time he cut off part of his left ear following a breakdown in his friendship with fellow artist Paul Gauguin. After this he suffered recurrent bouts of mania and depression (now thought to be symptoms of bipolar disorder), and eventually shot himself, dying in his brother's arms.

Amy Winehouse (1983–2011)

Five-time Grammy award-winning singer-songwriter Amy Winehouse linked her out-of-control drinking to bouts of depression. In a TV interview, she said: 'I do drink a lot. I think it's symptomatic of my depression. I'm manic depressive, I'm not an alcoholic, which sounds like an alcoholic in denial.' After her death in 2011, Amy's family set up the Amy Winehouse Foundation, which works to prevent the effects of drug and alcohol misuse on young people. See amywinehousefoundation.org.

Virginia Woolf (1882–1941)

Throughout her life, Woolf experienced drastic mood swings and, though these greatly affected her social functioning, her literary talent remained intact. Before filling her pockets with stones and walking into the river to drown, she wrote: 'I feel certain now that I am going mad again. I feel we can't go through another of those terrible times. And I shan't recover this time ... ' She has been given a posthumous diagnosis of bipolar disorder.

Catherine Zeta-Jones (born 1969)

Diagnosed with bipolar disorder in 2011, actress Catherine Zeta-Jones has said about her illness: 'Finding out that it was called something was the best thing that ever happened to me! The fact that there was a name for my emotions and that a professional could talk me through my symptoms was very liberating. There are amazing highs and very low lows. My goal is to be consistently in the middle.'

Q93. Can a diagnosis of bipolar disorder ever be a positive thing?

Kay Redfield Jamison is a leading researcher into bipolar disorder and Professor of Psychiatry and Behavioral Sciences at Johns Hopkins University in the USA. In her best-selling book *Touched with Fire: Manic-Depressive Illness and the Artistic Temperament,* she shows how bipolar disorder can run in artistic or high-achieving families. And in her autobiography *An Unquiet Mind,* Jamison writes in a poetic style about her own experiences of the illness, from her darkest days in hospital right through to the benefits she believes having bipolar can bring:

> I honestly believe that as a result of it I have felt more things, more deeply; had more experiences, more intensely; loved more, and been loved more; laughed more often for having cried more; appreciated more the springs, for all the winters; worn death 'as close as dungarees' – appreciated it – and life – more; seen the finest and the most terrible in people, and slowly learned the values of caring, loyalty and seeing things through.

Others emphatically agree that a bipolar diagnosis isn't necessarily all doom and gloom:

> When I first met my partner he was on the tail end of being high. He was a really charismatic man – a funny, intelligent, great, exciting person to be around. He was my Mr Fun. After six and a half years together, there's still something quite wonderful about my boyfriend. It's a real shame if people do get put off because of a bipolar diagnosis. I would rather have met him and suffered the highs and lows than never have met him.
>
> *(10)*

> My partner David swept me off my feet. He's so loving and adorable. He has more energy than anybody I've ever known. I have a daughter from a previous marriage, Cassie, and she really liked him straight away. He has a very gentle way. Kids love

him, mainly because he acts like one himself. In fact, Cassie had to do a 'Who's Your Hero' project at school a few years ago. She talked about her dad. 'No matter how poorly he is (he's got manic depression), my dad still loves me and spends time with me,' she said. It cracked me up. I was in tears. My two children really know how to work him a treat. One great story is that Cassie wanted a kitten. David said, 'No way, we're not having a kitten.' Cassie just said to her brother, Dom, 'Wait till Dad's manic.' Sure enough, they waited and asked again when he was manic. He took them straight to buy one. And now we have a cat!

(JACKIE)

It's very mixed how I feel about bipolar. Unless you've experienced a hypomanic phase, you can't possibly know how wonderful bipolar can be. That feeling does almost make it worthwhile. It's such a good feeling. No narcotic would give you that kind of feeling.

(PAUL)

The great thing is that people with bipolar can be so funny when they're on a high. I don't mind having bipolar now it's under control. I like being high. I'm very creative, I get a lot of work done, and me and my partner can have a real laugh – I think she quite likes it. I'm bipolar and Jane's a great listener!

(DAVE)

My philosophy is that you can learn to live with bipolar. It's a pain in the ass, but it really is possible to turn it into something more positive. All my friends love me to bits.

(SHARRON)

The positive thing about bipolar is that you tend to look at people differently. People with bipolar are far more sympathetic and compassionate towards others – far more forgiving because we know we're forgiven more easily. We suffer fools gladly. I talk to the stranger on the bus. I always say, 'There but for the grace of God.' You never know how far this illness can take you. People with bipolar years ago would have been tied to a chair and left there. That thought frightens me. At least I'm bipolar in the twenty-first century, rather than the nineteenth!

(DEBBIE)

Q94. *What does the future hold for bipolar disorder?*

(Over the last few years, I have become far more alert to the possibility that a patient's depression symptoms may be masking bipolar disorder. I probe more deeply and ask more questions about behaviours, especially with 'revolving door' patients who have recurrent depressive episodes, and often discover red flags (such as hypersexuality or excessive spending during 'happier' periods) that trigger my bipolar radar. I have certainly diagnosed more patients with bipolar disorder in the last five years than at any time in my 27 years as a family doctor – and I know that many colleagues have shared the same experience. It is encouraging too that a lot of patients now ask about the possibility of bipolar disorder, having discussed it with a family member or identified a family history. So when I think about the future for bipolar disorder, I'm optimistic that understanding of the condition will continue to grow across the medical profession and amongst the general public, so that more patients receive the right diagnosis, and the correct treatment, much faster.)

(DR JO WILLIAMS MB, CHB, GENERAL PRACTITIONER IN THE UK SINCE 1992)

(I am hopeful that over the next few decades, advances in research, in genetics and neuroimaging in particular perhaps, will transform our understanding of this illness so we can make some real progress improving prediction, prevention and treatment. Science is giving us the tools for understanding – and I really believe that we have to understand better the complex causes of this condition to bring benefits to those who experience it. I am also optimistic that in a generation's time the stigma around mental health will be considerably reduced. I am believer in the cancer example – in the early 70s, cancer was almost considered a defect of character, a death sentence you couldn't talk about: 'The Big C'. Then we declared the 'War on Cancer' and put billions of dollars into research. That made a massive difference to understanding its causes and developing better treatment, and led to improved prognosis (it's no longer a death sentence) and over time public perception has changed. The stigma has gone. I hope the same will happen with mental health.)

(PROFESSOR IAN JONES, PROFESSOR OF PSYCHIATRY AT CARDIFF UNIVERSITY AND DIRECTOR OF THE NATIONAL CENTRE FOR MENTAL HEALTH)

' In the near future, I would like to see more effective treatments for people with bipolar disorder that have fewer side effects. Plus, I'm hopeful there will be better physical healthcare for people with severe mental illness. Third, I think the role of mental health pharmacists will change so they do more outreach work with GPs and psychiatric nurses in primary care. '

(DR IAN MAIDMENT, SENIOR LECTURER IN CLINICAL PHARMACY AT ASTON UNIVERSITY)

' We need to see more public education about bipolar disorder and more general understanding of the illness. We also need more funding into treatments and services. Compared to Canada, Europe and Australia, services in the UK are seriously under-resourced. We need some huge changes in policy to reflect the reality of the huge cost to people who are sufferers and their families, and to the country as a whole. What I'm excited about is our study supported by the EU which aims to predict who's going to respond to lithium. At the moment about a third of people respond really well, about a third of people have a partial response and about a third don't respond well at all. Currently we can't predict which group someone with bipolar is likely to be in. Our five-year research project is going to measure everything possible – family history, individual symptoms, brain scans, adherence, markers in blood and saliva samples – so that we can spot predictors of response. In five years or so, we'll have a much better understanding of who lithium is and isn't likely to help. '

(PROFESSOR ALLAN YOUNG, DIRECTOR OF THE CENTRE FOR AFFECTIVE DISORDERS AT KING'S COLLEGE LONDON)

' Psychological support will be offered to everyone with bipolar disorder in the future; there will also be more focus on learning skills to help prevent relapse. '

(DR SARA TAI, SENIOR LECTURER IN CLINICAL PSYCHOLOGY AT THE UNIVERSITY OF MANCHESTER)

' We're in the midst of a transition from institutional care to more family based home care. We've still got a long way to go, but eventually it will be recognized that the family is essential in maintaining the health of the individual. '

(IAN HULATT, MENTAL HEALTH ADVISOR, ROYAL COLLEGE OF NURSING FOR 13 YEARS)

' I hope bipolar disorder will be taken more seriously by policy makers sooner rather than later, as the major personal and public health problem it is. The current neglect is shameful. However, more importantly, I hope the brightest and the best scientists are drawn to study bipolar, so that in a better future we will have ways of preventing its worst manifestations and treating better what remains. '

(*PROFESSOR GUY GOODWIN, SENIOR RESEARCH FELLOW AT THE UNIVERSITY OF OXFORD*)

' Understanding different coping approaches is going to be very important in the future. I think that although people with a bipolar diagnosis have plenty of problems, and there's lots of evidence of that, they also spend significant parts of their lives coping extremely well. And so I think as therapists we can learn to get better at building that up. And that's partly based on the psychological principle that it's easier to increase the frequency of a behaviour that's already there than it is to create a new one. '

(*PROFESSOR STEVEN JONES, PROFESSOR OF CLINICAL PSYCHOLOGY AND CO-DIRECTOR OF THE SPECTRUM CENTRE FOR MENTAL HEALTH RESEARCH AT LANCASTER UNIVERSITY*)

We fervently hope that in the future:

- No one ever says 'James is bipolar,' but 'James has bipolar' instead. Why should an illness define the person?
- The stigma and prejudices attached to mental illness are eradicated – and understanding and compassion replace them.
- Anyone who has a loved one diagnosed with bipolar disorder is given unlimited support, information and understanding from health professionals, friends, other family members and the community in general.
- Everyone diagnosed with bipolar disorder is offered psychological treatments from the outset as this greatly improves the chances of positive outcomes.

- Self-management programmes are available for everyone with bipolar disorder.
- Holistic care plans – including diet, exercise and complementary therapies – are routinely recommended for those with a mental health condition.
- All GPs and psychiatrists take more care when diagnosing non-bipolar depression because the wrong treatment (i.e. prescribing antidepressants without a mood stabilizer) may trigger or worsen the course of bipolar illness.
- A bipolar diagnosis isn't seen as someone's worst nightmare; it's considered a challenge – yes, like a diagnosis of diabetes or asthma might be, but a challenge that doesn't rule out the possibility of living a fulfilling, successful and happy life.

Extra resources

Action on Addiction

TEL: 0300 330 0659

WEB: www.actiononaddiction.org.uk

Action on Postpartum Psychosis

The national charity for women and families affected by postpartum psychosis.

TEL: 020 3322 9900

WEB: www.app-network.org

Adfam (families, drugs and alcohol)

TEL: 020 3817 9410

WEB: www.adfam.org.uk

Alcoholics Anonymous

HELPLINE: 0800 9177 650

WEB: www.alcoholics-anonymous.org.uk

Association for Nutrition

TEL: 0203 795 8823

WEB: www.associationfornutrition.org

Association of Reflexologists

TEL: 01823 351010

WEB: www.aor.org.uk

Bipolar Scotland

TEL: 0141 560 2050

WEB: www.bipolarscotland.org.uk

Bipolar UK

HELPLINE: 0333 323 3880

WEB: www.bipolaruk.org

British Acupuncture Council

TEL: 020 8735 0400

WEB: www.acupuncture.org.uk

British Association for Behavioural and Cognitive Psychotherapies

TEL: 0161 705 4304

WEB: www.babcp.com

British Association for Counselling and Psychotherapy

TEL: 01455 883 300

WEB: www.bacp.co.uk

British Association for Psychopharmacology

WEB: www.bap.org.uk

British Complementary Medicine Association

TEL: 0845 345 5977

WEB: www.bcma.co.uk

British Psychological Society

TEL: 0116 254 9568

WEB: www.bps.org.uk

British Wheel of Yoga

TEL: 01529 306851

WEB: www.bwy.org.uk

CALM – Campaign Against Living Miserably

HELPLINE: 0800 585858

WEB: www.thecalmzone.net

Care Quality Commission

TEL: 03000 616171

WEB: www.cqc.org.uk

Carers Northern Ireland

TEL: 028 9043 9843

WEB: www.carersuk.org/northernireland

Carers Scotland

TEL: 0808 808 7777

WEB: www.carerscotland.org

Carers UK

TEL: 020 7378 4999

WEB: www.carersuk.org

Carers Wales

TEL: 020 7378 4999

WEB: www.carersuk.org/wales

Community Advice & Listening Line

Offers emotional support and information on mental health and related matters to people in Wales.

TEL: 0800 132 737

WEB: www.callhelpline.org.uk

Drinkaware

TEL: 020 7766 9900

WEB: www.drinkaware.co.uk

Elefriends

A safe, supportive online community where you can listen, be heard and share your experiences with others.

WEB: www.elefriends.org.uk

Food for the Brain

TEL: 020 8332 9600

WEB: www.foodforthebrain.org

Harmless

User-led organization for people who self-harm, and their friends and families.

WEB: www.harmless.org.uk

Independent Healthcare Providers Network

TEL: 020 7799 8678

WEB: www.ihpn.org.uk

Inspire

Local services to support the mental health and well-being of people across Northern Ireland.

TEL: 028 9032 8474

WEB: www.inspirewellbeing.org

Institute of Psychiatry, Psychology & Neuroscience

TEL: 0207 848 0002

WEB: www.kcl.ac.uk/ioppn

International Federation of Aromatherapists

TEL: 0208 567 2243

WEB: www.ifaroma.org

Lifelink

TEL: 0141 552 4434

WEB: www.lifelink.org.uk

Lifesigns

User-led self-injury guidance and support network.

WEB: www.lifesigns.org.uk

Maternal Mental Health Alliance

Coalition of UK organizations which support women during pregnancy and in the year after giving birth.

WEB: www.maternalmentalhealthalliance.org

Mental Health Alliance

Coalition of more than 75 organizations which advocates for fair implementation of the Mental Health Act in England and Wales.

WEB: www.mentalhealthalliance.org.uk

Mental Health Foundation

TEL: 020 7803 1100

WEB: www.mentalhealth.org.uk

Mental Health Review Tribunal

WEB: www.gov.uk/mental-health-tribunal

Mental Health Review Tribunal (Wales)

TEL: 0300 025 5328

WEB: www.mentalhealthreviewtribunal.gov.wales

Mentally Healthy Schools

WEB: www.mentallyhealthyschools.org.uk

Mind

INFOLINE: 0300 123 3393

WEB: www.mind.org.uk

Mind Cymru

TEL: 029 2039 5123

The Mix

Helpline and online support for people aged 16–25.

HELPLINE: 0808 808 4994

WEB: www.themix.org.uk

Mood Swings Network

TEL: 0161 832 3736

WEB: www.moodswings.org.uk

Narcotics Anonymous

HELPLINE: 0300 999 1212

WEB: www.ukna.org

National Hypnotherapy Society

TEL: 01903 236857

WEB: www.nationalhypnotherapysociety.org

National Institute for Health and Care Excellence (NICE)

TEL: 0300 323 0140

WEB: www.nice.org.uk

National Institute of Medical Herbalists

TEL: 01392 426022

WEB: www.nimh.org.uk

National Self Harm Network (NSHN)

Closely monitored, survivor-led forum for people who self-harm, and their friends and families.

WEB: www.nshn.co.uk

Papyrus

Confidential support and advice to young people struggling with thoughts of suicide, and anyone worried about a young person.

HELPLINE: 0800 068 4141

WEB: www.papyrus-uk.org

The Patients Association

HELPLINE: 020 8423 8999

WEB: www.patients-association.org.uk

Place2Be

Children's mental health charity providing in-school support and expert training to improve the emotional well-being of pupils, families, teachers and school staff.

TEL: 0207 923 5500

WEB: www.place2be.org.uk

Rethink Mental Illness

TEL: 0121 522 7007

WEB: www.rethink.org

Royal College of Psychiatrists

TEL: 020 7235 2351

WEB: www.rcpsych.ac.uk

Samaritans

HELPLINE: 116 123 (open 24 hours in the UK and Republic of Ireland)

WEB: www.samaritans.org

SAMH (Scottish Association for Mental Health)

Provides general mental health information about local services for people in Scotland.

WEB: www.samh.org.uk

SANE

HELPLINE: 0300 304 7000

WEB: www.sane.org.uk

Scottish Intercollegiate Guidelines Network (SIGN)

TEL: 0131 623 4720

WEB: www.sign.ac.uk

SelfHarmUK

A pro-recovery charity committed to improving the lives of anyone impacted by self-harm.

WEB: www.selfharm.co.uk

Self-injury Support

Information and support for women and girls who self-harm, including a self-harm diary and local support groups.

HELPLINE: 0808 800 8088

WEB: www.selfinjurysupport.org.uk

Society of Homeopaths

TEL: 01604 817890

WEB: www.homeopathy-soh.org

Talk to Frank (confidential drugs advice)

HELPLINE: 0300 123 6600

WEB: www.talktofrank.com

Time to Change

Anti-stigma campaign jointly run by Mind and Rethink.

TEL: 020 8215 2356

WEB: www.time-to-change.org.uk

UK Reiki Federation

TEL: 01264 791 441

WEB: www.reikifed.co.uk

The UK Society for Play and Creative Arts Therapies

TEL: 01825 761143

WEB: www.playtherapy.org.uk

YoungMinds

PARENTS HELPLINE: 0808 802 5544

WEB: www.youngminds.org.uk

UNITED STATES OF AMERICA

American Herbalists Guild

TEL: 617 520 4372

WEB: www.americanherbalistsguild.com

American Psychiatric Association

TEL: 888 357 7924 (in the US and Canada)

202 559 3900 (outside the US and Canada)

WEB: www.psych.org

American Psychological Association

TEL: 800 374 2721

WEB: www.apa.org

Bring Change 2 Mind

Organization that raises awareness and works against the stigma that often surrounds mental health.

TEL: 415 814 8846

WEB: www.bringchange2mind.org

Depression and Bipolar Support Alliance

TEL: 800 826 3632

WEB: www.dbsalliance.org

Foundation for a Smoke-Free America

TEL: 310 577 9828

WEB: www.anti-smoking.org

Mental Health America

TEL: 703 684 7722

CRISIS LINE: 1 800 273 8255

WEB: www.mentalhealthamerica.net

National Alliance for the Mentally Ill (NAMI)

TEL: 703 524 7600

HELPLINE: 800 950 6264

WEB: www.nami.org

National Institute of Mental Health (NIMH)

TEL: 1 866 615 6464

WEB: www.nimh.nih.gov

National Suicide Prevention Lifeline

TEL: 1 800 273 8255

WEB: www.suicidepreventionlifeline.org

www.mcmanweb.com

Founded and run by American John McManamy, who has a bipolar diagnosis, this website offers information and advice on living well with bipolar disorder, research articles and online forums.

CANADA

Alliance for the Mentally Ill (Quebec)
TEL: 514 486 1448
WEB: www.amiquebec.org

Canadian Mental Health Association
TEL: 416 646 5557
WEB: www.cmha.ca

Canadian Network for Mood and Anxiety Treatments
WEB: www.canmat.org

Mood Disorders Association of British Columbia
TEL: 1 604 873 0103
WEB: www.mdabc.net

Mood Disorders Association of Manitoba
TEL: 1 800 263 1460
WEB: www.mooddisordersmanitoba.ca

Mood Disorders Association of Ontario
SUPPORT LINE: 1 866 363 6663
WEB: www.mooddisorders.ca

Mood Disorders Society of Canada
TEL: 613 921 5565
WEB: www.mdsc.ca

Organization for Bipolar Affective Disorder (OBAD)
TEL: 1 866 263 7408
WEB: www.obad.ca

AUSTRALIA AND NEW ZEALAND

Balance
Promotes the well-being of those affected by mental health issues.

TEL: 06 345 4488

WEB: www.balance.org.nz

Black Dog Institute
Medical research institute dedicated to understanding, preventing and treating mental illness.

TEL: 029 382 4530

WEB: www.blackdoginstitute.org.au

Mental Health Foundation of New Zealand

TEL: 09 623 4812

WEB: www.mentalhealth.org.nz

The Royal Australian & New Zealand College of Psychiatrists

TEL: 1800 337 448 (for Australian residents)

1800 443 827 (for New Zealand residents)

WEB: www.ranzcp.org

SANE Australia

HELPLINE: 1800 18 7263

WEB: www.sane.org

WORLDWIDE

Alcoholics Anonymous

To find AA groups outside the UK, visit www.aa.org

International Association for Suicide Prevention (IASP)

WEB: www.iasp.info

International Society for Bipolar Disorders

WEB: www.isbd.org

Narcotics Anonymous

To find NA groups outside the UK, go to www.na.org

Very Well Mind

International site crammed with information and articles about mental health, including bipolar.

WEB: www.verywellmind.com

World Federation of Societies of Biological Psychiatry (WFSBP)

TEL: 49 40 670882 90
WEB: www.wfsbp.org

Glossary

Addiction – the condition of being addicted to a particular substance or behaviour

ADHD (attention deficit hyperactivity disorder) – a range of problem behaviours, such as poor attention span, impulsiveness, restlessness and hyperactivity, often diagnosed in children

Adrenaline – a hormone secreted by the adrenal glands that stimulates and boosts motivation

Advocate – a volunteer who helps those with mental illness communicate their needs, explore their options and get things done

Amino acid – the brain's messengers found in protein-rich food

Antidepressant – a drug prescribed to alleviate depression

Antipsychotic – a drug prescribed to alleviate psychosis, mania and hypomania

Approved mental health professional (AMHP) – a nursing professional who's trained and qualified to participate in the decision to section someone

Atypical – a class of antipsychotic drugs

Bipolar disorder – a mental illness characterized by mood swings

Borderline personality disorder (BDP) – a mental illness characterized by fear of abandonment, intense emotions, unstable relationships, blame and paranoia

CAMHS (child and adolescent mental health services) – health services for those under the age of 18

Capacity – the ability to understand information and make decisions about your life

Care plan – a list of action points decided upon and written down by the person with bipolar and their support team to plan for the future

Care Quality Commission – the independent regulator of health and adult special care in the UK

Carer – a person who cares for someone who's unwell or elderly

Catatonic – when someone stays frozen in one position for a long time; repeats the same movement for no obvious reason; or is extremely restless, unrelated to medication

Chronic – persisting for a long time

Comorbidity – when two or more conditions exist in one patient

CPA (Care Programme Approach) – a care plan specifically designed for someone who's been in hospital to ease their transition back to their life outside

Crisis Resolution and Home Treatment (CRHT) team – provides 24-hour support for anyone experiencing a mental health crisis

CTO (Community Treatment Order) – after being sectioned and treated in hospital, a doctor can apply for a CTO where certain conditions have to be met in the community, such as living in a certain place and having certain medical treatment

Cyclothymia – where depressive and manic symptoms last for two years but are not serious enough for a diagnosis of bipolar disorder

Depot injection – a slow-release, slow-acting form of an antipsychotic medication administered by injection in a carrier liquid

Depression – a low mood and a loss of interest and pleasure in previously enjoyed activities

Diagnosis – the identification of an illness by means of symptoms

Diagnostic and Statistical Manual of Mental Disorders (DSM-5) – the fifth edition of a manual published by the American Psychiatric Association, used in the UK and the US for categorizing and diagnosing mental health problems

Discrimination – unfavourable treatment based on prejudice

Disruptive mood dysregulation disorder – a childhood condition of extreme irritability, anger, and frequent, intense temper outbursts first described in DSM-5

Dissociation – feeling disconnected in some way from the world or from oneself

Dopamine – a neurotransmitter that transmits signals between nerve cells

Dual diagnosis – where a diagnosis such as bipolar disorder is accompanied by another clinical condition, such as alcohol addiction

EIP (Early Intervention in Psychosis) – this service works with someone the first time they have psychosis

Essential fatty acids – healthy fats such as omega-3, important for healthy communication between brain cells

FFT (family focused therapy) – a type of therapy where the main goal is to teach patients and their families about the nature of their illness

General practitioner (GP) – a family doctor who treats people in the community

Grandiosity – the delusion of high rank or superiority

Hallucination – the apparent perception of an object, person or experience not actually present

Holding power – a legal process in place to allow a doctor to detain and assess a patient in hospital for 72 hours while they decide whether an application for a section needs to be made; a psychiatric nurse can exercise a holding power for up to six hours until a doctor can begin the assessment

Holistic – treating the whole person, including mental, emotional and social factors, rather than just the symptoms of a disease

Hypomania – a persistent mild elevation of mood

Hypothyroidism – a condition where the thyroid gland doesn't produce enough of the hormone thyroxine

Index of suspicion – a list of symptoms and/or behaviour a health professional needs to look out for to make a diagnosis

Informal patient – anyone who agrees to admit themselves to a psychiatric hospital voluntarily

Insomnia – habitual sleeplessness

Mania – an unnaturally high euphoric mood

Manic depression – a synonym for 'bipolar disorder', although the term is less frequently used today

Mixed features – where symptoms of depression and mania occur at the same time

Monoamine oxidase inhibitors (MAOIs) – a type of antidepressant

Nearest relative – the patient's closest family member who has certain legal rights

Neuroleptic malignant syndrome (NMS) – a rare but potentially life-threatening adverse reaction to neuroleptic/antipsychotic drugs

Neurotransmitters – chemicals that relay nerve impulses between brain and body

NICE (National Institute for Health and Care Excellence) – an independent organization responsible for providing national guidance on the promotion of good health and the prevention and treatment of ill health in the UK

Nicotine Replacement Therapy (NRT) – gum, patches, lozenges or tabs loaded with nicotine for quitting smoking

Occupational therapy – the assessment and treatment of physical and psychiatric conditions using specific, purposeful activity to prevent disability and promote independent function in all aspects of daily life

OTC (Over-The-Counter) – medicines that can be bought at any pharmacy or chemist without a prescription

Paranoia – thinking and feeling under threat even though there is no or very little evidence that this is true

Peripartum onset – where mood episodes begin during pregnancy or in the months after giving birth

Personality disorder – another name for the mental illness borderline personality disorder, or BDP

Pharmacist – a person qualified to prepare and dispense pharmaceutical drugs

Prescription – a doctor's written instruction for medicine to be taken

PRN – an abbreviation of the Latin term *'pro re nata'*, which is used on a prescription to mean 'take when needed'

Prophylactic – preventative

Protocols – official rules for a procedure or treatment

Psychiatrist – a person qualified in the study and treatment of mental illness

Psychologist – a person qualified in the study of the human mind and its functions

Psychosis – a loss of contact with external reality

Puerperal psychosis – a condition where symptoms of confusion, hallucinations and a total loss of reality can happen suddenly, often after childbirth

Quality and Outcomes Framework (QOF) – a governmental 'points' system for general practitioners (GPs) in the UK

Rapid cycling – experiencing more than four mood swings in a 12-month period

Rapid tranquilization – when medicines are given to a person who is very agitated or displaying aggressive behaviour to help calm them quickly

Schizoaffective disorder – a mental illness characterized by psychosis, mania and depression

Schizophrenia – a mental illness characterized by delusions and retreat from social life

Seasonal affective disorder (SAD) – a type of winter depression characterized by the need to sleep and eat carbohydrates

Section – compulsory admittance to a psychiatric hospital or ward

Selective serotonin reuptake inhibitors (SSRIs) – the most commonly used type of antidepressant in the UK

Self-harm (also known as deliberate self-harm or DSH) – hurting oneself as a way of dealing with very difficult feelings, painful memories or overwhelming situations and experiences

Serotonin – a 'neurotransmitter' known as the brain's happy chemical

Serotonin and noradrenaline reuptake inhibitors (SNRIs) – type of antidepressant that acts on the brain chemical noradrenaline as well as serotonin

Service user – someone who is a patient or other user of health and/or social services

Stigma – a sign of disgrace or discredit, which sets a person apart from others

Suicide – intentionally killing oneself

Thyroxine – the hormone produced by the thyroid gland that controls the way the body uses energy

Toxin – a poison

Treatment-emergent mania/hypomania (TEMH) – hypomania or mania that emerges only when a patient has been given an antidepressant

Tricyclic – a class of antidepressants

Tryptophan – an amino acid found in certain foods

Ultradian cycling – experiencing daily mood swings

Unipolar – a word used to describe depression where only low moods are experienced (not the high moods also experienced by those with bipolar disorder)

WHO (World Health Organization) – the specialized agency of the United Nations founded in 1948 that is concerned with health on an international level

Withdrawal symptoms – the unpleasant physical and emotional reaction that occurs when an addictive substance or behaviour is no longer taken or carried out

Index

Abbott, Paul xv–xvii, 254
acupuncture 193
acute admissions wards 153
Adam Ant 254
advance decisions 112–14
advocates 127–8, 166
age 25, 111–14
alcohol 45, 46, 47, 204, 219–22
Alcoholics Anonymous (AA) 220–2
AMHP, see approved mental health
    professional
anti-anxiety drugs 89, 93
anti-stigma campaigns 16
antidepressants 86, 89, 92–5
antimanics, see mood stablizers
antipsychotic drugs 89, 91–2
anxiety 26, 38–9, 65
    and medication 89, 93
approved mental health
    professional (AMHP) 161, 172–3
Armstrong, Clare 235
aromatherapy 193

aspirin 222
atypical features 27

Beethoven, Ludwig van 254
Bell, Kristen 16
benzodiazepines, see anti-anxiety
    drugs
bipolar disorder 132, 263–6
    and addiction 45–6
    and causes 48–9
    and definition 21
    and diagnosis (adults) 261–2
    and diagnosis (children) 55–7
    and employment 237–41
    and families 235–7
    and mixed features 37–8
    and name 22–3
    and physical health 46–8
    and pregnancy 242–3
    and stigma 229–35
    and students 244–7
    and symptoms (adults) 25–8, 38–41

bipolar disorder (*cont.*)
  and symptoms (children) 57–9
  and testing 52–3
  and types 23–4
  see also depression; hypomania;
    mania; treatment
Bipolar Disorder Research Network
  (BDRN) 53
blood pressure 185
blood tests 47, 89, 90–1, 92
borderline personality disorder
  (BPD) 43–5
brain, the 42, 45, 200
Brand, Russell 231, 255
breakfast 203
Bring Change 2 Mind 233
Bruno, Frank 255
Byron, Lord 255

caffeine 203, 216–19
calcium 207
Calm – Campaign Against Living
  Miserably 143
Campbell, Alastair 16
Campfire 150
cannabis 224–5
capacity 112–13
cardiovascular disease 46, 47
care co-ordinators 120, 126
Care Programme Approach (CPA)
  179–80
Care Quality Commission (CQC)
  73, 74, 116, 156–8, 250
carers, *see* family members

Carey, Mariah 255–6
catatonic features 27
Catherine, HRH Duchess of
    Cambridge 232
CBT, *see* cognitive behavioural
    therapy
childbirth 49, 243
children 54–9, 86, 126–7,
    235–7
  and treatment 108–11
chocolate 216, 217, 218–19
choline 211
Close, Glenn 233
CMHT, *see* community mental
    health team
Cobain, Kurt 256
cocaine 225–6
coffee 203, 216–18
cognitive behavioural therapy
    (CBT) 19, 76–82, 85, 108
community mental health team
    (CMHT) 84, 118
Community Treatment Orders
    (CTOs) 181
comorbidity 28
complaints 126, 249–51
complementary therapies 192–6
Connor, Gillian 86
coping mechanisms 144–9
Cornwell, Patricia 256
cough medicines 222
counselling 19, 83
Craddock, Nick 55, 63
creativity 31–2

Crisis Resolution and Home
   Treatment (CRHT) team
   123–6
cyclothymia 19, 24, 72

debt 247–8
decongestants 222
DeGeneres, Ellen 16
deliberate self-harm (DSH) 41
delusions 34–5, 36
depot injections 100, 246
depression 23, 25–6, 61–2
   and coping mechanisms 73
   and definition 28–31
   and diagnosis 64
   and driving 253
   and early warning signs 81
   and family members 144–5
   and medication 89, 93–5
   and mindfulness 197
   and psychosis 37
   and sleep 188
   see also SAD
diabetes 46, 47, 72
diet 198–206; see also nutrition
discrimination, see stigma
driving 252–3
drugs, see medication; recreational
   drugs
DSM-5: 23, 26, 242

early warning signs 79–81, 103, 121,
   140
ecstasy 226

electroconvulsive therapy (ECT) 71,
   104–6
employers 237–41
England 249
environment 48–9
Equality Act (2010) 238
essential fatty acids 210–11
exercise 47, 108, 191–2

family focused therapy 82–3
family members 50–2
   and children 235–7
   and coping mechanisms 144–9
   and early warning signs 103
   and hospitals 173–7
   and 'nearest relative' 172–3
   and sectioning 162–3
   and suicide 136–42
   and support 121–2, 128–31, 133–6,
      150
   and therapy 82–3
Fast, Julie A. 22, 134, 149
fatty acids 210–11
film 15–16, 152
finances 34, 247–8
Fink, Candida 70
fish 200
Fisher, Carrie 234, 256–7
folic acid (folate) 207, 242
food, see diet; nutrition
fruit 200–1
Fry, Stephen xviii–xx, 22, 231, 257
funding 115–16

gambling 45
gaming 45–6
gender 24–5
general practitioners (GPs) 63, 64, 84, 116–18, 246
genes 48–9, 50–3
Goodwin, Guy 88, 89, 265
gross professional misconduct 251

hallucinations 35
Harmless 143
Harry, HRH Duke of Sussex 16, 232
head injuries 49
Heads Together campaign 232–3
hearing voices 36–7
herbal remedies 212
heroin 226
high security special hospitals 154
holding power 160
Holford, Patrick 206
holistic therapies, see complementary therapies
homeopathy 194
hormones 49
hospitals, see psychiatric hospitals
Hulatt, Ian 155, 156, 177, 264
hypomania 23–4, 31–2, 89
hypothalamus 42
hypothyroidism 90–1

ibuprofen 222
'Improving Access to Psychological Therapies' (IAPT) programme 84
insight 67

insurance 119, 158–9, 251–2
intensive care wards 153
International Association for Suicide Prevention (IASP) 143
International Classification of Diseases, The 74–5
internet 17
iron 207

Jamison, Kay Redfield 261
Johnson, Dwayne 'The Rock' 16
Jones, Ian 53, 71–2, 87–8, 263
Jones, Steven xxi–xxii, 52, 76, 79, 265

ketamine 95–6
Ketter, Terence 63
Kinderman, Peter 77, 81–2
Kraepelin, Emil 22
Kraynak, Joe 70

lasting power of attorney (LPA) 248–9
legal advice 114
'legal highs' 227
Leigh, Vivien 257
Lewis, Martin 247
libido 28, 40
life expectancy 46
Lifesigns 143
lifestyle 65–6, 184–5
and stress 185–7
see also diet; exercise; sleep
light therapy 96, 107–8

lithium 47, 48, 88, 89–91, 117
Lovato, Demi 231, 258
LSD 226–7

McManamy, John 42, 87
magnesium 207–8
Maidment, Dr Ian 101, 170, 215–16, 222–3, 264
manganese 208
mania 23, 25–6, 61
  and antidepressants 94–5
  and diagnosis 64–5
  and driving 252
  and early warning signs 79–81
  and episodes 32–5
  and medication 89, 98
  and sleep 188–9
  see also hypomania; psychosis
manic depression 22–3
massage 194
MBCT, see mindfulness
medication 17–18, 19, 71, 86–93
  and CBT 77–8
  and children 110
  and driving 253
  and forgetting 99–100
  and herbal remedies 212
  and new developments 95–6
  and over-the-counter 222
  and pharmacists 170–1
  and pregnancy 242
  and prescription drugs 223
  and psychiatric nurses 121
  and schizoaffective disorder 43

and students 246, 247
and time period 97–9
and weight gain 100–2
and Zyban 215–16
  see also antidepressants; lithium
meditation 196–7
medium secure units 153–4
melancholia 27
menopause 49
Mental Capacity Act (2007) 112–14
Mental Health Acts 165
  1983: 161, 164
  2007: 106, 110, 166–7
mental health charities 149–51
mental health history 65
Miklowitz, David 75, 130–1
Miller, Dr Michael 54, 110
Mind Meal 204–6
mindfulness 196, 197–8
mixed features 26, 37–8
money management 34, 247–8
mood diaries 78–9, 103–4
mood stabilizers 89, 93–4
mood swings 24
  and CBT 77, 79
  and early warning signs 79–81
  and stress 185–7
Moodgym 85
Morriss, Richard 72, 116

National Health Service (NHS) 84–5, 157–8
  and complaints 251
  and funding 115–16

National Self Harm Network
(NSHN) 143
National Suicide Prevention Lifeline
143
neuroleptic malignant syndrome
(NMS) 92
neuroleptics, see antipsychotic
drugs 89
neurotransmitters 201
NICE 73–4, 75–6
and age 111–12
and ECT 105
and family support 128
and medication 89
and RTMS 107
and support 117–18, 124
and weight gain 101–2
nicotine 45, 46, 213–16
'No Health Without Mental Health'
programme 84
Northern Ireland 250
nurse therapists 122
nutrition 47, 108
and supplements 206–11
see also diet
nuts 203

obesity 46, 47
Obree, Graeme 259
occupational therapists 171
O'Connor, Sinead 258–9
older people 25, 111–14
omega-3/6: 200, 210
online resources 85, 102, 150–1

overspending 34
oxytocin 96

pain relief 222
Papolos, Demitri 58–9, 110
Papyrus 142
paranoia 35
pathway of care 66–9
Patient Advice and Liaison Service
(PALS) 249
peripartum onset 28
personalized treatment 72
pharmacists 170–1
physical health 46–8
Plath, Sylvia 259
post-natal depression 29, 243
postpartum psychosis (PP) 243
Pourasghar, Daniel 150
pregnancy 28, 90, 242–3
prescriptions 247
prevention 72–3
private treatment 85, 119, 158–9, 251
processed food 202
protein 201–2
Psychiatric Genomics Consortium
(PGC) 53
psychiatric hospitals 110, 152–8,
181–3
and children 236–7
and complaints 250
and discharge 179–81
and families 173–7
and 'informal' patients 160
and patient care 168–71

and private treatment 158–9
and sectioning 160–4, 166–8
and smoking 178–9
psychiatric nurses 120–3, 169–70
psychiatrists 119
psychological therapy 71, 73, 75–6, 84–5
    and family focused 82–3
    and group 83
    see also cognitive behavioural therapy
psychologists 119–20
psychosis 27, 35, 43
    and medication 89
    and postpartum 243

Quality and Outcomes Framework (QOF) points 117

rapid cycling 27, 48
recreational drugs 45, 46, 47, 49, 223–8
reflexology 194–5
Reiki 195
relationships 147–8
repetitive transcranial magnetic stimulation (RTMS) 71, 107
respiratory disease 46
review meetings 174–5
risk management 121, 139–40
Rowling, J.K. 16

SAD (seasonal affective disorder) 41–3, 96, 107–8

St John's wort 212
Sajatovic, Martha 112
Samaritans 142
Sarkhel, Dr Arghya 192
schizoaffective disorder 43
Scotland 74, 250
Scott, Jan 78
Scottish Intercollegiate Guidelines Network (SIGN) 74
seasonal patterns 28, 41–3
    and light therapy 96
    and treatment 107–8
sectioning 160–4, 166–8, 180
seeds 203
self-esteem 28
self-harm 28, 36–7, 41, 136, 143–4
Self-Injury Support 144
self-management techniques 71, 102–4
Selfharmuk 144
serotonin 212
sex 45; see also libido
sexual behaviour 167–8
side effects 89, 105
sleep 49, 89, 187–90
smoking 178–9, 213–16
social media 17, 150–1
solicitors 166, 167
speed 227
stigma 16, 229–35
stress 49, 185–7
students 244–7
substance abuse 28, 45
sugar 203

suicide 38, 136–43
supplements 206–11
support 18, 115–28
  and family members 128–31,
    133–6
  and mental health charities
    149–51
  and self-harm 143–4
  and suicide 142–3
symptoms 134–5
  and prevention 72–3
Syrett, Michel 67

Tai, Dr Sara 73, 76, 86–7, 110, 264
  and family members 128–9, 134
tea 203, 216, 217–18
Teach, Dr Mary 78
teachers 126–7
television 15–16
therapy 71, 73, 75–6
  and family focused 82–3
  and group 83
  and light 96, 107–8
  and nurses 122
  and occupational 171
  see also cogntive behavioural
    therapy; complementary
    therapies; electroconvulsive
    therapy
Thornicroft, Sir Graham 229
thryoid gland 48, 90–1
treatment 17–18, 19, 71–3
  and addiction 46
  and BPD 45

and children 108–11
and CTOs 181
and ECT 104–6
and guidelines 73–5
and older people 111–14
and SAD 107–8
and self-management 102–4
see also medication; pathway
  of care; private treatment;
  psychiatric hospitals;
  psychological therapy; support

unipolar disorder 29, 46, 93
United States of America (USA)
  119, 120, 126
  and families 131
  and involuntary hopitalization
    163
  and stigma 233
university 244–7

Van Gogh, Vincent 259–60
vegetables 200–1
vitamins 206, 208–9, 211
voices 36–7

Wade, James 233–4
waiting times 84–5
Wales 250
warning signs, see early warning
  signs
water 203
Wax, Ruby 198, 233
weight gain 100–2

Wessely, Simon 165
William, HRH Duke of Cambridge
  16, 232
Williams, Dr Jo 263
Winehouse, Amy 260
Woolf, Virginia 260
workplaces 237–41
World Federation of Societies
  of Biological Psychiatry
  (WFSBP) 75

yoga 196
Young, Allan 95, 264

Zeta-Jones, Catherine 260
zinc 210
Zyban 215–16